Saint Mary Mazzarello
The Spirit of Joy

Saint Mary Mazzarello
The Spirit of Joy

Domenico Agasso

Translated by Sr. Louise Passero, FMA

BOOKS & MEDIA

BOSTON

Library of Congress Cataloging-in-Publication Data

Agasso, Domenico.
  [Maria Mazzarello. English]
  St. Mary Mazzarello : the spirit of joy / Domenico
Agazzo ; translated by Sr. Louise Passero, FMA.
      p.   cm.
  ISBN 0-8198-6989-9 (paper)
    1. Mazzarello, Maria, Saint, 1837-1881. 2. Christian saints—
Italy—Biography. I. Title.
BX4700.M43A3213   1996
271'.97—dc20
[B]   96-4557
                                                     CIP

Original title: *Maria Mazzarello Il comandamento della gioia*

Cover Credit: André Derain, *Paesaggio del mezzogiorno*
Photos from SEI Archives

Copyright © 1993, SEI—Società Editrice Internazionale
English edition copyright © 1996, Sr. Louise Passero, FMA

Printed and published in the U.S.A. by Pauline Books & Media,
50 St. Paul's Avenue, Boston, MA 02130.

Pauline Books & Media is the publishing house of the Daughters of
St. Paul, an international congregation of women religious serving
the Church with the communications media.

1 2 3 4 5   99 98 97 96

Contents

Introduction

She seemed to be the presence of God. This is one of the many things said of her while she was alive. It was a way of alluding to her capacity of multiplying herself, so as to be present at the right time, in the right place, for the right problem in her adventure of molding characters. Certainly, Mary Mazzarello did this, with her capacity for seeing and understanding, for nipping problems and difficulties in the bud. This was already much for someone like her who, born in the poor countryside, unschooled, became a scholar at thirty-five years of age to learn how to write. Even in this way, hers was the great adventure of a woman fulfilled on the highest levels during the most adverse times.

She also seemed to incarnate that presence for a deeper reason. By her exceptional capacity of infusing joy into faith, she succeeded in communicating the exultant certainty of a God who loves and saves, rather than one who is to be feared as judge because of his verdicts. Inherited from her mother, her characteristic cheerfulness became a magisterial element in her. It became a serene theology spread with the festive language of one who, though ignorant of Latin and Greek, knew how, with St. Paul "to be of help to all of you for the progress and joy of faith."

Mary Mazzarello and joy—here we have the synthesis of her biography. But be careful. We are not in the presence of the happy candor of an elect and rare creature. Her life was a battle, and cheerfulness was the weapon for her victory against weakness, falsehood, a resigned spirit and mediocre goals. Cheerfulness means clear vision and courage.

In the pages of this book, following Mary Mazzarello during her brief yet full human existence, we don't remain in the past. We are in the present. This story fits into the chronicle of our times very well, these deluded and fearful years, with their annoyances of so many inept teachers, times which are thirsting for credible witnesses. By her life, this daughter of peasants, deprived of goods and the right to vote, can teach at the school of trust and hope for today's men and women.

What did Mary Mazzarello know how to do with the women of her times, those little peasants of the hillsides, as she walked in the footsteps of John Bosco, and used all of her personal talents for them? How did she bring them to fulfillment, one by one, conquering weakness and fear, urging them to march forward? She found them resigned to limited horizons—the countryside, the farm, the hills—and she made them capable of crossing any frontier. She guided them for only a few years, but it was enough to see them spread throughout Italy, find a welcome in France, and finally travel to the then remote Latin America. They became leaders wherever they went.

In these pages Mary Mazzarello's adventure is lived together with that of the girls who were the first to bear, under her guidance, the name of Daughters of Mary Help of Christians. They were born in an Italian mountain village called Mornese. Today, their field of activity is the world.

Chapter One

The sermon dragged on and the bored little girl wasn't paying much attention to it. Punctual and attentive, she liked going to church. But she couldn't bear the long, pious talks, perhaps because there weren't many good preachers. The Piedmont area of Italy in the 1800's had two types of homilists: the pious exhibitionists of the pulpit, literati dedicated to "a sublimity of style or ingenious invention" which the people could not understand, and the thundering catastrophics who "claimed that they could only move the faithful by their noisy bravado and threatening tone." So complained the 17th century pastor, Francesco Bernardi, in one of his treatises on Christian doctrine.

Actually, the child's parish church at Mornese in upper Monferrato had better preachers, even future bishops and cardinals. But for her the sermon was always a heavy duty. It was like a long march with a knapsack on her back.

But when it was time for catechism, she became another person. Questions, answers and explanations were her daily bread. She won the doctrine contests and beat all the others. Best of all, she pushed herself forward to explain things to her peers and to give answers. "Always be ready," Peter the apostle exhorted the early Christians, "to respond to whosoever asks the reason for the hope which is in you." Perhaps these exact words were still unknown to her, and she was ready simply because from the time she was a little child she had questioned her father about God and humanity, about the "reasons for hope," and she loved his short, clear answers. He was her first catechist. Now, among her companions, it was she who tried to answer, accepting Peter's invitation even before she knew the text existed. She had hardly begun to read and did not know how to write, since only boys attended the village schools.

Mary Domenica was born on May 9, 1837 in one of the sectors of the municipality of Mornese called the "Mazzarelli." It had about 1200 inhabitants and was located on the border of Liguria. She was baptized on the same day she was born, by the pastor, Fr. Lorenzo Ghio. Her father was called Joseph and her mother, Mary Magdalen Calcagno, was a native of Tramontana, a village in the diocese of Genoa, not far from Mornese. Mary Domenica was the first of ten children. After her came Mary Felicita, born in 1839; Mary Catherine, born in 1841 and who died in 1842; Mary Magdalen, born in 1844 and who died after a few months; Dominic, born in 1846; Mary Filomena, born in 1848; Joseph, born in 1850; Mary Assunta, born in 1853; Mary Magdalen, born in 1857 and who died after a month; and finally Nicholas, born in 1859.

The Mazzarello family were farmers with a bit of their own land and another piece which they sharecropped. Toward the end of 1848 or the beginning of 1849, Joseph transferred his family to an important property which he had been sharecropping for some time, the Valponasca farm, about three quarters of an hour walk from the village. As did other properties of the area, it belonged to people of the patrician class of Genoa. The owners were the family of the Marquis D'Oria and the farm dominated a hilltop and vineyard. The great local resource was wine, an excellent product which usually found its way to Liguria by means of the mule trains which passed through.

When Mary Mazzarello was born, Mornese was a municipality in the district of Castelletto d'Orba, province of Novi, diocese of Acqui, division of Genoa, according to the old administrative order cited by Goffredo Casalis in his *Historical Dictionary of the Kingdom of Sardinia*. From the former Ligurian domination, important signs remained of the rapport between work, commerce and strong cultural ties. In these cities, those who were inclined toward professional studies usually went to Genoa; the priests were almost all from the archbishop's seminary at Genoa.

The territory and the people of Mornese play a major part in the story of Mary Mazzarello because it was not merely her native land with its tender memories, but it was also her battlefield. She is now a saint of the Church as teacher and cofoundress (with Fr. Bosco) of a women's congregation which is among the most dynamic of our times: the Daughters of Mary Help of Christians. Today, they are an active force of thousands throughout the world. This undertaking began in these vineyards, these forests, these houses and this church. She lived here for forty-two years, and died at age forty-four. Here she found her first guide in Fr. Dominic Pestarino, another native of Mornese. Here she formed her first major confederation, the first group of collaborators. These were girls destined to live a more or less ignored and obscure life. She transformed them into protagonists, guides and leaders. In the footsteps of Fr. Bosco, she changed their lives and horizons, without breaking with their native environment. This is one of the most original distinguishing features of the undertaking: the girls accepted the call to a supernatural ministry by remaining in their village and listening to her. She described their mission beyond oceans and continents with joyful, soft words, in the sober dialect of the hills and vineyards.

We must, therefore, know this land and this human environment. They were people with few means, little instruction and no right to vote. They were secluded people. The great ways of communication did not touch Mornese. Important events always happened somewhere else. When Mary Domenica was born, the most rapid connection between Turin and Genoa was still the mail coach, which, with many changes of horses, traveled the distance in twenty-five hours. At the time of her youth, the old people remembered a painful spectacle which had taken place in 1799 in the fields of Mornese—wounded and ragged French soldiers fled before the Russians commanded by General Suvorov, after the fall of Novi Ligure. For a brief moment, history touched the houses and vineyards of these peaceful people.

They also recalled the more recent events of the two periods which Pope Pius VII spent at Savona: the first from 1809 to 1812 as prisoner of Napoleon, under the surveillance of the military with a few faithful persons and some traitors; and the second, joyful occasion, in 1814 upon the fall of Napoleon, at the return from compulsory exile in France. In memory of the long adventure, Pope Pius VII instituted an annual feast in honor of Our Lady, invoked under the title of "Help of Christians," *Auxilium Christianorum,* to be celebrated on May 24, the date of the pope's return to Rome.

After three decades, that pontifical decision had some effect even in Mornese, where, in 1843, a votive chapel was built in honor of Mary Help of Christians. (Later, on the wall of a house of Via Valgelata, a Marian painting estimated to be from about 1814, but not after 1841, carried the inscription *Auxilium Christianorum.* Perhaps it was painted in fulfillment of a vow by survivors of the Napoleonic Wars.) At that time, little Mary Domenica Mazzarello was six years of age and still lived in the section of the Mazzarelli, not far from the little chapel built by the people in 1836 during the cholera epidemic.

As a result of the epidemic, the eldest of the Mazzarello brothers and his wife died, leaving two children. During those times, even poor families frequently assumed the consequences of great calamities on their own, because of the lack of public assistance and even because of a strong concept of dignity and decorum. So the two little children went to the homes of paternal uncles; Joseph welcomed Domenica, the older child, and Nicholas took in the second child, Mary.

The Suspicions of Charles Albert

A few weeks before the birth of Mary Mazzarello, on Thursday, April 4, 1837, the new Bishop, Modesto Contratto, made his official entry into Acqui. During the following June, the city had nothing less than the visit of the king, Charles Albert of Savoia Carignano, absolute sovereign of five million subjects. Surrounded by authorities he stopped, among other places, at the famous thermal baths; in the cathedral, he paid homage to St. Guido, patron of the diocese. It was a historic day for the citizens, and for many people who had come from the countryside.

However, to the untrusting eyes of the sovereign, the city and the diocese seemed somewhat suspicious, and during the visit he must have attentively scrutinized the ecclesiastical environment. At times, monarchs feel that they are both bishop and pope, or even anti-pope. Charles Albert strongly suspected that the city and the diocese harbored widespread and active Jansenism. It was a very dangerous sect, according to him, and a close accomplice of the secret societies which plotted to corrupt the pillars of established order, both on the sacred and secular levels.

Perhaps many pastors and priests of Acqui did not know that the king kept an eye on them even after the visit. Between the end of 1837 and the beginning of 1838, he wrote the

Réflexions Historiques in French, dedicating a page to these supposed Jansenists of the diocese: "They present themselves with great purity and rigidity of principles and virtues.... Under the now deceased bishop of Acqui, Bishop Sappa dei Milanesi, they had succeeded in introducing themselves into his diocese. That holy old man, possessing a great goodness and bent under the years, no longer feeling the strength to resist the evil, begged me to allow him to give up his diocese. Many pastors, having drunk of those principles and showing a great austerity, distanced their parishioners from the sacraments, making them feel that they were not worthy. In some municipalities only a small number of individuals could receive Communion, and then only at Easter time. Once the people were distanced from the sacraments, lack of religion and corrupt habits took over...the new bishop of Acqui has now put things in order in a most satisfying way."[1]

In Piedmont, the Jansenists were clerics who sustained the doctrine of Port-Royal, in conflict with both the Holy See and the throne; they were teachers of morality, scholars and pastors. Later, during the decline of this movement, those who were rigorous by nature concerning morality and sacramental absolution, and who for these reasons discouraged frequent access to the sacraments, continued to subscribe to Jansenism.

This habit of receiving Holy Communion only at Easter time was taking root also in Mornese. To approach the sacrament at other times and to receive it often was an inadmissible extravagance. This is the way things were and there was no way that Fr. Lorenzo Ghio, the elderly, almost blind pastor, could remedy the situation.

A young priest from Mornese, Fr. Dominic Pestarino, whom we have already mentioned, changed the situation. Born of a well-to-do family in 1817, he had studied theology and had been ordained in Genoa. It seemed as though he would be destined to work there, with responsibilities in the seminary and in priestly ministry. He formed valued friendships with priests a little older than himself, which helped his formation. Among them Joseph Frassinetti stood out. Ordained in 1827, he was noted for his publications and was nominated prior of Santa Sabina in Genoa. (He also had three brothers who were priests and a sister Paula, foundress of the Sisters of St. Dorothy, who was destined to be canonized by Pope John Paul II in 1984.) Other companions in studies were John Baptist Cattaneo, and the younger priest, Louis Sturla, the future cardinals of Reggio and Alimonda.

They were the outstanding figures among the young clergy, concerned that religious observance had become sterile in habitual practice. To give it new life it was necessary to begin from the beginning, that is, from the teaching of Christian doctrine, and to instill a new familiarity with the sacraments. So it was that they reconnected with St. Alphonsus de Liguori, cultivating in the people trust and love in God's mercy for all. Trust, hope and confidence were to be stimulated with the help of the sacraments. Therefore, it was necessary to receive Holy Communion not only at Easter, but at other times, often, even every day.

Here Frassinetti and his friends came up against the "rigorists." With other ecclesiastical authorities, they had been formed to an austere type of moral theology which had long been in force. In the confessional they confused many of the faithful by denying, suspending or delaying absolution. Because of this, there was scant possibility to receive Communion. A barrier had been formed between the people and the Eucharist.

"Benign" and "rigorous" priests opposed one another. Yet, this was not enough. In the renaissance spirit which had begun, even the difference in doctrine became a political encounter in Genoa, Turin and elsewhere, involving the clergy in the hopes and fears, the passions and adversities of the moment. The "rigorous" priests were regarded by their "benign" confreres almost as heretics of the Church and destroyers of the State. Conversely, every "benign" priest was judged by the others to be a hopeless reactionary, an enemy of Italy, dangerous to the Church, and a friend of the Jesuits, who were then being accused of every evil.

In Genoa, the conflict was further embittered by the traditional republican ferment, which the followers of Mazzini had rekindled in a national unitarian sense. This time also saw acute social unrest. In 1847 during his Genoese sojourn, Charles Albert had been heartily welcomed by the liberals who asked for a constitution. But an elderly seaman who had been admitted to speak with him had said: "Your Majesty, after you have pleased these gentlemen, think a little about the poor people."

Thus, when the Italian constitutional movement took off, the demand for liberty in Genoa was more severe and seasoned with Jacobite ingredients. The first was the attack against the Jesuits, who were immediately expelled, as were the "benign" clergy as friends of the Jesuits. Even the catechetical and formative works created by the Frassinetti group were suppressed. They had to leave Santa Sabina and hide in the houses of friends. Leaving Genoa, Fr. Sturla reached Arabia, and started missionary work in the territory of Aden.

It was not enough. A delegation was immediately sent to Turin to ask Charles Albert to expel the Jesuits from the whole kingdom. The fiery delegates, without being aware of the fact, instead gave Camillo di Cavour the opportunity of beginning his public life. As A. C. Jemolo wrote: "In January of 1848, the Genoese delegation arrived in Turin to ask for the expulsion of the Jesuits.... [Cavour] observed that if a danger had to come about, it would have been better to have it for something more serious than the emptying of some convent, and obtained, instead, that they ask for a constitution."[2]

In 1847 even Fr. Dominic Pestarino had left Genoa. From

what we know, he must have tranquilly said good-bye to the prospect of a fairly good career, given the quality of his preparation. He did not go elsewhere and did not follow other projects. He simply decided to go to Mornese. Upon his arrival he told his fellow villagers: "I was offered various places, but I will remain here in your midst, if you give me the work I'm looking for." At first he did not even have an official placement in the parish, but that didn't matter. He could live on his family means, since the Pestarinos were fairly well off. The pastor, Fr. Ghio, had illnesses and was satisfied with letting him carry on. Thus, the *previn* ("little priest" in the local dialect), at thirty years of age, became the new voice in the parish of Mornese. Even ten-year-old Mary Mazzarello came to church to listen to him.

Holy Communion, Almost a Scandal

At ten years of age the child, like her peers, already knew a little bit about the life of an adult. Without the hope of any type of schooling, she entered the work force as soon as possible. Above all, she cared for her younger sisters and brothers and helped her mother at home. Very soon, she began to work in the vineyards with her father and the farm hands. The schedule of the good weather was linked to the course of the sun.

When she was about eight years old, she was away from home for a while. Her parents allowed her to go to their childless relatives, the couple John Baptist Bodrato and Catherine Pestarino, to keep them company. Frequently, living away from home could last for an extended time, transforming it into a type of adoption. Perhaps the Bodratos had thought of something similar for her, since they accepted and treated her as a daughter. Catherine, the wife, also dedicated herself to Mary's Christian formation. Perhaps it was even too much: prayers and more prayers, visits in church which almost became a sojourn, and then certain showy devotions which placed her in an embarrassing situation. As she would say much later: "I liked to be good, but without staying all those hours in church and without making it so evident to others." So after a few months she willingly accepted the decision of her parents, who recalled her to help with her younger siblings.

The transfer to the Valponasca farm changed the life of the Mazzarello family, with the distance from Mornese which grew in the wintertime when snow and ice blocked the shortcuts. In those moments the great building seemed like a type of fortress, high and isolated above the modest valleys. Within, the little community of the family continued to grow, dominated by the voice of the mother. Mary Magdalen Calcagno was expansive and cheerful (Mary Domenica inherited this). She liked to joke, but at times she carried on excessively with advice and counsels. She liked to talk. Joseph, the father, was more concise in speech and commanded obedience with few words.

From both parents Mary Domenica and the other children received their first religious formation. Her father, in particular, began to explain those points of Christian doctrine which he knew. In the *Cronistoria* of the Institute of the Daughters of Mary Help of Christians we read: "She learned [the catechism] from her father's lips, when she was still too small to go to the parish church. This went on as long as her dad could answer her demanding questions. She was not satisfied with any sort of reason, but when faced with a problem, she wanted to see it through."[3]

With her father's help, Màin (as she was called at home) began her personal battle against illiteracy. She fought long and hard, with measured, slow successes. At first, with great effort, she learned to read. Writing was not even thought of, and arithmetic meant being able to do sums using her fingers.

During Lent, her mother accompanied her to catechism lessons with the pastor, Fr. Ghio. Then Fr. Pestarino came along and began his peaceful revolution in the area of religious practice. Instead of making abrupt changes, he completed, added and enriched. Above all, he explained. He explained to young people and the elderly the real reasons for the gestures which many made merely out of habit. He had the gift of making himself understood by the people of Mornese. He was one of them and knew them intimately. After some time, there was a surprise. Someone in the crowded parish church dared to go to Communion, even outside of Easter time. Then, gradually, others began to imitate him. It was as though they only needed a push. Among the first to accept frequent Communion was Joseph Mazzarello.

His daughter Mary Domenica, as we have said, began to go to catechism lessons. Coming from the farms, at first she was not considered to be at an advantage because she was "Mary Domenica from Valponasca." Even in small villages there is some doubt about the ability of those who live in the countryside. At Castelnuovo d'Asti a teacher accused the student John Bosco of having copied in class because his work was too well done for "someone who comes from Becchi," a few hovels scattered among cows and chickens. When little Mary Mazzarello stood out for her quick learning and exact answers, some marveled: "How bright the little one is...and to think, she comes from a farm...."

On September 30, 1849, she received the sacrament of Confirmation at Gavi, from Bishop Aleramo Pallavicini. With regard to her First Holy Communion, her biographies had long placed it in April 1848, when she was eleven years old. However, new documents found in the parish archives of Mornese give the correct date. It was in 1850 that Mary Domenica Mazzarello received the Eucharist for the first time, and "we may hold as most probable that it was during the first days of April." We owe this correction to the research of Maria Esther Posada, in her volume *Attuale perché vera.* According to her information the erroneous date previously indicated may come from a mix-up of names. In April 1848 the register states that "Domenica of Valponasca" received her First Communion. This was not the future saint, but rather the orphan cousin who had been welcomed into the home of Mary Domenica.

Maria Esther Posada observes: "We should not marvel at the reception of First Holy Communion at almost thirteen years of age if we think of the practice of the times, a practice which began to weaken at Mornese due to the renewal brought by Fr. Pestarino, formed at the more decisive Frassinetti school which proposed frequent, even daily Communion."[4]

This period of Maìn's life coincides with the events following the first war for Italian independence. Two failed military campaigns tragically concluded in the Austrian victory at Novara in March 1849, which forced Charles Albert to abdicate in favor of his son Victor Emanuel II and go into exile in Portugal. On the day on which Mary Domenica received the sacrament of Confirmation at Gavi, the Marquis Brignole Sale of Genoa, new ambassador of the Sardinian kingdom in Austria, left for Vienna. The two governments had made peace and had reestablished diplomatic relations.

In the autumn of 1849, Charles Albert, unexpectedly, was once again spoken of in upper Monferrato. People went to see his last "passing," in a coffin bearing the royal crown. He died at Oporto on July 28, 1849. During the first days of October, the warship *Monzambano* carried the body to Genoa. The funeral cortege moved toward Turin on horseback, traveling a week with stops at Pontedecimo, Ronco Scrivia, Novi Ligure, Alessandria, Asti, Poirino, Carignano and finally, Superga, where he would remain forever.

The lost war brought new renunciations for the kingdom, on both sides of the mountains, on land and in Sardinia. Great resources had been destroyed. It was necessary to restore the balance of the State by hard sacrifices, and also to pay the war indemnity to the Austrian victors. That was not all. Upper Monferrato also felt an event which had happened in Genoa at the end of March 1849, after the defeat of Novara. Wicked voices spread the news of an imminent Austrian attack against the city. A revolution broke out against the monarchy and against the Piedmontese. These were terrible days; some officials were arrested at the onset. Others were killed, after having attempted resistance. Finally, a division of the army "reconquered" Genoa as though it were an enemy city, and there were shootings, looting and brutalities on both sides. The consequences devastated the economy of the city and the Ligurian and Piedmontese back countries.

At this time Maìn was already a steady worker. She was so strong that she could keep up with the men, and a few of them had problems keeping up with her. She worked like this year after year, and she became famous for it in the village.

Not all days are the same, however. She had her moments of fatigue and impatience with certain long or petty, interminable tasks. For example, bending over the earth, she had to tie the new vines which sprouted. She had done it over and over again, but one day "the vines were endless," as she herself later admitted. So in order to finish more quickly, instead of tying the vines, she cut them away.

But she could not keep it a secret. She went to tell Fr. Pestarino, and found a severe welcome. The "little priest" was inflexible. Here's how she told the story in the *Cronistoria:*

"You should have heard Fr. Pestarino! How he scolded me! I didn't think it was such a serious matter, since we had so many vines. Yet, he said 'who knows how much they were worth and what they could have become.'"[5] It was an invaluable lesson in ethics.

Neither Fear Nor Sadness

Actually, the priest did not make allowances for Màin, even though he saw her making sure progress. Take confession, for example. She didn't like it and didn't feel like going. It was another allergy, like her aversion to the sermons. Yet, she had the example of her mother, who was assiduous in going to confession, as were the other girls. It wasn't easy. Once she understood its importance, she made firm, decisive strides, but without much enthusiasm.

It was not a sudden change, because Màin did not like making a scene. Later, the duty of confession would be enriched for her, becoming a serene necessity, and sometimes a dramatic urgency. Once she even ran over the hillsides looking for a confessor. But it wasn't like this at the beginning. Then confession was a heavy effort which she imposed upon herself. It was an act of adult will. She reasoned: "I don't like it very much, but I have to do it."

Fr. Pestarino never seemed to give up on her undeniable success, her sure results. He continued expecting much from her. More and more, almost with a special obstinacy he called her to difficult and unpleasant trials, to measure and test the gifts which he was discovering in her. Trusting and exacting, he placed before her continual challenges even in little things, making her understand that certain results are not open to all, but definitely to her: "You can do more, and therefore you must."

They were carefully reasoned and motivated challenges, with clear goals for a girl who always had to understand what she was doing. Guided in this way, she arrived at explaining to herself the reason for certain serious commitments which the priest imposed on her. At first glance these commitments were incomprehensible, bizarre and even ridiculous, such as renouncing innocent touches of finery in her dress, and "aging" her bright new boots with grease, to conquer the weakness of showing them off.

(Don Bosco worked among his boys in the same way: the masons, the porters, the stragglers whom he collected along the byways of Rome and the very young clerics to whom he gave heavy duties. Something sparked in one and the other when they heard his voice or read in his eyes those words: "You can do it.")

Ferdinand Maccono, biographer of Mary Mazzarello, worked with eyewitnesses of his time. He questioned her surviving peers, a few companions of her spiritual adventure, male and female relatives and people from her village. Through their testimony we see the girl of the Valponasca come alive and grow. Between one remembrance and another, one episode and another, it becomes a testimony of transformation.

Mary Domenica Mazzarello was a girl like so many others, subject to the same rude pedagogy of the life of the poor, to the same enthusiasms and discouragements and life crises. But at the same time, the many testimonies about her merge to describe something new from which her hidden personality emerges, which is manifested in flashes, in brief moments, in a gesture, an exclamation. This ordinary girl was moving toward an unknown future, through ordinary ways.

In her we see a leader, with a character which we already know. She was a leader who did not seek after command, and one who acted with uniform naturalness, without dramatic moments which she detested. Even when she would be in a position of command, this was the style of her orders: she recommended "cheerfulness, obedience and working without 'gena' [fear]...never sadness which is the mother of tepidity. Be courageous and make these dear, dear sisters happy."

Mary Domenica was revealing an ever more refined capacity to call people to herself and to help them walk along with her. The ever attentive Fr. Pestarino watched over this growth, guiding her energies and smoothing this sometimes rough metal. The work of formation began with her behavior toward those closest to her, the people in her home, her brothers and sisters, her cousin Domenica who lived with them, and friends and fellow townspeople.

The witnesses questioned by Maccono say: "Fr. Pestarino wanted her to bear with their defects without complaint; never avoiding anyone because of antipathy; not distancing herself from any companion due to diversity of character or natural repugnance...moderating her too lively and authoritarian character; not allowing impatient acts or words to escape her, even though she was working alone; she was to be calm and humble; she should treat all with sweetness and charity."

These precepts were not imparted to one who was by nature a model of submission and meekness. For her, instead, it was unthinkable to remain neutral, in any situation or dispute. She would say what she had to say quickly, expecting agreement, and a contrary opinion would cause her temper to flare up. She would become, as the *Cronistoria* tells us, "flushed, with a marked trembling of her lip." This is why Fr. Pestarino kept a tight rein on her, much as the farmers did with fiery colts.

But he never needed to urge her to participate in Holy Mass. She went daily, going down from the Valponasca early in the day, in any kind of weather. Mass was celebrated early because the people had to get to work. The participation of the faithful was still good, even though it was not possible to distinguish between passive, habitual attendance and solid conviction. She, certainly, was well aware of what she was doing. She made an effort to have her companions of those early morning walks, her cousin Domenica, her sister Felicina (Mary Felicita) and other girls who joined them in the village, understand it also. The most assiduous among them was Petronilla Mazzarello, who had the same surname but was not a relative. She was a year younger than Mary. The daughter of a school teacher, she knew how to read and write. They had made their First Holy Communion together and their friendship lasted a lifetime.

Going from the farm to the church was a stupendous walk during the good season, which invited them to run and jump along the hillsides, over fields and through woods in the enchanting dawn. It was much more difficult during the winter. Shortcuts were cut off, and therefore the road was longer. They faced rain, snow and mud, and the church was so cold that the wooden clogs which they wore, having become soaked, would freeze to the pavement. They had to leave early during the difficult season, and at times they arrived at church to find the door still locked. Then they took refuge in a nearby house or stable, waiting for Mass. At other times, the girls lit small bonfires to warm themselves.

Fr. Pestarino called the faithful to church even during the evening hours for prayer meetings and Eucharistic benediction, according to the custom of the times. Mary could not go down to the village another time, but she found a way to participate in these events. Let us allow the admirable simplicity of Ferdinand Maccono to describe this: "She observed that the house had, on the western side, a little window which looked out toward the parish church, and she would go to that window. Seeing the reflection of the far off flicker of the lit candles, she would unite herself to the people in thought and she adored Jesus, and thanked him for the good day and asked his blessing."[6] After a while, her mother noticed this habit, and then the whole family would go to that window for evening prayers.

This is a little fact of domestic history, but it indicates that Maìn was becoming a point of reference for her family in its life of piety. She did not pressure or insist on this, perhaps she didn't even think about it. In all simplicity, her habit "of the window" was pleasing to all in that house. The impetuous girl had experienced in a small way the persuasive vigor of the calm sweetness which Fr. Pestarino recommended.

Her familiar influence in the area of religious practice was also due to another fact: she had learned to read. She was always seen with a book in her hand, even during the pauses in work (just like Johnny Bosco in the pasture). She always had ready a quotation from the *Imitation of Christ* or St. Alphonsus de Liguori *(The Practice of Loving Jesus Christ, Eternal Maxims),* or even from the 17th century book *The Exercise of Perfection and Christian Virtue,* by the Jesuit Alfonso Rodriguez, the lives of saints and other texts to which Fr. Pestarino was gradually introducing her.

Books, printed material, instruction—Fr. Pestarino was one of those who could see clearly, even in moments of confusion. In the Piedmontese statute, one of the fundamental victories was freedom of the press. It brought about discussion, criticism and encounters and it experienced the defects of every new undertaking: animosity, impatience, inexperience, verbal outrage. A great political battle raged which involved the Church with the "revolutionary laws," first against ecclesiastical immunity and then for the suppression of religious orders, with the confiscation of their goods. In the press the controversy had passionate tones on both sides, and anticlerical polemics often became a frontal attack against religion and its principles. During the early years, the Piedmontese bishops often addressed collective documents to the faithful, to exhort them to keep far from these newspapers.

Today, reading about certain furious and coarse attacks against the faith, and certain anguished complaints of pastors and believers, gives one a dramatic, misleading sensation, as though the "gates of hell" had conquered. There was, instead, an extraordinary mix of things both new and old, of sunset and dawn. Certain usages connected with the "religion of the State" (such as the signs of mourning in the army on Good

Friday) were abandoned or suppressed. Yet the great leaders of 19th century sanctity were already on the scene. The seeds of ideas were planted, the embryos of the works of social Catholicism of the last century. All this happened in the midst of anticlerical furor. (We probably owe them our thanks!)

In the midst of the complaints about the attacks on the Church, some people thought concretely about accepting the battle, giving life to a Catholic press, ready to fight. One of the most attentive was Fr. Bosco. In 1851 he began to publish *The Friend of Youth,* but it did not go well. The magazine folded after only a few months. He tried again in 1853, starting *Catholic Readings,* a pocket-sized monthly magazine which spread first throughout Piedmont and then all Italy.

In Genoa, Joseph Frassinetti, the learned priest who knew how to mold himself with singular efficacy into a popular publicist, quickly accepted the battle. His texts were brief, edited in the style of the times, but he had a capacity for simplification which rendered them accessible to all. Among the most popular, *A Girl Who Wanted to Belong Completely to Jesus,* was widely read in Mornese. Then there were *Spiritual Friendships, Imitation of St. Teresa of Jesus, The Art of Becoming a Saint, The Jewel of a Christian Family.* All were good "companions for the journey," even for the future of Mary Mazzarello. There were also timely biographical sketches of contemporary Christian figures.

To Believe Even When You Are Alone

Old and new things were everywhere. In 1844 Charles Albert approved the project to build in Piedmont a network of railroads which would link Turin with Genoa on the one side and with Lago Maggiore on the other, having Alessandria as a junction. Two years later, the young Camillo di Cavour was excited over the project of a railway from Turin to Chambèry:

"This line...will be the point of union of the north and the south, the place in which the people of the Germanic and Latin races will come to exchange products and lights, an exchange which will profit principally the Piedmontese nation, which already participates in the quality of the two races. It is a marvelous perspective, a magnificent destiny."

One of the first lines on which thousands of workers began was the Turin-Genoa line. Every step of its progress was celebrated as they went along: Trofarello, Asti, Novi...in August 1853 the newspaper *The Corriere Mercantile* of Genoa still spoke of an incident with horses and carriages: "The stagecoach of the Bonafous Line overturned as it descended from Giovi, and it is feared that some of the travelers were seriously wounded." But under Giovi the tunnel was ready for the train which on December 6, would make its first direct journey from Turin to Genoa, with Camillo di Cavour and a few ministers of state on board. Even this time the little village of Mornese was left out. The great work barely touched it, but it was an enormous advantage to have the stations of Arquata and Ronco Scrivia at hand and thus be able to arrive quickly at Genoa and Turin.

It seemed as though new things almost always come to the countryside from the city, and a few people complained about it. But in this 1853, which saw the great novelty of the train arrive at the sea, in Mornese a small novelty was coming to life, which was destined to favor another of historical import.

The novelty, still at the beginning, was a twenty-one-year old girl who spoke to a priest. Her name was Angela Maccagno. She lived with her widowed mother, helped in the parish and knew the grief of the priests and faithful for so many dangers against the faith. But she was convinced that "fleeing from evil conversations" was not enough. She had been gradually meditating on an idea, mentioning it to the priest, Fr. Pestarino. Now the idea had become a more definite proposal in the great plan.

Angela explained to Fr. Pestarino, "Wouldn't it be wonderful if, in these troubled times for the nation, while sects are agitating the people and subverting them against the Church and religion, there were women who would bear arms against arms. To work, that is, without noise and without having anyone know, to bring God back into families and the State, to make the Church and the pope, so badly treated during these painful years, loved once more?"[7]

It must have been a beautiful day for Fr. Pestarino. His efforts at catechetical and pastoral updating had not only won followers, but it had even inspired projects. Angela Maccagno's idea consisted in creating at Mornese a "pious union" for girls who decided to live a certain type of consecration. Without becoming sisters, they would pronounce a temporary and renewable vow of chastity, and obey a priest called their director, or a companion designated by him. Their aim was to transform themselves into an exemplary community, in models of lived faith, detachment and silence. Angela said that these young people were to be "more detached from the world than those who live in retirement." They were to have no direct rapport with men, "not even to convert them." Through prayer and example they were to bring back those who had left their religious practice and, beyond this, there were to be only discreet interventions through sisters, wives and mothers.

They were to practice modesty, reserve, amiability and patience. With regard to firmness of faith, they would be inflexible: even though "all were to become cold in religion and piety, the sisters were to remain firm even at the cost of persecution from relatives, friends, people or even religious who preached to the contrary." The sisters would have no special habit, but would dress like everyone else. They would continue to live with their families (except in the case of one who remained alone in the world; then the director would make arrangements for her).

They would also have a name. Since the dogmatic pronouncement on the Immaculate Conception was near, in her honor these girls would call themselves "The Daughters of the Immaculate." Fr. Pestarino had Angela prepare a rule of life, which he then sent to Fr. Frassinetti in Genoa for definitive drafting. Meanwhile, he didn't waste time. Fr. Pestarino founded the little group of the first Daughters, who were only five in number: Angela Maccagno, Maria Arecco, Rosina Mazzarello, Giovanna Ferrettino and finally, sixteen year old Mary Mazzarello. What about her friend, Petronilla Mazzarello? The "little priest" was not sure about admitting her to the group, at least not in the beginning, because she did not seem sufficiently mature for the type of life which was projected. Her piety was sincere, but she was still too exuberant and noisy. Then, too, Petronilla was only fifteen years old. From this moment on, however, one of Maìn's commitments was to help her to mature, in a friendly way, by example and good counsel, but also with playfulness—it was the pedagogy of the smile.

The group met in the house of Angela Maccagno who lived with her mother. There was no proselytizing, no haste. The preparation of these first members was essential. Under the guidance of Fr. Pestarino, they learned the practice of spiritual reading, and studied the religious situation and practices of their day.

In approximate, contemporary terms, the group had something of a nucleus of animation, something of pastoral counseling. All, naturally, was according to the form of the times, focusing primarily on example and on quiet counseling. The definitive rule was still missing. (Fr. Frassinetti had lost the original text, and would also lose the copy which came from Mornese.) Yet the little association soon became a vital reality in the church and in families. A new enthusiasm was noted in parish life and it was the work of the small semi-clandestine group, the Daughters.

During the same period and in the same climate of secrecy, on January 25, 1854, a similar event was taking place in Turin. There, it was among men, and the cleric Michael Rua summed it up for history this way: "We, Rocchietti, Artiglia, Cagliero and Rua, gathered in the room of Fr. John Bosco. We proposed, with the help of the Lord and St. Francis de Sales, to attempt the exercise of practical charity toward our neighbor, arriving at making a promise, and finally, if possible and convenient, of making a vow to the Lord. From that evening on those who proposed to follow this exercise were called *Salesians.*"

Some things disappear, while others take their place. The government of Turin was preparing, by the Rattazzi Laws, to suppress 331 houses of congregations and 4500 male and female religious, and to confiscate their goods. In silence, other new things were coming to life, like a mustard seed, at Valdocco and Mornese. They took place with delightful seriousness in both cases. Angela Maccagno said they wanted to work "without anyone noticing," and Michael Rua wrote their aim was "to carry out a practical exercise of charity."

Other events shook Europe. In March 1854 the Crimean War broke out, with Russia on one side and the English, French and Turks on the other. Even Piedmont would take part in 1855, contributing to the victory, and bearing its share of the combat and the cholera, along with a general disorganization which multiplied sufferings. In the *London Times* one could read the scandalized description of the war zone which W. H. Russel wrote: "Men advanced painfully and stumbled in the mud with whispered curses, or they allowed themselves to collapse on an outcrop of rock, exhausted, images of filth and unspeakable misfortune. At times, along the way, an exhausted, worn out soldier was overcome by illness and the sad vision of a dying comrade struck the passersby. This was even worse because help was impossible and the situation hopeless."[8]

A letter written by a Piedmontese soldier to his family summed up the extremity of the situation: "Here we do nothing else but die from morning to night."

For the Church, 1854 was the year of the dogmatic definition of the Immaculate Conception of Mary, pronounced by Pius IX on December 8: "The doctrine according to which the Blessed Virgin Mary, from the first moment of her conception, because of a particular grace of predilection on the part of Almighty God, in view of the merits of Jesus Christ, redeemer of the human race, was preserved from every stain of original sin, was revealed by God and must, therefore, be held firmly and immutably by all the faithful."

During this time a notice was sent from Genoa for the girls of the Mornese group. Fr. Frassinetti had found the draft of their rules and had rewritten the text and completed it, but without changing the substance. What is more, he was so pleased with Angela Maccagno's idea that he decided to imitate it and thus a pious union with the same name and the same scope was born in Genoa.

On December 9, 1855 at Mornese the little group officially initiated its life governed by the definitive rule, with a ceremony in the small chapel of Fr. Pestarino's house. It was a clandestine ceremony, according to Angela's initial recommendation: to work united and hidden, imitating in good what others do "in secret unions promoting evil...united from country to country, from city to city."

Only once did they appear in public together solemnly. On May 20, 1847 Bishop Contratto of Acqui approved the rules. On the 30th of that month, the bishop went to Mornese, and met them formally in church, in the midst of all the people. Then they returned to their hidden, silent work.

Chapter Two

Let's take a look at Mary Mazzarello's behavior in the group. She seemed to have found what she was looking for: a type of new family with certain rules, closely bound to the life of the parish, to the activity of the apostolate and to the practice of charity. It was a family unto itself, small and reserved, which did not, however, separate its members from their natural families. It was as though the Valponasca had been enlarged so that it could hold all the people of Mornese. The Union of the Daughters of the Immaculate was becoming more deeply (and gradually more cordially) a part of the lives of all.

The director and confessor of all the Daughters, Fr. Pestarino, was the head of the group. Officially, Angela Maccagno was like everyone else, part of it. Because of her maturity and level of culture, and because she had begun the group, she had a strong influence over the others. In practice, all treated her as the superior; Mary Mazzarello also did so with great tranquillity.

She was already quite different from the combative Main of just a short time before, who would blush at the first contradiction. Her capacity for self-control had grown; she knew how to control herself. At first sight one would say that she had been born to be a Daughter of the Immaculate, which she did effortlessly. But this was not true. Her serenity was a daily conquest; it required the daily victory of her will. It was an experience which she would later be able to transmit to her sisters in her letters: "Be attentive in conquering yourselves; if not, all will become heavy and insufferable, and like an infection, malice will rise in your hearts."[1] The knowledge of reading, gained in long, weary evenings at the Valponasca, now gradually multiplied other occasions for enrichment. The spiritual direction of Fr. Pestarino and, through him, that of Fr. Frassinetti, was and continued to be the "support" which sustained the growth of the vine. Then, of course, there was the vine itself: she, with all her vigor. She decided on certain fundamental steps simply, without much fanfare. We would say that it was almost with great ease, if we did not know that behind every step lurked a vast and at times tormented background of examination and research. Once she had made a decision, however, she never gave up. It was to be done, and that was it; there was no changing her mind, no self-complacency.

A document of this incisive capacity for decision can be found in the *Cronistoria,* with reference to the vow of chastity. Even before the Union of the Daughters of the Immaculate was born, she found herself among a group of friends discussing the fact that some intended to make the vow temporarily, and that Fr. Pestarino was encouraging or discouraging individuals case by case. "Mary, who was there in the midst, stood up and said: 'I don't understand why we have to ask permission for this for a certain time. I didn't ask anyone anything and I made it once and for all. I don't think I did anything wrong.' She was then about fifteen years of age."[2]

"I didn't ask anyone anything." Experts in the field of virtue would probably have something to say about humility and submission, which were not very evident here. But Mary

Mazzarello did not pretend to be an angelic creature; she was who she was. Her example could be imitated or not, but it showed her style; certain responsibilities are to be taken on one's own.

Fr. Pestarino's pastoral activity was devoted in great part to the families, especially to the mothers. Now, having seen the work of the Daughters of the Immaculate, he decided that they could assume this task. (In the microcosm of Mornese this was a clerical delegation not only to the laity, but to women. These were deep roots of a "novelty" so solemnly heralded today.)

Every Daughter of the Immaculate assumed responsibility for five mothers from a group put together by Fr. Pestarino, called the Union of Christian Mothers. They met regularly for prayer, spiritual reading, succinct conferences by the one in charge, and for much conversation on family situations, problems with children, exchange of experiences and suggestions. Mary Mazzarello was greatly interested in this work and gradually, her sayings and counsels began to circulate among the homes of Mornese. Everything about this girl, the youngest of the Daughters of the Immaculate, was authentic.

She had another victory: Petronilla Mazzarello became part of the group. This happened through dialogue, trust and counsel which Mary disguised in her lighthearted wit and contagious joy. Gradually, Petronilla came to resemble Mary, wanting to be one of the Daughters, and Fr. Pestarino allowed his former objections to fall. They were together again, with many roads awaiting their steps.

These roads could have been threatened at any moment by unforeseen chasms, even during this time of hope. Petronilla, shaken, discovered something which seems incredible: Mary Mazzarello, her friend, her counselor in difficult moments, the girl of joyful certainty, had fallen victim to a grave crisis. She who had trust and enthusiasm even for others was now a prisoner in a tangle of coldness and tedium.

A symptom of her surrender was that she gave up on joyfully approaching daily Communion. With an almost unbelievable fall into the old ways, Mary was ensnared in the old arguments of Jansenism; that is, she feared that those who approach the sacrament too frequently will allow their fervor to dry up and will even lack respect for the sacrament. She felt a weakening of her trust in self; she was overcome by a dark sense of her unworthiness, a kind of weariness, while she continued in her usual practices in a gray, mechanical way.

Her condition was described by Maccono on the basis of testimony given at that time: "She went through great anguish of spirit for some time, and began to feel an unusual sense of apathy, never experienced before. She prayed, but felt no comfort whatsoever; she went to Communion, and her heart seemed as cold as marble; she carried out the same practices of piety, but her former consolation had disappeared. God had withdrawn himself."

It was like crossing a desert, the night of the spirit which the great mystics had experienced and described. For her it was an unexpected blow. She knew nothing of these things which had come upon her so suddenly, and she was incapable of reacting. She could do only one thing: she told Petronilla everything.

Her friend could give her only one piece of advice: "Run to Fr. Pestarino." It was, naturally, the first idea which came to her mind at the early signs of the crisis, but she had done nothing, treating it as simply scruples and fear. Petronilla's voice, instead, urged her to take the step, which was, in itself, the first reaction of her will. The experience with the "little priest" helped her to free herself, and then she confided to Petronilla: "It's all over and I am as peaceful as before. How I suffered! Now I am content."

She reserved it as a precious experience for when she would be called upon to teach others how to avoid the ravines.

She did so without speaking like the Doctors of the Church, but was just as efficacious in her cordial simplicity: "Remember," she would write to a sister, "it is not enough to begin, you must continue to fight always, every day. Our self love is so refined that when it seems that we are a little ahead in something good, it makes us trip and fall."

The Black Year of the Epidemic

In autumn of 1857 Angela Maccagno temporarily left Mornese and went to Genoa. This was suggested by Fr. Pestarino who had an idea. He wanted to have an elementary school for girls in the village. Angela, the most instructed among the Daughters of the Immaculate, attended the "School of Method" in 1857-58 in Genoa. She returned to Mornese with the license of elementary school teacher for the lower grades. Thus the project was realized. The municipality decided to start the elementary school for girls and entrusted it to Angela Maccagno on August 11, 1858. Francis Bodrato was named teacher for the boys' school, since he had studied the course of methodology at Chiavari, finishing his studies on October 6, 1858. On November 12, he received his teacher's license for lower elementary grades.[3] Bodrato succeeded Francis Mazzarello, Petronilla's father, who, though not having completed the course for a formal license, had been teaching at Mornese.

At the beginning, however, the village did not know where to put the girls' school; there were no facilities. Maccagno then taught in her own house, which had a large room that could serve as a classroom. The Daughters of the Immaculate occupied the same desks on Sunday, when the new teacher held class. "Naturally, even Mary Mazzarello went," reports the *Cronistoria.*

Angela Maccagno's prestige in the village and among the

members of the Pious Union grew because of her teacher's license. Mary Mazzarello's admiration for her grew also. It was almost a type of voluntary dependence which the others laughed at. Her mother was also a little disturbed about this behavior. It seemed as though now Mary was less her daughter and would continue to consult with Angela even in minor things such as the color of a scarf or blouse. Mary accepted the teasing of her companions well enough; after all, she was the youngest. Even her mother managed to play down everything without much effort; there was no motive for resentment or jealousy. Everyone knew how devoted Maìn was to her family and the household duties. It was enough to see her efforts with Petronilla Mazzarello, and to see her cut back even on the time spent in church to help her sisters-in-law, who had so much work to do.

Once they called her *bula* (arrogant) because of her leadership qualities. Now it seemed that she enjoyed stepping back. She sought advice from Angela because she saw her dedication to that which we would today call a commitment for human and Christian advancement. Angela spread examples and encouragement of faith among the Daughters and at home; she brought instruction to those who never had it and opened her home to all in need. One could learn much by watching and listening to her.

This is how Mary learned humility as an exact science which does not bear with exceptions or variations; to deviate is to make a mistake. "Make a friend of humility and learn her lesson," she wrote one day to a sister. "Humble yourself without discouragement and then go forward courageously." She was frugal in speech and writing. Instead of long dissertations, she briefly urged humility and courage of action. It was her teaching and life story. The *bula* of adolescence urged her not to repress her native impulses, but to master them and to direct them, so as to move forward.

In 1858, a historical year for Mornese because of the birth of the girls' school, something new also happened in the life of the Mazzarello family: they went down from the Valponasca to live in the village. While all were out, thieves had come to the farmhouse, and they had stolen 700 lire, quite a sum for those times (the teacher Maccagno was paid only 250 for the entire scholastic year). Papa Mazzarello felt concerned about the safety of his family, and so he decided on the move, buying a house on Via Valgelata in Mornese.

In 1859 war broke out: the Piedmontese of Victor Emanuel II and the French of Napoleon III battled against Austria. There were recruitments, loans to the government for war expenses, requisitions, prohibitions of commerce...and a railway movement never seen before.

This was the first war of the train. Many French regiments traveled by train from Paris to Marseille. Then they reached Genoa by sea, and once more took trains toward Alessandria, Vercelli-Novara-Mortara, together with those who arrived with other convoys from Susa and Turin.

This time was not like 1848-49. This time the mayors received government notices of victory: Magenta, Solferino-San Martino. Their victories came at a dear price, especially the second, a double battle fought of the feast of St. John on June 24. It was the bloodiest day of the whole Italian *Risorgimento* (renaissance) with almost 5,000 deaths and 20,000 wounded between both sides.

The battles stopped, but not the course of independence. Many other telegrams with wild announcements reached the mayors, until that conclusive one of March 1861 which announced the birth of the Kingdom of Italy.

In 1859 something happened which was not reported in any newspaper. On Sunday evening, December 18, Don Bosco gathered a group of seventeen priests and clerics in his room at Valdocco. Together they made a decision reported in the

minutes of the meeting: "The members gathered together decided to erect a Society or Congregation which...proposed to
promote the glory of God and the well-being of souls, especially those most in need of instruction and education." After a
decisive "trial" on January 26, 1854, on the evening of December 18, 1859, the Pious Society of St. Francis de Sales was
born at the oratory of Valdocco, already a center of instruction
and education with its first schools and workshops.

Completely unknown to Mary Mazzarello, that evening
of 1859 put into motion something which radically concerned
her. It was something which would later reveal itself fully to
her, and would take every atom and energy of her existence.

Meanwhile, painful moments were being lived in
Mornese. In 1860 a typhoid epidemic spread suffering and
terror. Many people died, because at that time it was difficult
to prevent the illness. Relatives of the Mazzarellos also fell ill;
these included a seventeen-year-old cousin, Joseph; his mother
and father and an uncle; and four patients in the same house,
with the most serious among them a mother and her son. They
appealed to Fr. Pestarino and his Daughters of the Immaculate,
"who," says the *Cronistoria,* "had as their rule, the obligation
to assist the sick women of the village"—only the women.

Fr. Pestarino went to Mary's parents to ask them to send
her as a nurse to her relatives; they, especially the mother,
wanted her to come. Her parents reacted frankly to that request. Her mother pronounced a clear, unyielding no, because
her daughter was indispensable at home, and the risk was too
great. The father had at first also refused, then relented to a
degree. While he wouldn't send Mary to that house, he
wouldn't oppose her decision to go.

Mary had definitely decided not to go and she explained
why. It did not deal with taking care of only women; there
were also boys and men in that house, a situation which found
her disturbed and unprepared. She faced the danger of infec-

tion; she did not minimize her fears. She almost felt that she had already contracted the disease. However, she found the right words to answer Fr. Pestarino: "If you want, I'll go, even though I am sure that I'll catch it." She did not lose contact with reality, but she had decided that her will must not prevail over the call to service. In her humble response, perhaps the priest saw echoes which came from afar, from the Lake of Tiberias, on a day of unlucky fishing. Yet, we cannot help but think also of the Garden of Olives.

Death Knocked at the Door

"Yet, I'm sure that I'll catch the disease." Though she repeated these words more than once, she still went to that house. She stayed there for a whole month, working full time for the healthy and the sick, until it seemed as though all were healed, even the mother who had been the most seriously ill. She worked wonders among those relatives, and they could not thank her enough. There was no end to the admiring descriptions of her work as nurse for the sick and governess for the younger children who did not fall victim to the typhoid. Her cousin, Joseph, tells us that he was surprised at her "jovial ease." He hadn't expected it, having seen Mary only from afar, absorbed in prayer in church. There, instead, in her field of work, she showed not even the shadow of the feared embarrassment or worry.

Mary returned home with the gratitude of the whole family, but also with the dread typhoid in its most serious form. The illness struck on the day of the Assumption with a high fever, and it nailed her to bed for fifty-two days, with grave crises which brought her to death's door. She received the last sacraments and a crown of flowers was ordered for her funeral.

The Daughters of the Immaculate took turns in caring for her; the doctor had given up hope. Mary felt close to death and she prepared herself as for an important task. It was like when she was at the Valponasca, and during the evening hours they sharpened sticks to be used in sustaining the fragile vines. With the typhoid (and even without) many people died at her age, twenty-three. The girl with whom Angela Maccagno stayed in Genoa was only twenty; Rosa Pedemonte died from the "subtle illness" (tuberculosis). Mary had met her at Mornese where she had come with Angela, still hoping that the good air of the hills would cure her. Rosina lived twenty splendid years. It was enough for her to realize herself as Mary was doing. With this thought, Mary prepared herself for death, attentive to its coming. In her room everything had to be in order and ready for *that* moment.

But the moment did not come. Her fever fell and the doctor declared her to be convalescing. He warned, however, that she was still not out of danger because of her general physical condition.

In fact, Mary stayed indoors for the whole winter of 1860-61. Her cure came with the springtime. She rose from her bed another person. She was not, nor would she ever be, the vigorous young woman who feared no effort in the vineyard. At twenty-four years of age she found herself fragile and vulnerable. She found that she could not call up her previous energy. There would be no more long runs over the hills to gain a half hour for prayer, no more working during the night to have an hour free in the morning.

Prepared to die, she suddenly returned to life. However, she seemed to find herself destined to an unexpected, different kind of life, one with limits which she had never imagined.

In *Attuale perchè vera* Maria Esther Posada writes: "The illness cut off the strength of the young Mary Mazzarello and gave her the opportunity of having an in-depth experience of her physical, psychological and spiritual fragility. In the depths of this experience she found the strength to take up only a trusting abandonment to God, understood and known in a new light. This strength and this light were nothing more than the virtue of hope which, infused in Baptism together with that of faith and charity, acquired greater vigor and luminosity in the purifying moment of the trial."

Mary Mazzarello, in fact, during her first visit to the parish church after the illness, prayed "in a new light," and serenely asked: "Lord, if you have willed to give me still some years of life, grant that I may pass them ignored and forgotten by all, except you."

Ignored, forgotten...but not resigned. She was alive, and had an idea which she felt like a calling. It had been germinating in her mind for a while now, and had grown slowly during the long days of her convalescence.

The idea was about those children whom Angela Maccagno was teaching to read and write. It was a wonderful accomplishment, but they had to do more, to develop them by also teaching some useful work, occupying themselves with the religious formation of later years. This was the substance of the idea—*to dedicate one's life.*

(For Mary there was also a vision of the Mornese countryside; a mysterious event which seemed to have indicated this undertaking to her. But when she confided it to Fr. Pestarino, his reaction was quick and conclusive: enough with these fantasies. I don't even want to hear about them.)

Feet firmly planted on the ground, Mary explained her project to Petronilla. It was a spring morning in 1861. From Turin, Victor Emanuel II, now king of Italy, governed 22,000 subjects. At Valdocco Don Bosco was expanding his oratory and school, spending 100,000 lire to buy and adapt the Filippi house. The two girls of Mornese had gone to the "borders of the fields" to talk, and Mary's project came up: the two of them should go to the men's tailor, Valentino Campi, to learn the trade, so they would later be ready to start a workroom-school. "We will be able to support ourselves...*and we can also spend our whole lives for the good of young girls."* It was the turning point of their existence, announced with the least possible number of words.

They began to work after Easter 1861. By day they went to the tailor's shop and by night they sewed at Angela Maccagno's house. At the beginning of 1862, they left Valentino Campi to set out on their own. Truthfully, they had only mediocre success, because they were still so green. May presented them with a new opportunity. The only seamstress of Mornese had gone to live elsewhere. So it was that Mary and Petronilla remained alone in the field, changed into "seamstresses for ladies," inheriting the clientele. Most important of all was the fact that some of the mothers brought their little girls to learn to sew. All of the families of Mornese trusted them.

Finding a location presented a problem. It had to be large enough for the number of students. They wanted a bright, sunny building near the church. After some unsatisfactory attempts, a suitable place was found in the house of one of Angela Maccagno's brothers. It was for rent, which had to be paid punctually. The apprentices paid a modest fee in money or materials, and then there were the proceeds from the work on new or repaired children's clothing. The clients were fairly numerous.

With regard to the religious formation of the children, Mary remembered the weight of certain long sermons and the endless pious practices to which she was subjected as a child. This is why she simplified matters even here: brief individual prayer upon entering, before a little statue of the Immaculate, and a certain freedom to chat while they worked. When the conversation lagged, it was she who would reanimate the group with a brief reading (especially from the lives of the saints) or a song in honor of Our Lady. There was no fixed time or schedule; she was interested in seizing the moment of highest interest between one conversation and another.

Naturally, Mary and Petronilla were still part of the Daughters of the Immaculate. This group had grown in number and other pious unions with this title had arisen in a few cities of upper Italy. Interest grew for this new type of consecration, and then they discovered that it was not really new. In the 16th century, groups like theirs had been organized, among them the Ursulines, founded by Angela Merici of Desenzano sul Garda, who died in 1540.

Starting out alone, Angela had dedicated herself to the education of poor children. Later, the undertaking became permanent with the help of many young people, who by 1535 constituted a group living under a rule, becoming the "Humble Company of St. Ursula," called Ursulines. Their principal task was to educate girls in a Christian manner, teaching them a trade, and assisting the sick who had been abandoned by their families.

This movement was not looked upon with favor by all because it revolutionized feminine religious life. At that time being a "consecrated woman" meant always and only "a woman in a convent." This, instead, was different. They had neither convent nor habit, dressing in lay clothes, nor did they depend on any male religious order. Furthermore, the Ursulines did not leave their families; they had no church or chapel of their own, but chose to pray with others instead.

They didn't last because they were changing too many things. The Ursulines were forced to abandon that which made them unique and to become a cloistered congregation. It was thought that only in this way could a woman attain personal sanctity. This brought an end to an inspired attempt to answer the call to a direct apostolate and the practice of charity among the sick and suffering of those times.

Pope Pius VII rendered justice to Angela Merici by canonizing her. On July 11, 1861, Pius IX wrote a document inviting a renewal of the spirit of the Ursulines, updated according to new needs.

The gifted Fr. Frassinetti had discovered Angela Merici's life. He immediately adhered to the Holy Father's exhortation, placing himself in accord with Fr. Pestarino for a renewing of the Daughters' rule. In the *Cronistoria* we read that he "modified the first rule of Mornese, blending it with that of St. Angela, adapting it to the times, and formed one alone, which was printed during that year with the title: *Rule of the Daughters of Holy Mary Immaculate under the protection of St. Ursula and St. Angela Merici.*"[4]

The new rule stated that a "prioress" should be elected to be the head of a community. But the Daughters of Mornese had already had this in Angela Maccagno, and they only had to continue, since all approved. The group now called themselves the "New Ursulines," but they continued to use the original name for some time.

"It Would Be Better to Heat the Broth"

Mary's parents and Petronilla's brothers-in-law were not too keen on this idea of the girls becoming seamstresses. It was only the beginning, however; they would see many other new things. The two girls found it perfectly natural that the little workroom would have other persons and problems. More and more came and were accepted without worrying about "compatibility." Everyone and everything was all right.

A widowed peddler in Mornese was left with two little girls, six and eight years old. He found it difficult to care for them and to go to the market, so he asked Mary and Petronilla to take them in, and they did so. At first the children were cared for only during the day, going to stay with their grandmother at night, but the father preferred that they remain even during the night. Fr. Pestarino gave permission, and Petronilla stayed with them, first in the house where the workroom was situated, then later in the house across the street, where two rooms had been rented. Soon another guest arrived; it was Petronilla's fourteen-year-old niece, Rosina Mazzarello.

In 1863 we find a little workroom, a small hospice, and soon after, a meeting place for girls. Every Sunday Mary and Petronilla gathered the girls of the village in the workroom and little courtyard. Many came, drawn by their popularity and that unique opportunity to be happy together, with all of the novelties that Mary invented to allow them to enjoy themselves. Ferdinand Maccono emphasized her special gift of animator during those occasions: "She was not afraid of noise, nor the racket they made nor any other disturbance, as long as there was no danger for body or soul."

Certainly she hadn't decided, premeditated and planned to act in this manner. This was simply the way it was, and with the girls she could act no other way. A comparison comes immediately to mind: this was the same way Don Bosco, whom Mary Mazzarello did not yet know, acted with his boys.

In 1863 Don Bosco set his hand to two unusual initiatives: the creation of a minor seminary, with the support of the bishop in Mirabello, in the diocese of Casale; and the construction of the great sanctuary dedicated to Mary Help of Christians. At the moment, his institute had 600 resident students with five classes of high school, shops for tailoring, bookbinding, shoemaking, wood and iron working and printing, along with the school of music. For him, one of the most beautiful moments of the day was that of noise, when the courtyards and playgrounds of Valdocco were filled with yelling boys.

Though there was a diversity in volume and number, Mary Mazzarello enjoyed the same contentment with the noise and laughter of the girls at the Maccagno house, in the small courtyard which could be called an oratory. She didn't call it this because she didn't even know the word. When the weather permitted, she organized outings to more open, freer surroundings. Even this was one of Don Bosco's famous customs.

Maìn's popularity grew even more (but along with it, a lack of understanding on the part of others) when she invented a carnival. Carnival or *Carnevale* in Italian, was a time of dancing and carousing just before Lent of each year. The parish priests warned the people about the consequences of rowdiness and uncontrolled behavior. In many places, they invited the faithful to penitential functions in church during the time of the celebrations.

Maìn's strategy was completely different. Instead of prohibitions, she sent out invitations to celebrate the carnival with her. There would also be dancing among the girls. She found a concertina and someone to play it and the Maccagno house was filled with the sounds of laughter and dancing in the courtyard and workroom. She even prepared a carnival feast with the flour, eggs and wine which families donated for the occasion.

After this, the young people of Mornese followed Mary into Lent, when she conducted catechism classes. They also celebrated various liturgical days throughout the year, such as the Marian celebrations, the feast of St. Aloysius Gonzaga, and novenas.

At the time of the month of May, the *Cronistoria* had a serious but extremely telling note about the poverty of the countryside in religious practice: "The pastor, Fr. Ghio, from the very beginning was somewhat opposed (to the solemn celebration of the Marian month) because the poverty of the church could not bear the increased expense for a greater use of candles. Fr. Pestarino asked the faithful for help and 'a woman began to offer candles, and her example was immediately imitated by many.' In this way at the function of the closing of the month of May, the whole church was illuminated, and there were enough candles left over to celebrate all of the special feasts of the year."[5]

So much activity required a continual expenditure of physical energies, and Mary Mazzarello didn't have as much as previously. She had been weakened and had to make the most of what she had. Petronilla, still strong, helped very much in the various tasks, but it was a difficult trial for Mary because the idea of having to reduce her efforts had never even occurred to her. For her "to dedicate her life to the children" was not merely one activity among so many others. It was a radical choice made once and for always, like the vow of perpetual chastity.

"Dedicating herself to the children," meant teaching sewing, welcoming orphans, organizing outings and carnivals. It was done without counting the cost, which meant also spending hours with the mothers, involving herself in their worries and family sorrows. If there was no time to go home for meals, she fixed them herself in the workroom, with the children.

At other times she had no time to take part in the specific moments of common prayer of the Daughters of the Immaculate. There was no contest when choosing between the children to be cared for and a conference of the Pious Union. Even Fr. Pestarino insisted: "Don't ever lose sight of those little ones, for any reason." With all her experience in helping with the younger children at home, Mary was the logical choice to help care for them.

Her spiritual journey had already brought her to see with a greater vision, to discern necessities beyond the letter of the rule. She was definitely a Daughter of the Immaculate, but she knew that fervor could not be nourished by formal fulfillment with eyes closed and merely pious observance. Perhaps without knowing it she had instinctively understood a famous counsel of the 14th century mystic John Ruysbroeck: "Even though you are rapt in ecstasy like St. Paul, if you hear that an invalid needs some warm broth or any other help, I would suggest that you come down for an instant from your ecstasy to heat the broth." She heated milk and dried clothing.

All of this, however, did not find favor with the older members of the Daughters of the Immaculate. It seemed an unacceptable transgression of the rule that Mary and Petronilla were apparently to be separated from their families and isolated in their rooms. It seemed almost as though these two had formed a new mini-community, with Mary as superior. Other Daughters, however, admired Mary very much. So now there were two currents of thought in the Pious Union.

At the end of 1863 the two currents became two separate parties, because Angela Maccagno's three year term as prioress was over, and the Daughters were called upon for an election. For the first time, one part of the group put forth the name of Mary Mazzarello as a candidate for the office. It was a bitter situation because of how it came about and what was feared. For the moment, Fr. Pestarino's intervention solved the problem, and Angela Maccagno retained her well-earned office. Being elected prioress was far from important in Mary Mazzarello's thoughts, and therefore she lost no time. Let those who started that electoral campaign know that it was a mistake, and that internal dissensions always bring ruin.

1863 was also a disturbing year in politics. During that summer a surprising number of duels were fought with swords and guns. Those most involved were officials, so much so that the Ministry of War had to speak out against the participants. But disputes also broke out among functionaries, veterans of the Garibaldi brigades and nobility. Finally, on June 21, after a heated argument in the House of Deputies in Turin, the duel of all duels was fought, a sword fight between Marco Minghetti, President of the Council, and his predecessor, Urbano Rattazzi, who was lightly wounded.

Instead, Mary Mazzarello's future and that of the Salesian universe was being decided in a dialogue between two priests. Fr. Pestarino met in conversation with Fr. John Bosco. We do not know exactly when the two met. It seems to have been toward the end of the summer of 1862, but the locale and circumstances vary according to the sources. Some speak of Don Bosco's stopping in Acqui; others tell of a conversation on a train from Acqui to Alessandria. Others claim that the priests met in Genoa, in the home of Fr. Frassinetti. To this day we don't have a decisive answer to the question.

What matters, however, is that it did happen. Fr. Pestarino already knew Don Bosco because of what he had done in Turin, because of the *Catholic Readings,* and through what was said of him at ecclesiastical meetings. There is no doubt that such a specialist of youthful humanity as the *previn* of Mornese would have spoken a little of the initiatives of his parish, especially of the Daughters of the Immaculate, who were also in contact with Fr. Frassinetti and Fr. Sturla, friends of Don Bosco. Then, too, there must have been a special mention of what those two special Daughters, Mary and Petronilla Mazzarello, were doing with their quasi-hospice, quasi-oratory and workroom-school.

A cordial proposal came from that first encounter: "Fr. Pestarino, come to see me at Valdocco some day." So it was that one day the priest from Mornese boarded the train as he had often done before. Now, however, he was going toward a new destination; after Genoa, he would even reach Turin.

Chapter Three

In 1862 Don Bosco was forty-seven-years old. On May 14, he was once again surrounded by his first followers in the usual room at Valdocco. It was close quarters for twenty-two people, twenty-two Salesians who had committed themselves by vows of poverty, chastity and obedience, accepting Don Bosco as their superior. He made a prophecy: "Twenty-five or thirty years from now, if the Lord continues to watch over us as he has done, our society, spread throughout the world, will have thousands of members."

Now there was one more member—Fr. Dominic Pestarino of Mornese. He had come to visit Valdocco and saw one marvel after another, like so many others before him who had discovered a city of young people in the Turin lowlands, which had once been a refuge for misery and dens of iniquity. Upon meeting Don Bosco, he spoke of Mornese and of the activity there, including the work of the Daughters of Mary Immaculate, Mary Mazzarello and Petronilla. He confessed a desire: he wanted to come to Don Bosco and become a Salesian.

At first, Don Bosco gave him a cordial, affirmative answer, but he well knew what Fr. Pestarino meant for the people of Mornese. Therefore, there would be no transfer to Turin. The *previn* would remain where he was most needed: with the new work, with those girls, with those projects.

So it was that Fr. Pestarino returned to Mornese re-energized. He could transmit to his fellow villagers a message of esteem from the "famous Don Bosco," as the newspapers called him. He could also give Mary and Petronilla two medals of the Blessed Mother and a brief, written message: "By all means pray, but do all you can to impede even one venial sin." We read this in the *Cronistoria,* along with the fact that Fr. Pestarino went back to Mornese "...lighthearted and as happy as though he had discovered a gold mine." Mary and Petronilla also must have felt lighthearted and happy because of the medals, but even more so because of the message: do good to young people. They felt that Don Bosco was on their side, even though they had never met him.

Carnival time in 1864 rolled around, and Mary once more organized the recreational activities. She had bought a concertina for the girls' dance, but she also set about creatively varying the diversions, so that this was not the only attraction.

The festive celebration cut into the attendance at the other local carnival dances, and the irritated young men of the village played tricks and frightened Mary's friends. Inconsequential stories were exaggerated, and new accusations were levied by other Daughters of the Immaculate: this is the result of the dances; this is what happens when Mary Mazzarello is left too free; this is when we have disorder and quarrels.

It wasn't only the dance. Other events inflamed the souls of the Pious Union. The two Daughters who had been authorized by Fr. Pestarino to conduct a workroom and hospice (Mary and Petronilla), had become four. Teresa Pampuro, in her generosity, had decided to stay with them during the day.

When she had been alone and infirm, according to the rule of the Pious Union and at the request of Fr. Pestarino, Petronilla had stayed with her overnight. Teresa, who was one of the older members, had never taken part in the criticism against Mary, but had rather sought to help her because she saw that she had so much work to do and suffered ill health.

A fourth girl arrived, Rosina Mazzarello. She had previously been accepted as a guest, but had now decided to stay permanently with Mary and Petronilla, to "dedicate herself to the care of children," like them.

The four young women started to live a type of common life. They had dinner together, and then Mary also began to stay overnight, gradually leaving her family. She was well aware of their suffering; bitter conversations raged at home. However, she felt that she had to do this to realize the full gift of self to an eternal goal.

This point is clear: the activity and quasi-common life of Mary's group were very different from the original aims and strict rule of the Pious Union. Certainly, every new initiative had Fr. Pestarino's explicit permission, but according to many Daughters, the priest, director of all, should not give privileges to a few. Because of this state of ideas, the souls of the Pious Union were on a rocky road.

To avoid an imminent crisis, the "little priest" called Mary Mazzarello to a severe trial. It was not because he believed her to be wrong. He had always helped her, knowing that she was on the right track with her simple, expansive idea of a charity which must be free. It was a charity which is by nature free because the rule must serve charity. Fr. Pestarino knew that this girl, though physically worn out by typhoid, was still the strongest, and therefore he placed upon her the burden of pacifying the Daughters. She alone was asked to sacrifice herself.

To end the extensive complaining, he announced that

Mary, because of fatigue, would temporarily leave her tasks. He obliged her to withdraw to a type of "house arrest" at the Valponasca, where her father and brothers, Dominic and Joseph (14 and 18 years old) continued to work the vineyards. She would come to the village on Sundays for Mass. Petronilla and Teresa Pampuro would take her place in the workroom for an unspecified time.

Mary obeyed immediately, without protest. She did not speak or discuss the matter; she simply went. After the solitude of her illness, she now faced more time alone. This time, however, it was more painful, because it seemed in the eyes of others that she was being "punished." Besides that, being at the Valponasca reminded her of times past when she had still been vigorous and strong. Looking at the vineyard where she could no longer work, she felt useless and powerless.

She accepted everything without self-defense or recrimination. She did not play the role of victim. Yet, these Daughters of Mary Immaculate of Mornese were not a severe religious order, with a long, rigorous novitiate for mature, cultured persons. This Pious Union, after all, was just a confraternity of good peasant girls who lived at home, and being together was fairly optional.

But not for her. In her eyes, this membership had all the obligations and requirements of a total, definitive choice. It was like that vow of chastity which she had made once and forever, without asking anyone for suggestions. Not even for a second did she think of absolving herself from any kind of prohibitions which the priest imposed on her, while leaving the others alone. This was another of Mary's characteristics, like her cheerfulness: she had the capacity of feeling the enormous, invincible, committing power of a free act of her will. She knew how to be coherent at any cost.

This Mary Mazzarello of Valponasca had something of the radicality of the youthful behavior of the 20th century; she was adverse to compromise, capable of paying a price to serve a principle; she conserved fidelity.

The Valponasca was quiet during the many hours when her father and brothers were working in the fields. She, too, was quiet as she drew close to the window and gazed out over the fields to the village which was prohibited to her. She spent her days in reading and pious practices, with their variety of precepts and invocations for every hour of the day and every event in life, in preparation for the last instant. She was also faithful to the so-called "exercise for a happy death" approved by Pope Pius VII which realistically described one's last agony, accompanied by invocations for divine mercy.

"When my imagination, agitated by horrible and fearful phantasms will be oppressed by mortal sadness...when I will have lost the use of all my senses, and the whole world will become nothing for me, then, merciful Jesus, have pity on me...."

On Sunday she sat quietly on one side of the church, and those who so desired could impute an attitude of guilt to her. St. Aloysius Gonzaga, the saint whose devotion she spread in Mornese, was compared to raw iron to be molded by the blows of a hammer. Now it was Mary who was feeling the blows, and she didn't like it. She couldn't accept them as caresses, nor did she enjoy the suffering, but neither was she afraid of it. She understood; she knew its purpose.

It was not merely a matter of restoring peace among the Daughters of the Immaculate; this was a minor, contingent reason. She understood that the blows were a preparation and a test for the future.

As Maria Esther Posada notes in her small volume of the letters of Mary Mazzarello: "The origins of her apostolate are intimately connected with suffering, with that kind of suffering called misunderstanding. Silence, lived in an atmosphere of trust, free of rebellion prepared her for the beginning of an authentic, ecclesial mission."[1]

The villagers were unhappy with Mary being sent away. As was expected, the girls of the workroom suffered from her absence and considered her to be a victim of injustice. A few even invented excuses to visit her at the Valponasca. They weren't alone. Even the mothers of the children went to Fr. Pestarino to tell him of their daughters' displeasure over the fact that Mary had been sent away.

So it was that after a month and some days, the "little priest" invited Mary to return to the village, to once again take up the direction of her little group.

Don Bosco Sets Mornese Afire

Finally, Don Bosco's day in Mornese dawned. During his visits to Valdocco, Fr. Pestarino, with a certain right, insisted that Don Bosco come. He had officially become one of Don Bosco's sons, and frequently took part in meetings at Valdocco while continuing his much-needed mission in Mornese. For his part, the founder of the Salesians found his days overflowing with obligations. He was sought after from all sides. Pope Pius IX frequently called him to Rome, and there he also met with prelates and aristocrats. Then there was the time he spent caring for the boys at Valdocco. How could one dare to ask him to hunt through the distant forests for entire days?

Yet, the little priest knew that this was very possible in Don Bosco's mind, that he was ready to go to Pius IX, but he was also ready to miss two or three trains as he stood in a fog-shrouded station, speaking with an aggressive, discouraged gang leader whom he would make one of his own boys, Michael Magone.

The repeated requests brought success. At the end of the summer of 1864, he went to Genoa by train with a hundred of his boys. On the return trip, he and the boys would make a stop at Mornese.

1864 was an unhappy year for Turin. On January 19, the city, especially the poorer sector, had lost one of its most generous supporters. Marchesa Julia Falletti di Barolo died— the foundress of the Sisters of St. Ann, of nurseries, schools and hospitals, protector of the imprisoned. Actually, her death did not raise a wide political clamor, because Julia di Barolo was not on the side of the dominant political party. The spontaneous mourning of thousands of people in Turin who had been helped, understood, saved by her, gave the funeral the dimension of city-wide mourning. The final good-bye saw an army of the forgotten and undernourished, and even suspects on whom the police kept an eye, fill the center of the city.

At the end of summer, the worst happened. It was an almost unbelievable tragedy. Halfway through September, the government under the Bolognese, Marco Minghetti, joined that of Paris in the "September Agreement." This obtained the withdrawal of the French *presidio* from Rome, in exchange for the Italian commitment not to attack (but rather to defend, if necessary) the pontifical territories. In an additional document, Turin's government committed itself to transfer the whole kingdom to Florence, the capital.

All of this was done without first informing the people of Turin, who took the news very badly. They found themselves displaced by Florence as the capital of the province. They lost prestige and economic resources with the departure of the court, the government and parliament, the diplomatic corps, central offices and high military command. On September 20, a tumult erupted in the center of Turin. An unfortunate order resulted in the gunning down of dozens of people. The king and his ministers lost a sense of reason and one of them spread the word that he was wearing protective armor against the knives of the people of Turin.

But calm was restored because of the people, not the guns. So it was that Don Bosco and his boys could leave Turin tranquilly and arrive at Genoa on time. Once the visit was over, they returned by train to the station of Serravalle Scrivia. From there, they walked to Mornese, with Don Bosco leading them on Fr. Pestarino's white horse. They arrived on the evening of October 7 and stayed until October 11. The villagers were greatly impressed by this troop of boys who had come from Turin, with their liveliness and enthusiasm, their band and their singing in and out of church. Mornese had never seen anything like it. Don Bosco and his boys were welcomed, fed and housed by all of the inhabitants who offered food, lent pots and pans and helped to cook and serve.

Mary Mazzarello participated in all the preparations for the event and was then an attentive spectator. She didn't miss a word of Don Bosco's sermons or talks; she found a way of being wherever he was speaking. Ferdinand Maccono wrote: "For her, it seemed as though Don Bosco's words were like an echo of an inexpressible language which she felt in her heart. It was like a translation of her very sentiments, like something which had been yearned for and had now finally come."

At this time no one even suspected that the founder of the Salesians was thinking about involving women in his work. The male society was still defining itself as it journeyed toward definitive approval on the part of the Holy See. If anyone had an inkling of this problem, they certainly would not have looked for answers among the poverty and illiteracy of the countryside. They would only find more problems there.

Yes, there was a problem in Mornese. Fr. Pestarino owned a beautiful piece of property in Borgoalto, and, with the agreement of the municipality, he wanted to build an institution which would be useful to the village. Don Bosco's visit provided him with an opportunity to speak of this, examining ideas and projects. With his advice, they came to a decision: the most useful establishment for the village would be a school for the boys of Mornese. It would provide a necessary means for instruction.

Everyone was well aware of this necessity. From 1861-71, the young Kingdom of Italy would dramatically lower the rate of illiteracy, but it would not eradicate it completely. The State spent very little for the people's instruction, leaving it almost completely up to the local government. There were probably enough schools for future lawyers, doctors and teachers, but there were far too few technical and professional schools. In 1867, a state deputy asked the governors: "What have you done for technical schools? How many farmers, industrialists, men of commerce have you provided for a nation which needs them so much?" The nation would soon arrive at the point of abolishing the Ministry of Public Education.

During his trips Don Bosco continued to hear about the same needs and requests: elementary and professional schools. In every village he found boys who wanted to go to his schools. He accepted ten from Mornese.

The whole village was enthusiastic about the idea of a school. Fr. Pestarino offered to help the volunteer workers with food, and they received permission from the bishop to work even on Sundays. Almost all the families sent someone or offered financial assistance and material. On October 21, the excavation for the foundation was begun. Don Bosco sent some Salesians who were expert in building (construction never ceased at Valdocco) to direct the work. Bricklayers were hired and the auxiliary force of the Mornese residents brought the necessary materials for the work at Borgoalto. Women and girls had the task of collecting the stones they found in the vineyards, piling them up along the roadside, then later carrying them in carts to the construction site.

Petronilla tells us of this feminine contribution in the *Cronistoria:* "This is how we did it. Early in the morning after Mass we hurried home to start the day, then one of us, (usually Mary) would go out into the street with the resident students, clapping their hands. The other girls would come out of their

houses, and together they would go to places they had previously "scouted" for stones. Then the women would come. Fr.
Pestarino would see to it that men and women had breakfast in
different groups. Toward 11 AM, work was halted and all went
to Mass.[2]

Compassion and Skepticism

On June 13, the first stone of the school was in place. It
was a solemn celebration with the mayor, a few neighboring
pastors, and a band which came from Lerma. During the preceding April, the cornerstone was laid at the sanctuary of Mary
Help of Christians in Turin with Amadeus of Aosta present,
the second son of Victor Emanuel.

During the carnival of 1865 a dance for the girls was not
held because there was too much work; neither was it held in
1866. There was official mourning during this year because of
the death of the twenty-year-old Prince Oddone, Duke of
Monferrato, fourth son of the king. Rumors of war spread
throughout Italy. Prussia and Austria teetered on the brink of
war, and the Italian government made a pact with the Prussians
to gain Venice.

The call to arms began and the countryside was stripped
of young men during the season of greatest work. On June 6,
the conflict between Prussia and Austria erupted. On July 3,
the Austrians were beaten at Sadowa and the armistice was
signed on July 26. The decisive Austrian victory at Custoza
and at Lissa on the Adriatic Sea prolonged the war with Italy
for fifty-three more days. Since Italy was allied with the
victorious Prussia, it still held Venice, with the help of Napoleon III.

In Salesian history, 1866 was also memorable because of
certain words of Don Bosco to Fr. John Baptist Lemoyne, then
director of the school at Lanzo. It happened on the feastday of

St. John the Baptist, patron of Turin, when everyone celebrated Don Bosco's feastday, even though his patron was
actually John the Evangelist.

Observing the illumined playground and listening to the
music and songs of the boys, the two priests allowed themselves to reminisce about the modest beginnings, now sur-
passed by a great reality. Fr. Lemoyne himself tells us about it
in the *Biographical Memoirs of Don Bosco*. "I was a bit hesitant at first, then I ventured: 'How about the girls? Aren't you
going to do anything for them? Don't you think that if we had
an institute of sisters, founded by you, affiliated to our Pious
Society, it would be the crowning touch to our work? Couldn't
they do for girls what we are doing for boys?' I had hesitated
to put forth my idea, because I was afraid that Don Bosco
would have opposed it. He thought for a moment and then, to
my surprise, said: 'Yes, this too, will be done. We will have
sisters, not now, but later on.'"

This was the first operative announcement, after years of
thinking about it. While the suggestion was still an uncertainty,
it was hopeful. This hope became a pronouncement on the
feast of St. John in 1866: "We will have sisters."

What was Mary Mazzarello thinking about during those
years? We don't know much about it, and we can even understand how hazardous it was to attempt new projects during
these times which seemed endless. It was a time of apprentice-
ship in the tailor shop, with the children to be cared for, the
workroom, the difficulties and friction among the Daughters of
the Immaculate...and with hunger.

During the process of canonization, a few witnesses recalled some of her brief sayings and allusions during this long,
precarious time. At times Mary alluded to an institute for girls,
or she spoke of a "pious union for girls," but with no further
clarification, Some of her listeners felt that she was already
leaning toward a real, actual religious family, "because she

spoke to us of the habit which we would wear" (Maccono). The original intent on the Mornese level—to gather children so as to educate and instruct them—now seems to have developed itself slowly into something which was not a project, but would have conserved a local dimension; however, it also seems to point to a more certain and guaranteed duration of time, to stability.

A significant and decisive step was taken in this direction during the autumn of 1867. Fr. Pestarino had built a new house facing the parish square. It was constructed mainly at his own expense, but also with the generous help of Angela Maccagno and others like Petronilla Mazzarello and Teresa Pampuro. It was a large, comfortable building which he used during the winter months because of its proximity to the church, but it was destined for a very different end. Encouraged also by Don Bosco, he wanted to place there those Daughters of Mary Immaculate who wanted to live a common life. They would carry out their beneficent works: workroom, hospice, oratory. The house would be all for them, rent-free.

That was what they expected when the priest left it empty, even during the winter. The move would take place as soon as possible, in October 1867. Mary Mazzarello, Petronilla, Teresa Pampuro and thirty-five-year-old Giovanna Ferrettino moved into the new headquarters. The children of the peddler had returned home, but in their places were the residents Rosina Mazzarello, who was Petronilla's niece, and two girls from the nearby village of St. Stephen: Maria Grosso and Maria Gastaldi.

For Mary Mazzarello, entering the new house meant leaving her family definitively. Parents, brothers and sisters lived in a climate of "tears and desolation" at this detachment. Her sister Felicita said that she had never seen her people so upset. We're not talking about a family who sees a daughter going off to become a sister, because even though they often do so in tears, there's a certain secure institutional aspect. Mary, instead, was walking into the arms of hunger, and she was doing so in the village where all could see her, with all the gossip against a family who could allow such a thing.

She played it all down. It's true, she wouldn't be living at home, but she would always be in Mornese. And as for food...well, when there was not enough for all, she would go to her parents, brothers and sisters to ask for help. "I'm sure that she'll come, and it will be soon," Felicita must have thought. She knew the situation. She knew that the little group could not put together both dinner and supper, even though their meals for the most part consisted of polenta [cornmeal mush]. "And even when they had this," she wrote, "they often didn't have the firewood to cook it."

The new house was called the House of the Immaculate, and they retained the name of Daughters of the Immaculate. Those, instead, who chose to live at home and had Angela Maccagno as their superior, took the name of Ursulines, drawn by Fr. Frassinetti from the life of Angela Merici. Their new rule gave them St. Ursula as their patroness.

When we speak of the house of the Daughters, we need to keep in mind the feelings of the Mazzarello family for Mary. It was a fact that these girls were precious for the people, however, the idea of life in common, maintaining themselves, wasn't too convincing. Some were compassionate, others smirking, but all were curious and were interested in seeing how many of the girls would last.

In order to sustain the tiny work, Petronilla was assigned the task of looking for sewing commissions even in the surrounding villages. Then, too, every now and then, someone would dash to her family in search of flour or vegetables. During the inclement season, they would rise before dawn to gather firewood on the property of relatives or parents.

At the school construction, the chapel and a few rooms

where Fr. Pestarino was to live were finished and ready for use. Don Bosco arrived from Acqui on the evening of November 9, 1867, to bless the chapel. He came early because he had been called to the bedside of the dying Bishop Modesto Contratto, but it was too late. Upon his arrival he found that the bishop had already breathed his last.

After the funeral, the people of Mornese welcomed him. He arrived in a carriage and passed between a great bonfire and fireworks. The construction site at Borgoalto was illumined. They led him to a special seat, and from there he listened to poetry and words of welcome. Since the evening had grown very cold, further activities were curtailed.

During the following days, between functions, sermons and gatherings, he found time to speak privately with Mary Mazzarello and her few companions. It was a meeting completely bereft of any solemnity. All stood under a portico whipped by icy winds. The *Cronistoria* tells us that Mary did not place herself in front of the group. She wanted to be in the back, "hidden so that she could freely grasp every word. Ordinarily very pale, she became more and more flushed with joy and deep feeling as Don Bosco spoke. She had listened with clasped hands as though in fervent prayer, and lowered eyes which shone with agreement. At that moment it seemed as though her whole soul vibrated in unison with that of Don Bosco, in the understanding that she was receiving the light of a sure life."[3]

All Addressed Her Respectfully

The girls of the House of the Immaculate were now quite distinct from those of the Ursulines; all they had in common was Fr. Pestarino as their spiritual director. They made an annual vow of chastity, but did not assume the commitment of stability in the house. Those who wanted to leave could do so freely.

The time had come to put someone in charge of the operation. Until now, it had moved forward with Mary and Petronilla assuming roles similar to those of the consuls of the Roman republic, who made decisions on their own. Now Fr. Pestarino invited all to elect a superior, one of their number chosen from among the insiders and the externs.

This was done on a Sunday. Mary Mazzarello was elected unanimously and accepted without any special emotion. Petronilla said: "I want to be the first to address you respectfully." This feeling was also unanimous, and Mary felt that she must quickly accept this change. She understood its value. These young women fighting cold, hunger and the ironies of life, poor peasants without even a religious habit or any other distinguishing mark, wanted to address their superior formally, out of respect for themselves and in order to lend a tone of seriousness to their undertaking.

It was a decisive action in the face of the murmuring and whispers of the village. "They adopted that tone of respect with such deference, that without words they impressed even those who were less favorably inclined toward them."

However, they never thought of recording the action or of leaving a written note of this first election. Because of this we do not know the exact date when Mary Mazzarello became superior. We only know that it took place on a Sunday, some time after Don Bosco left Mornese.

Mary Domenica Mazzarello was thirty-years-old when she became superior. It was the age when life choices had already been made, either for marriage or another way of life. Those thinking about becoming religious would have already done so at this age. But what about her? What did guiding the Daughters of the Immaculate mean for her? In this group she found lifelong friends and acquaintances and a few promising, new members. Others had been sent by pastors and by Don Bosco himself, to test their vocations. Some succeeded, and others did not. For some, life in the house was too difficult, and the companions too ordinary and ignorant.

Also, we don't read prodigious accounts about saints who gathered crowds of faithful and followers in a brief time. From the outside there seemed to be a modest balance. These girls and women were rendering a precious service to the families of their village, which had no more than 1,200 inhabitants. This was all well and good, but was it worth the suffering and all the physical difficulty with cold and malnutrition? The habit—or penance—of eating polenta morning and evening, exposed all to the risk of pellegra, which in northern Italy annually strikes tens of thousands of persons, even leading them to insane asylums.

Was it worth bearing the burden of the vows, even though temporarily? Mary Mazzarello's response, naturally, was yes, it's worth the trouble. But she also knew that this renunciation and suffering for years and years, this indigence which was humiliating at times, was literally and truly a suffering in the eyes of others. It was like having to ask for advance payment for work. And there were no great rewards, from a human perspective.

The life of the countryside had, however, taught her time-lessness and patience, by the means of incessant care of the vines throughout the year so as to have a harvest. Then, too, every family lived through the autumnal stomach aches of those children who drank the must of the grapes, believing it had already become wine. Yet, it wasn't so. To have wine you need more work and longer periods of waiting in dark cellars. It is also this slowness which makes wine, and woe to those who would hurry the process. During these years, Mary's strength lay in knowing how to value and appreciate being hidden. She succeeded so well that her friends felt fulfilled and "promoted" in what they did, without measuring the weariness. It was an authentic joy, enriched by immediate and long-term hope: to have new rooms, more work. They also learned how to raise silkworms, later selling the cocoons to raise funds for the school.

Mary continually reminded them of Don Bosco's words. That little talk under the porticoes, those messages which occasionally arrived from Valdocco, entrusted to Fr. Pestarino, made them feel the winds of newness and enriched their everyday acts, bringing greatness within reach of all. "You can."

It was as though Don Bosco thought of them day and night. Mary and her companions did not know exactly the extent of his exceptional position among the Italian clergy and the political world. The government consulted him about episcopal nominations, about which there was a very strong conflict with the Vatican. Pius IX also confidently consulted him on the same question. On at least a couple of occasions we can see a dozen dioceses covered because of his mediation. When he traveled through Italy, he was kept in sight by friends and foes alike, because wherever he went, something always happened. All that mattered for the Daughters of the Immaculate were the times he came to Mornese or the messages and exhortations which arrived from Turin.

At Valdocco, instead, he was overseeing the conclusive moment of the great work of Mary Help of Christians. The magnificent construction already stood out in the Turin skyline, but for a brief moment he was almost resigned to the fact that the work would have to stop because of the extreme financial burden. The problems with money had become very serious, not because people didn't want to help, but because the Italians had all become more impoverished.

The State's debt for the war of independence had come due. The government was looking everywhere for money. In 1867, a new law of suppression and confiscation hit many existing religious and ecclesiastical institutions. These confiscated buildings became courts, schools barracks, offices, jails

(Regina Coeli, the Mantellate, St. Victor, etc.). This way the State saved itself enormous expenditures. But it did not take in funds, at least not as quickly as it needed them, because the auction of ecclesiastical lands entailed time-consuming procedures.

It was then decided to move on to privatization, giving over many public activities like the management and construction of railways. Even the tobacco monopoly was privatized. What hit all citizens, however, beginning from the weakest, was a "broad-based tax" on such items as flour, bread and cornmeal. The latest tax was on milled goods. It went into effect at the beginning of 1869 and it seemed planned to exasperate the poorer classes. In fact, it unleashed the first, important social movements from the time of Italian unity.

There were no "movements" at Mornese, in upper Monferrato, but there was still bitterness. The tax continually renewed and exacerbated the hatred. The usual trip to the mill with grain or corn was an occasion of anger for the farmer. The tax was to be paid immediately, before the flour could be brought home, and he did not always have the money. In that case, he had to pay in merchandise, leaving part of the flour with the miller. The scene of the angry, furious farmer trudging home with a half-filled sack was a common sight: "Look at what I have left, between paying the miller and that cursed tax."

This money served to pay the State's debts and public works. With the money coming in from the mills, hundreds of kilometers of railway were constructed and new roads were built, especially to the South. But the mill tax also aggravated the farmer's misery. Urged on by hunger, many people emigrated, especially to the Americas.

Mary Mazzarello and her friends chose a terrible time to support themselves by their work, to care for the sick and the children, living on prayer and polenta. It was also bad timing on Don Bosco's part. The grandiose construction had to be completed and paid for just as the adventure of the work with the young women was beginning.

Those at the House of the Immaculate knew nothing, but he continued to think about his project. He had not said "We'll have sisters" by chance. He would confide to young Fr. Francesia that the moment had come to provide for the women. He would also be more precise: it dealt with "establishing a pious congregation which would do for girls that which the Salesians do for boys" *(Cronistoria)*.

He was coming to the idea of a true and proper religious family for women. It was another new task for his hands, as though he didn't already have enough. Fr. Francesia marveled and was preoccupied about this accumulation of projects. "My dear Don Bosco, don't you ever stop taking on new work?" The reply? "The Lord knows that I am seeking his glory, and he will help me. If he sees any humanity creeping in, he will know how to get rid of it."

John Bosco was not like Gideon, son of Joash, who asked for signs and proof of God's favor, before going against the Midianites. No, he was the man of resigned dynamism, which means act first, with an upright conscience, placing yourself in the Lord and his judgment, whatever it may be.

We don't know if Don Bosco and Mother Mazzarello ever spoke about Gideon and the Midianites. Certainly, the priest from Becchi went into the field of action without asking for guarantees, because he felt it was necessary. The girl from Mornese did the same, also thinking and saying that it was beautiful.

All Looked to Mary

The consecration of the sanctuary of Mary Help of Christians took place on Tuesday, June 9, 1868. Bishop Alexander Ricardi of Netro celebrated the first Mass at the central altar.

He had been archbishop of Turin for a year, taking over a diocese which had long remained vacant. A four-meter gold-plated bronze statue of the Madonna stood on the cupola of the sanctuary. A circular inscription ran around the inside of the cupola: *Hic domus mea, inde gloria mea.* The actual words were not taken from the Old or New Testament, nor from some Father of the Church. Don Bosco had seen these words in a dream many years before, when the place of the sanctuary was a field belonging to someone else. Later, walking though the grass, he told his dream to a group of boys, saying that a sanctuary of undreamed-of proportions would rise there.

Now the sanctuary was there, and so were Don Bosco's boys, 1,200 of them, who could look up and see the words which he had dreamt: "This is my house, from here my glory will go forth." The choir sang the solemn Mass composed by John Cagliero, a farmer's son who had been brought to Valdocco by Don Bosco, at the time of his dreams.

A group of forty persons from Mornese who had come by train were among the crowds at Mary Help of Christians that day. Many had given up their work in the dead of summer to be there. For some reason, Fr. Pestarino, usually so attentive and considerate, did not bring to Turin some girls from the House of the Immaculate. Why? At least Mary and Petronilla could have gone with him to see something, at least once.... The *Cronistoria* explains: "In the group from Mornese there were only men, no women. So the priest had to tell them 'I would bring you two, but where would you stay?'"

In the spring of 1869, however, he brought a new, cheerful Don Bosco back to the village and to the Daughters. Two months before, on February 19, the Holy See had given definitive approval to the Salesian Society. From now on, it would be governed by its own superiors, answering only to Rome. Independent from bishops, it could operate throughout the world. It was now an institution of the universal Church.

This decree from the Congregation of Regulars sanctioned by the Holy Father relieved Don Bosco of another enormous burden. He had won, notwithstanding the unfavorable political atmosphere on the one side and the consequent pessimism of the Vatican on the other. Now he was ready to do new things.

During his stop at Mornese, he encouraged the builders of the school, preached, heard confessions and received the visits of the people as he usually did. As an extra, he reserved much attention for the Daughters of the Immaculate. He looked after them and studied them. A few were too bent over in church and he advised them that they should "be upright, only bowing their heads." He held some conversations exclusively for them, but without alluding to projects or a new foundation. He didn't say a word about this.

But he did do something unusual. He wrote about twenty short pages for them, casually spelling out "a daily rule." He told them to go to daily Mass, "that celebrated for the people at sunrise," and as to the time spent in church "thirty minutes but not more than forty." He insisted on the regularity of their daily actions, work, prayer, reading and silence on Saturday in honor of Our Lady.

Notes on work followed, both on the personal and community level. Meanwhile, "Love work, so that each will be able to say to herself: 'I support myself by the sweat of my brow.'" Further, "Constant work on one's nature, to form a good, patient happy character, to make virtue lovable and living together easier."

We would have loved to have been there, among the Daughters, watching them as they listened to these counsels, seeing their looks concentrate little by little on Mary Mazzarello's face, hearing him speak of "happy, patient character"; so patient and happy as to "render virtue amiable." Don Bosco was right, but these stupendous counsels at the House of the Immaculate were already law, placed in act by the person who was sitting in the last row, Mary.

Every time he came to Mornese, Don Bosco *brought* something, but he also *found* something which attracted him. He found the novelty of these girls and women gathered around "Mary from Valponasca." It was a group which absorbed the novelty of its intuitions, nourished by the spirituality of Joseph Frassinetti, seen in his works or heard in his voice when he preached at Mornese. Fr. Frassinetti died in January 1868, but Mary kept his publications, never letting them go.

Don Bosco came to Mornese again on May 8, 1870 for three days. The official occasion was the first Mass of Fr. Joseph Pestarino, Fr. Dominic's nephew. However, in the *Cronistoria* we read: "He did not lose sight of the hidden goal of his frequent visits to Mornese. In fact, he had many private talks with Fr. Pestarino and spoke repeatedly with the Daughters, who, naturally, during those days were responsible for all that went on in the house. In this way, without becoming aware of the fact and without even thinking about it, they could give sure proof not only of what they knew how to do, but also of their natural, serious attitude."[4] On December 8, 1869 Pope Pius IX opened a meeting at St. Peter's which would later be known as Vatican Council I. It was the most crowded in history, with the participation of seven hundred bishops. It would accomplish little, however, because of the Franco-Prussian war and the taking of Rome in September 1870. Its work would be remanded to autumn, then suspended, never to be taken up again.

Don Bosco was not a conciliar father, and therefore he did not enter the hall. At the beginning of 1870, however, he was at Rome for the usual question of episcopal nominations. He had the opportunity to meet many bishops and theologians of the Council during heated moments. The discussion was on the proposal of affirming in the most solemn way, by dogmatic definition, the infallibility of the pope when he speaks *ex cathedra* on a question of faith or morals. There were three currents of thought among the council fathers: those in favor of the definition, those against it and the "not opportune," that is, those who tended not to be adverse to the definition, but held that the moment for the proclamation of the dogma was "not opportune." Approval would later be given after many debates and with the absence of one side of the fathers in the decisive voting.

For his part, Don Bosco sustained the proposal; it seemed indispensable to him to reinforce the authority of the pontiff in this period of grave crisis in Italy between the State and the Church, and of widespread disorientation elsewhere. Therefore, upon meeting Pius IX in private audience, he encouraged him along this path. But at the same time, he sought to prepare him as he had done other times for the loss of Rome.

When Victor Emanuel II's army was about to march on the city, some said that the Pope should stay in Rome and others said that he should leave in solemn protest. Pius IX asked Don Bosco his opinion, and heard him resolutely advise not to move: "The sentinel, the angel of Israel, should remain in his place and be on guard for God's rock and the holy ark."

This was also the year of the aforementioned revelation to Fr. Francesia, "We will have the sisters."

Pius IX Said: "Begin"

After the taking of Rome the Italian Catholics (including the clergy) divided themselves into three groups. The catastrophe-bound expected the fall of the Kingdom of Italy from day to day. The conciliatory sector with laity, priests and even cardinals wanted instead that Catholics should insert themselves into the new situation, honestly accepted, and openly intervene in politics as electors and elected. The third current was more widespread. It was made up of Catholics opposed to conciliation with the State, but also opposed to expectations of chaos. They were decided about the social commitment among the people still excluded from political activity, because out of twenty-two million Italians, only half a million had the right to vote. The great initiatives of Catholic social action would later come to light due to these principles.

And Don Bosco?

For many years now Don Bosco had traveled that way which his famous "dreams" had pointed out to him when he was very young, and he had made of them a grandiose reality. Nothing changed for him. This year of 1871, which seemed to some to be the first year the Church was "imprisoned," was a year of great progress for him. In his eyes the loss of the temporal kingdom didn't detract anything from Pius IX. No Piedmontese general could strip him of his quality of pope, of Christ's vicar, sufficient to himself in any condition or state. Therefore, there was little to cry about. Work needed to be done, and he, Don Bosco did it tranquilly, at Rome, Turin and Mornese.

Now we follow him during the months of the great new work.

In January and February, Fr. Pestarino was at Valdocco for the meeting of Salesian directors. He spoke with Don Bosco, and heard that the opening of the school at Mornese would take place "in a great way." There were concerns about the Curia of Acqui, which was against this novelty. But Don Bosco told him to go ahead, and the *previn* also bought a house near the construction to expand the work.

On April 24, 1871, Don Bosco called a chapter of the Salesian Society and declared that the time had come to think of the women. It was necessary to have oratories and schools also for girls, and therefore, they needed a congregation of Sisters who would carry out this work. For some time now he had received requests for this type of work from bishops, pastors and authorities. After this brief exposition, he invited his collaborators to reflect and prepare. "Give your answer in a month."

Shortly after, while they began to think about it, he went to Mornese. It was a brief visit, concentrated on the little group of women and girls around Mother Mazzarello. Don Bosco found no one putting on an act for his benefit. They presented themselves as they were, even with their internal problems. For some time now, a teacher sent by Canon Olivieri, a friend of Fr. Pestarino, had been living with them. She was a good woman, but nothing was good enough for her. Because of her diploma she wanted to be the guide in the house, change this, undo that. So it was that Don Bosco could also see how Mary Mazzarello managed a crisis, not seeking "any other primacy than that of work and sacrifice," as the *Cronistoria* says.

That rule which he had written for them the previous year had become the guide of the community. Mary made it well-understood by all, even by the little ones, in the workroom which Don Bosco had inspected very carefully. We read further in the *Cronistoria:* "When he confirmed that which he already knew, that Mary Mazzarello brought others to virtue and to God, making herself more loved than feared, he had to return to Turin with a well-formed concrete idea about the group of Daughters who would have been able to give shape to his expectations."

Still during the final days of April, and before having his chapter's answer, he turned to Sr. Maria Enrichetta Dominici, superior of the Sisters of St. Ann, to whom he had already spoken of his project for a feminine congregation. He now sent her the statutes of the Salesians in view of this work, accompanied by a letter. "Dear Reverend Mother, I entrust to your hands the rule of our congregation and ask you to have the goodness to read it and see if it could suit a religious institute. Feel free to leave out or add as you in your wisdom see fit for an institute in which the Daughters, before the Church, would be true religious, but would, in the eyes of society, also remain free citizens. I would be pleased if you would add those chapters or articles of the Rule of St. Ann which could be adapted."

At the end of May, there was a new gathering of the Salesian chapter to give their answer on the feminine congregation. All agreed: Rua, Cagliero, Savio, Ghivarello, Durando, Albera. Don Bosco concluded: "Good. Now we can hold it as certain that it is God's will that we also care for girls." Once having known God's will, he immediately followed a human initiative: "To come to a concrete solution, I propose that the house of Fr. Pestarino which is being finished at Mornese be destined for this work."

So it was that even the location was found. In fact, there could not be a boys' school in the house of Mornese. The Curia of Acqui was opposed to it because it would take students away from the minor seminary of the diocese. Therefore, the Daughters of the Immaculate would be placed there as a first step. The second would consist in making the proposal to them: "For those who would want to belong to the new institute, forming that first nucleus of a religious family which would open festive oratories and educational institutions for girls."

However, everything was still secret. Many things were being prepared for the new adventure, but Don Bosco wanted the pope to announce it. Toward the end of June he found himself before Pius IX, who listened attentively to the project, taking a few days before deciding. "We have to think about it carefully." When they later met in an audience, his assent was convinced and motivated. Yes, he told Don Bosco, it is necessary to found this family of Sisters "for the instruction and education of children," translating the Salesian initiative into a feminine sense: "Formulate the constitutions and begin the trial; the rest will follow."

There was no time to lose. On July 9, Fr. Pestarino was to arrive at Valdocco and it was necessary to give him good news along with a blow. The good news was that, in accord with the Holy Father and the Salesian chapter, they would have a congregation of sisters, called the *Daughters of Mary Help of Christians.* This was the blow: the headquarters of these religious would be located in Mornese, more precisely, in the building enthusiastically constructed by the people as a school for their sons. No, there would be no school, also given the opposition of the Curia of Acqui....

The idea of the sisters must have already been preoccupying Fr. Pestarino. Who knows where they would find the future teachers there, in the countryside, where there was already so much feminine illiteracy. But he was also tormented by another thought: "Now I'll have to inflict this enormous disappointment on my people: There will be no school; your efforts were useless; the projects you had in mind for your sons are canceled...."

It was not to be. Don Bosco was a leader and faced difficult persons and situations; he would be the one to inform the people of Mornese, personally and at the right moment. To the "little priest" there remained the task of finding the "cornerstones" for something which would be enormously great in the building at Borgoalto.

When he arrived in Mornese, he confided Don Bosco's astonishing intention: women in the school! On the contrary, he spoke vaguely of "Daughters," and it could be them, but who knows. It was necessary to keep quiet and to pray.

He let a few days pass, then he held another conversation with the two of them. It seemed that Don Bosco wanted to create a new congregation of sisters, to educate girls. It was also probable that the first would be chosen from Mornese, from the House of the Immaculate. There were no special reactions to the words, but he noted "a flash of light in Mary Mazzarello's eyes." He chatted on, saying that since Don Bosco had let his eye rest on this group, perhaps it was necessary to do something higher, to better oneself further, to get in step with the times. For example, perhaps it would be better to get used to speaking in Italian instead of dialect.

Chapter Four

Therefore, they had to learn Italian, because in the future, Daughters of Mary Help of Christians would come from all of Italy. They were not preparing for an event which would involve only Monferrato or Piedmont; the future sisters would have to "educate and instruct children" without territorial limits, where necessary and possible.

As Don Bosco explained to Mother Enrichetta, they would have the status of religious before the Church, but for civil law, they would be free citizens, freely associated, thus exempting them from the "destructive laws" which suppressed communities and appropriated goods. It was an idea suggested to Don Bosco by Urban Rattazzi, author of those laws which are still in effect.

In spring 1871, while the Salesians were making plans for the new congregation, older ones were disappearing at Rome at the hand of state functionaries, who were confiscating religious headquarters and convents. Among them were: Santa Maria in Vallicella of the Filippini, Santa Maria sopra Minerva of the Dominicans, Sant'Andrea della Valle of the Theatines and the house of the Signor della Missione at Monte Cavallo, including the gardens.

These were the "years of tearing apart," as defined by Arturo Carlo Jemolo, the first post-unity period when Italy "did not know how to take pleasure in the joy of the formed national unity, carried out with a prodigiously light effort."[1] The Church-State conflict was entering its most painful moment, with rowdiness on both sides, so much so that it seemed that all of Italy was focused there.

Other things were happening, many other things. Here we tell one of the adventures. A young girl from Monferrato, Mary Domenica Mazzarello, daughter of Joseph, was about to enter Italian history. Her objective was not a statue in the public gardens; it was a place in paradise among the just who were unknown and propertyless, *cum Lazaro quondam paupere,* as we sing in the obsequies.

We can sketch out a type of chronicle which parallels the great events between the Quirinal, the Vatican and surroundings, and the important yet hidden facts which concerned her and her small group. At Valdocco in May 1871, the project dealing with the Sisters matured, and at Rome, so did the Guarentigie Law, by which the State intended to regulate the position of the pope with respect to Italy, offering him guarantees for the exercise of his spiritual authority. Pius IX immediately rejected this along with all the rest.

The discussion on the laws had high points because of some interventions both pro and con, from the Chamber to the Senate. Outside, instead, they moved ahead by invective, such as that of Garibaldi (one among many) in August 1871: "The cry of all Italians, from the youngest to the eldest, must be 'War on priests!'" The head of the thousands gave free reign to his expressions, but in substance it was the same discourse made by the coldest and most lettered writers of the *Review of Italian Masonry:* The papacy, they said, "is the implacable enemy of our order" and the brothers should never stop being vigilant, because, after achieving temporal power, "it will rise more vicious and wilder than ever."

A rough symmetry of rancor was being built; on the one side, a good Italian must detest and fight the Church; on the other, a good Christian is one who awaits the ruin of the unified State. At times, Pius IX himself, who knew what the situation was, unnecessarily took part in dangerous polemics. On the same day, however, he was ready to carefully study with Don Bosco the problems of many dioceses without bishops, and to pay attention to the design of the new feminine congregation which the head of the Salesians had drawn up for him.

Ruggero Bonghi, one of the fathers of the Guarentigie law, complained in Parliament about the lack of "fire," of a "word" capable of awakening and undoing the residual power of the Church, which, according to him, had nothing else to say: "Every movement of life has been stopped in the Catholic Church."

He was not alone. In making this mistake, Bonghi expressed the view of many. He based his opinions on the ecclesiastical summit of the entire Catholic world; but he did not know it very well, confusing it with a procession of bishops. It was with great difficulty, therefore, that he was capable of intercepting the signs of vitality and newness which came from the world at this time: the railroad reaching those who were far away, and the excavation of the Frèjus tunnel, leading to the opening of the Suez Canal. He would never understand that even the conversations held in dialect among young peasant girls of Mornese, whether they were about the orphans to accept, or on the Sunday oratory for girls, or on the sewing workroom, were "life movements." These were conversations on *things which were not done and had never been done, but were now necessary.* "Life movements" could also describe this tiny group which understood the new requirements and in its own dimension sought to meet them.

Politicians often do not see beyond their own environment (those in favor, those opposed), considering it to be the center of the universe. They don't see situations, movements and changes, appeals and complaints of the society which they govern. Even politics becomes something at the top, and that's what happened especially during this time of very restricted suffrage.

The Chamber of which Ruggero Bonghi spoke was elected in November 1870 by merely 240,000 persons—in contrast to the 530,000 who had the right to vote—2% of the population. This elective parliamentary assembly (Senate membership was for life) represented one out of every hundred inhabitants; it was a sort of club where elected and electors knew everything, and governed together, making laws for all. A colossal majority of the villages found themselves taxed and not represented. They were poorly known, for the most part, by notable well-intentioned persons who frequently spoke of people in imaginary classifications, in a literal way.

As Pasquale Villari said after the defeat of 1866: "Italy must begin to persuade itself that there is at the heart of a nation something which is more powerful than Austria—our colossal ignorance; it is the unlettered multitudes, the bureaucratic machine, ignorant teachers, childish politicians, impossible diplomats, incapable generals, careless workers, patriarchal farmers, and a rhetoric which gnaws at the bone." Villari's talk was heavy and generalized a bit too much, but the rhetorical myopia was truly widespread. It prevented one from measuring, for example, the dimensions which the migratory phenomenon was beginning to assume, which is still today little spoken of in the Chamber, and for which there are still no laws. Yet, in 1871 there were 126,000 Italian expatriots, half the number of the persons who voted in the previous year's elections.

"The Daughters Will Rise Today"

Now we see the birth of the new family of sisters desired by Don Bosco. It was a "movement of life" in the Church of the 1800's, which was realized in the sign of silence. On the contrary, we may speak of a double silence. First of all, Fr. Pestarino guided the girls of the House of the Immaculate during the first gradual trials of their life which was already somewhat similar to those of sisters, introducing new elements every day. One of these was general silence during certain times of the day. This took place throughout the day, except for recreation time, and it was not met with much enthusiasm, so the norm was changed somewhat: one of the girls would read aloud from a book of spirituality, or the life of some saint, so silence, for the others, was not too burdensome.

The second type of silence was that of the birth of a true congregation of sisters, which would unleash pandemonium in many families. The whole village was also upset over the fact that women had taken over the school built for the boys.

Fr. Pestarino followed the changes, saying only what was indispensable: it was necessary that they learn new prayers, change their schedule and exercise themselves in the Italian language. He used a notebook compiled by Don Bosco with the outline of a rule for the future religious. It was a wearisome task, says the *Biographical Memoirs:* "With great difficulty he has sought to obtain the books of the Constitutions of the principal religious orders and congregations...and how many vigils, how much reading and written correspondence he carried out with eminent persons, who, with their doctrine and experience, were in a condition to communicate light to him. The task was even more difficult because his congregation had to assume external forms which distinguished it from others, stripping it of certain practices and usages which were too ascetical." As we have already seen, a particular help came from Mother Enrichetta Dominici, superior general of the Sisters of St. Ann.

Fr. Pestarino's other task was to observe the Daughters one by one, to see who would be able to succeed as a religious. He had a criteria which Don Bosco had given to him: those who are quick to obey even in the little things and accept observations serenely are for us.

During this preparation, life went on as usual at the House of the Immaculate: workroom, oratory.... The hospice was still in existence. In fact, in late autumn, Mary Mazzarello took in nine-year-old Rosina Barbieri, who had lost her mother and whose father could not care for her.

A girl also arrived who was "new" in every way. It was the beautiful, sixteen year old Corinna Arrigotti, whose mother had died (a maternal uncle had sent her to Don Bosco). She was the daughter of a wealthy, pleasure loving father. He was not only indifferent to religion but opposed it, yet he consented to allow her to go to Mornese, because there she could learn the piano. There was a piano in the house. It was no longer used by Fr. Joseph Pestarino, who was now residing at Canelli. Perhaps she would also be able to give lessons to some girls.

Corinna's elegance, attitude and language stood out against the rustic ways of the Daughters and their home. She was amiable and frank with all, but would hear nothing of prayers and devotions; in this she had really learned from her father.

So it was that Fr. Pestarino could observe an important test. No one among the Daughters pushed Corinna to the practices of piety, because this was what Mary Mazzarello wanted: friendship and cordiality with all, but no pressure or invitations to prayer or functions. Corinna was to decide for herself, if and when she wanted. This was what Mary recommended, and this was what all did, putting the guest at her complete ease.

Silently, the *previn* kept an eye on what was happening. Mary had the Daughters on her side, never giving orders, using few words and many smiles. With time, Corinna would draw close to the faith, gradually and voluntarily, and naturally, without much show. Mary helped her with conversations and timely silences, with her quiet, vigorous capacity for guiding to discernment.

On the whole, then, the priest was convinced that all of these young women of the House of the Immaculate would make good religious, in the spirit of the future Institute. Naturally, they had to work much on their specific formation, and also on cultural development. Yet, they possessed the basic gifts, and he prepared himself to joyfully inform the Founder.

But it fell to him, instead, to listen with anguish to Don Bosco's weak voice, to read what he dictated with his last strength. He had fallen unexpectedly. While visiting the new Salesian school in Varazze on December 7, 1875, Don Bosco was seized with strong pain, high fever and skin eruptions. It was a dangerous collection of signs for those times; death seemed imminent and Holy Viaticum was brought to him. The alarming news was sent to Fr. Rua in Turin and all the Salesian houses were notified. At Mornese, Fr. Pestarino gathered the Daughters and they prayed in a special way. Among the girls one confided to the priest that she had offered her life for Don Bosco, asking God to let her die in his place. No record explained who that "one," "capable of exercising so much influence on those around her" was, notes the *Cronistoria,* but "the name Mary Mazzarello immediately came to mind."

Slowly, the illness passed its crisis, leaving Don Bosco in a very weak state. He remained in bed for all of December, and was still there when at the beginning of 1872 he welcomed a delegation of heads of families representing all Mornese. Gathered around him, they listened to the unpleasant news about the school at Borgoalto. There were serious, perhaps insurmountable difficulties, said Don Bosco. Perhaps the sisters of a new Institute could go to live there. Naturally, the

Salesian schools would always be open to the boys of Mornese; Turin, Lanzo, Varazze.... But these things were not to be spoken of yet. It would be better to keep quiet now, to wait, to be patient....

The twelve delegates left, tormented by that secret. They knew well what would happen at Mornese when all knew. Fr. Pestarino was as disturbed as they were, even though he already knew about it. Meanwhile, however, since the illness was beaten, he gave his report to Don Bosco about the Daughters. This was finally a piece of good news. It would be possible to have a good group of sisters from the House of the Immaculate.

On Saturday, January 6, 1872, the feast of the Epiphany, Don Bosco responded to the report of the priest from Mornese without wasting breath on small talk. His voice was still weak, but the discourse was all action: "You may, then, begin that of which we spoke last summer in Turin. If you think it wise, upon returning to Mornese, gather the Daughters together and have them vote on forming a council (directive council). Also include those of the village who belong to the Congregation of the Immaculate or the New Ursulines."

Everything took place between the two of them, the sick priest and the healthy one. No one else was aware of what was going on. In Italy as elsewhere, the usual New Year's Day celebrations were held. Everywhere the members of the Diplomatic Corps were bringing best wishes to monarchs and heads of republics. Groups of the faithful and pathetic organizations of leading figures were still speaking about transferring the Holy See here or there outside Italy. In the little room of Varazze, smelling of medicine and teas, a new chapter of life in the Church was being born, a new way of being present to the world today and tomorrow.

"The world doesn't know it," says a moving selection from the *Cronistoria, "but Don Bosco's Daughters rise today."*

First Election and First Rejection

At the house of the Immaculate they still lived in a spirit of ambiguity. Mary Mazzarello and the others were convinced that Don Bosco wanted them to join an already existing institute (or one coming into being) somewhere else, and that soon they would be established at Mornese under its direction. They thought they were going to *enter* a congregation, and were unaware of the fact that they *were* the congregation.

Fr. Pestarino gave them the outline of the rule drawn up by Don Bosco for the Daughters of the Immaculate, and he also showed it to the New Ursulines of Angela Maccagno. In the house they gathered in groups around those who could read, asked explanations of this or that section, and stumbled on an unexpected expression: "the discipline." Here the expression did not indicate an attitude of obedience. Those who knew, explained that it dealt with a penitential instrument well known to ascetics. It consisted of a sort of whip made up of many small cords which were knotted or made up of small chains. "To give oneself the discipline" meant, in the language of the ascetics, to whip oneself with that implement with the intention of "making up for one's own sins and those of others, reanimating devout fervor, dominating the senses, keeping temptations far away."

"This, no!" The first to say it in her own way was Petronilla Mazzarello, but the others all agreed with her. It was not even to be spoken of.

Once the text of the rule was read, explained and commented on, each could privately confer with Fr. Pestarino as to whether or not she felt inclined to enter the new institute. The priest wrote down the decisions without commenting on them.

Mary Mazzarello immediately said yes, and her sister, Felicita, joined her. Petronilla, instead, hesitated. She was not sure that she could keep up with the schedule and rigorous

calendar. She spoke with Fr. Pestarino, telling him of her difficulties. He listened in silence, without a word or any sign of
insistence, leaving her more uncertain than before. Her "yes"
would come a little later, after having spoken with Mary.
Many years later, Petronilla remembered the event: "Mary
immediately accepted and embraced Don Bosco's proposal,
but I waited, and later accepted with other young girls who
were with us, even though they did not belong to the Daughters
of the Immaculate."

Now for the surprise. Fr. Pestarino explained that there
was no institute of the Daughters of Mary Help of Christians
that was already formed, with a Mother General and all that
went with it; they and they alone were the new Daughters. Don
Bosco had chosen the group of young women formed by Mary
Mazzarello to be the nucleus of the new congregation. This
was the reality and, therefore, the superior would come from
Mornese. As soon as possible, as Don Bosco had requested,
there would be a plenary session on January 29, 1872, the feast
of St. Francis de Sales. Even the New Ursulines, those who
lived with their families, would come and vote. Nothing was to
be spoken of outside.

On the established day, the meeting was held in the
House of the Immaculate, before a table with a crucifix illumined by two candles. Fr. Pestarino wanted to impress on all
the awareness of that which they were doing. First of all, the
Veni Creator Spiritus was recited with two lit candles, as the
cardinals did when they elected a pope, because this was an
ecclesial event. For the first time, twenty-seven women were to
elect the superior of the Daughters of Mary Help of Christians.

Angela Maccagno assumed the function of scrutineer and
then announced the results of the voting: twenty-one votes for
Mary Mazzarello, three for Petronilla, two for Felicita and one
for Giovanna Ferrettino.

The results speak for themselves, but the person elected
said immediately that she could not accept, and she would not

change her idea, even though it was said that the general wish was to be respected. Finally, Fr. Pestarino suggested (and she accepted) that Don Bosco himself should nominate the first superior. This proposal was accepted by all, but on condition that Mary remain head of the group for now, with the title of vicar. Petronilla was then elected second assistant, Felicita mistress of novices and Giovanna Ferrettino treasurer. Thus the leadership was formed with the participation of the New Ursulines who then continued to live as they were, with Angela Maccagno at their head. Finally, Fr. Pestarino recited a brief psalm sung at the vespers of the apostles: "All you people praise the Lord, all nations give him glory...because his love for us is strong, and the fidelity of the Lord will last eternally."

They extinguished the candles and the assembly dispersed with an almost furtive speed, like a gathering of conspirators. They could not speak yet; it was necessary that the village be unaware of what had happened.

These women and girls were now a congregation, even though they had not yet pronounced their vows. They needed a habit which would distinguish them as sisters. Fr. Pestarino passed along this order to Mary with the opportune indications. She closed herself up in a room to make the first model, described to us by Petronilla: "It was a brown habit, similar to that of the friars, but without a cord, and with a cape which reached to the elbow." There would also be a blue veil.

The rapid changes in the House of the Immaculate resulted in a bit of confusion. So many things changed by themselves. In the meantime, there was a distinction between those Daughters who had said yes to Don Bosco's proposal and those who had not yet decided or who had decided not to accept. (For example, the teacher who was so useful as an instructor did not become a sister because she had her own ideas on how they should live. Now she was getting ready to return home permanently.)

In 1872 they once again raised silkworms. We cannot

separate the origins of the Daughters of Mary Help of Christians from this industrious peasant activity in community life. During the period of raising them (about forty days between May and June), even the schedule of the house moved in time to the voracious silkworms and their needs. There were endless rhythms for providing food (mulberry leaves), for their cleanliness, and then there came the time of maturity of the installation of a "shrub" where the silkworm would go to close itself into a cocoon, and finally the harvesting and sale.

All of the Daughters had learned this task at home, and they knew what the "money from the cocoons" meant for the family economy. It was true that the families even had to get up during the night to care for the cocoons, but during a good year the sale could pay for a bride's dowry, help to buy a piece of land, or send a son to school. The House of the Immaculate had contributed toward the work at the school with the "cocoon money," and now, in the spring of 1872, it would pay for the new habits.

However, this could not be done in full secrecy. In the village something was beginning to give them away; people noticed certain indications of something new. Comments and suspicions arose, even without complete knowledge of the facts. It was simple, yet bitter. As we have already stated, the bishop of Acqui did not want a male Salesian school in Mornese; it could harm the minor seminary of the diocese by taking away the students. The problem which existed during the time of Bishop Modesto Contratto was certainly not solved during the interim, and maintained all of its seriousness during the time of his successor, Bishop Giuseppe Maria Sciandra. If the school was established now, there would be the risk of a bitter encounter with this bishop, and Don Bosco could not allow this. His relationship with his old friend and collaborator, Lorenzo Gastaldi, who had become archbishop of Turin thanks to him, was already becoming cold.

On the other hand, he did not want to expose the bishop of Acqui to the resentment of the people, to portray him as an enemy of the school. In short, they made a studied effort not to cause dissension. They avoided announcing immediately that a new family of sisters had been founded and would live in the building constructed for a school. They trusted in time, waiting for an appropriate moment.

In some way, this arrived in spring of 1872. A situation came to light which would justify the temporary movement of the group of women to Borgoalto, without creating alarm.

This is how it happened. It became necessary to knock down and rebuild the canonry, and the town agreed to the expense. Then, in council, they decided that the pastor (who was now Fr. Carlo Valle) should move to the House of the Immaculate for the duration of the work and the Daughters should move temporarily to the rooms which were ready in the building destined for a school.

All temporarily, they said over and over again. The move came about on May 23, and even the cocoons were carefully transferred to Borgoalto. All was done very discreetly, during the night, but it was impossible to hide the fact that the girls had taken over.

No Longer a Secret

The transfer to Borgoalto touched all, even the students of the workroom who continued to come regularly, as did those of the festive oratory. This latter group had grown in number, attracted by the amount of space within and without. Continual news and secrets of the village arrived by way of these girls, and the news was not good. No one was pleased with the women taking over the building destined to be a school. Few believed that it would be a temporary sojourn, as the town council had said. Bitter feelings spread and they made the worst accusations: "We have been fooled, they never really thought of this place for a school." The idea of betrayal became strong, and everyone blamed Fr. Pestarino.

He had to allow them to talk without defending himself, because if he told all, the Curia of Acqui would be implicated and he did not want to do this. There were also those who began to threaten by other ways—physical violence. It was then that some people began to react. Strong young men let it be known that they would take care of his safety, and that no one should even think of touching the *previn.*

The usual murmurings against the Daughters increased. Was it really true that they would become sisters, even though so many of them didn't know how to read? Their loyalty to Don Bosco's proposal seemed to be the wild ideas of four presumptuous women who would shortly find themselves starving to death. On the opposite side, some complained that they had been "taken away" from the village where they rendered so much service. Finally, a few families threatened to withdraw their children from the workroom, fearing that they would be led to become religious like the others.

There was enough reason to sow anxiety in the little group which already had so many problems of formation and even hunger. Here, with her humble title of vicar, a smiling, decided Mary Mazzarello took the reins.

It was a strange, delicate moment, between a first acceptance and a final commitment. They had to form themselves more or less on their own. Father Pestarino was ready to counsel, and Don Bosco had drawn up the master outline of a rule, but it was difficult for them to give real content to the carrying out of every duty, gesture, obedience. It was not like joining an established order with its history, seasoned members and "preceding experience." Here there was still nothing; it was like a ship guided by sailors (and a captain) who were seeing the ocean for the first time.

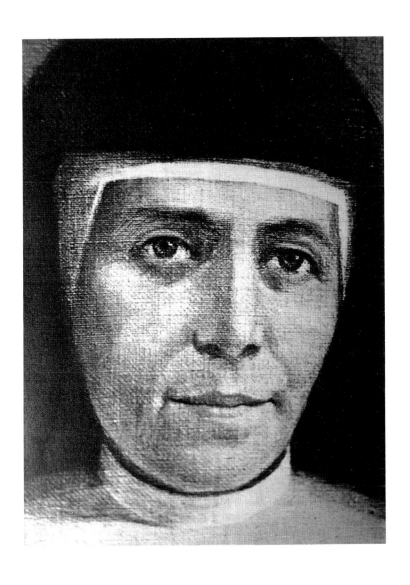

*St. Mary Domenica Mazzarello in a reproduction done
by Crida*

A panoramic view of Mornese

St. Mary Mazzarello's birthplace in Mornese-Mazzarelli

The parish church of Mornese

The Valponasca farm

The attic with the historic window

The school with the old well

The motherhouse at Nizza Monferrato

"Captain" Mary, however, knew the route even without maps or instruments. She knew that she had to communicate to her companions the greatness of the sense of the moment which they were experiencing. Greatness lay in the adversity to be overcome: that cloudy pessimism and mistrust which seemed to rise from the village toward the new house which was too big, the scarcity of everything, beginning with food. Discomfort stimulated them. Conquering it by work was also a step on the path of perfection. Those who worked well, also prayed well; those who were not afraid of commitment and fatigue were also not afraid of temptations and dangers. And they were never sad.

The girls had different capacities for work, and she was very careful about controlling the danger of competition. There were no classifications: "God does not take into account if someone did more work than another, but whether all used the talents which he gave them."

So it was possible to work in joy, that is, to rise to the privileged condition of children of God who knew how to do his will. Mary took every opportunity to keep them happy, and frequently, she was the leader of well-thought out projects in the direction of joy. For example, take the laundry. They now had the possibility of doing it at home, but it was better to continue as they had previously done, going to the Roverno with all the laundry as the people of Mornese did. In this way, the little group avoided the appearance of being set apart and withdrawn, and the work became an adventure, between the hills and the water. Bread and polenta eaten there had a different flavor, and there was no obligation to silence in this place. Work, play, joking all became one, and people felt like singing, even when getting soaked with cold water during the more difficult seasons. Mary made them feel that they were in God's presence when they washed clothes, split wood or hoed in the vineyards of Borgoalto, just as they were when they adored in chapel, between candles and the perfume of incense.

They knew how to read every new event in a spirit of trust in everyday events. That teacher who was a little bossy left, but another arrived from Turin a short time later. Angela Jandet held a teaching degree, and had been sent by Don Bosco. In the *Cronistoria,* we read how Mary observed her closely to understand her attitude: "She immediately set her to the test by giving her the task of a few little house registers in which contracted services were written, while she studied her character and her spirit."

There was another sign. Two Daughters of the Immaculate who had not shared the others' choice, Sr. Rosina Mazzarello and Maria Poggio, were now having second thoughts. Perhaps they were impressed by the serenity which they saw in the others day by day. Apparently, the conversations in the village had not bothered them, since now they asked Mary to be accepted into the group.

At this point everything was settled, with Don Bosco's consensus. The date of the first vestition was set for August. Those who already had made private vows would make profession with triennial vows, becoming real sisters. A few of the others, after the vestition, would become novices.

Don Bosco wanted to make the most of a coincidence. The bishop of Acqui, Bishop Sciandra, recuperating from pleurisy, came to convalesce at Borgoalto, Mornese. The "good air" of these hills was famous, and during the summer a small group of well-to-do people from Liguria came to spend their vacation here. Once Don Bosco heard the news, he set July 31 as the date for the spiritual retreat of the future sisters, after which the bishop would preside at the vestition.

Bishop Sciandra, called to rule the diocese at the suggestion of Don Bosco, wanted him to be present at the ceremony. Without taking into account his refusal because of commitments (and also because he was not well), the bishop sent his secretary to Valdocco to accompany him. Don Bosco arrived the evening of August 4, and the vestition was to be held the next day. The young people had been carefully prepared, practicing the gestures and words of the ceremony, but Don Bosco wanted to personally assure himself of everything. For example, did they know how to walk in church before and after having put on the religious garb, and in the midst of the people? He explained: bearing erect, eyes lowered, head high, a moderately slow step. He did not know if they had understood well, and said: "Look. You have to walk like this," and he acted out the part of a sister who had been vested, walking up and down the large room.

On the morning of August 5, we see them in the chapel of Borgoalto, before the bishop who was vested in ceremonial vestments, a group of priests and quite a few villagers: parents, brothers and sisters. Perhaps all did not agree with what was happening, but at least they came. They saw the girls enter in procession still dressed in lay clothing, each carrying her religious habit to the bishop who then blessed it. They left to change, and returned again in procession, walking the way Don Bosco had taught them, all dressed uniformly in brown and blue.

Mary Mazzarello was the first to recite the words of the solemn promise which would bind her for three years. Then the others followed, the first Daughters of Mary Help of Christians in history: the vicar Petronilla Mazzarello; Felicita Mazzarello; Giovanna Ferrettino; Teresa Pampuro; Felicina Arecco; Rosa Mazzarello, daughter of Stephen; Catherine Mazzarello; they were all from Mornese. Then there were Angela Jandet of Turin, Maria Poggio of Acqui and Assunta Gaino of Cartosio. Eleven sisters professed triennial vows, and to each of them the bishop gave a crucifix, symbol of their new state in life. The four novices who received a medal of Mary Help of Christians were: Rosina Mazzarello, daughter of Joseph of Mornese; Maria Grosso of S. Stefano Parodi; Clara

Spagliardi of Mirabello and finally the scintillating Corinna Arrigotti, whom Mary, as vicar, had guided on her return to the faith and then toward religious life. In her, the Daughters of Mary Help of Christians had their first music teacher, a necessary element for Salesian life.

On this Monday, August 5, 1872, the new feminine congregation was publicly presented for the first time, before the Church in the person of the bishop and the faithful, to the people of Mornese. The Sisters finished their religious exercises, after which, the *Cronistoria* tells us, "They entered into ordinary, everyday life of the Daughters of Mary Help of Christians, into the serene and active piety which could now be called Salesian. They consecrated themselves to the most faithful observance of those constitutions, which must bring the seed of the institute to the robust growth of the grain of mustard seed."

A Cold Glance at Don Bosco

This time Don Bosco came and went without a celebration. He no longer had triumphal entries on horseback, welcoming escorts, bells or an illumined village. During his quick stop at Mornese he had found coldness—respect, but coldness, bitter glances, closed expressions, no one drew near to speak with him. Fr. Pestarino had spared him the worse, keeping quiet about the accusations of betrayal and ill will which continued to run through the area. Certainly, a few words would have been enough to settle everything, putting the two of them in the clear, but then the conflict would fall upon Bishop Sciandra, and bishops had enough troubles. Therefore, it was necessary to allow themselves to be accused, and to keep quiet.

While Don Bosco was leaving, Mary Mazzarello had asked him when the real superior would arrive, since the congregation was now an established fact, and she was no longer sufficient.

Don Bosco told her not to worry, but to be tranquil, without adding, however, that he would send a superior. He only said "The Lord will provide." Therefore, Mary, for the present, did not have to worry, and for the future she was not to oppose those events which were already maturing. What was important, he concluded, was that they observe the rules carefully.

Observing the rule meant adapting to a strict daily schedule: "Rising and bedmaking" at 5:30 all year, then prayers in common and meditation at 6:00, followed by daily Mass at 6:45. At 7:30, work assignments were given out and ordinary tasks performed until breakfast at 8:00. Then they worked until noon, the time of the Angelus and the particular examination of conscience (ten minutes). This was followed by dinner and recreation. At 4:45 they had the "third part of the rosary and spiritual reading," then work again until supper time. Finally, at 9:30, they had a "visit to the Blessed Sacrament and the reading of the points of the next morning's meditation. From here, all retired in strict silence."

We have a detailed explanation about the food from Ferdinand Maccono: "At breakfast they had a little leftover bread or polenta; at dinner, bread and soup, polenta and salad or potatoes and vegetables. Occasionally they had milk, eggs, cheese or fish, which had been given to them as a gift or in exchange for work."

Frequently, their efforts to be self-sufficient were not enough, and the history of this first period is rich in food crises, resolved with the intervention of some family, time by time, and not only that of Mary Mazzarello. The relatives of the other Mornese natives helped, as did even strangers.

The resentment for the "failed school" remained sharp, woven through with skepticism on the success of this community dressed in brown. When they appeared in the village, a few Daughters suffered episodes of antipathy or derision.

Even Mary Mazzarello suffered all this, but when she felt

that it was not a danger from which to flee, she thought: "This is a test, and if we want to grow, we must face it." Therefore, the attitude of being under siege dissipated. She wanted no catacombs, no martyred attitudes, no closing themselves off from the village. They came and went as they needed, helped others when possible and responded to hostility with cheerfulness, which helped them to do good to all.

Mary's cheerfulness was the opposite of thoughtlessness. It did not take away anything. On the contrary, it took into consideration and interpreted adversities, but without fear or illusions. "To be cheerful," she would later write to a sister, "we must go forward with simplicity, not seeking satisfactions, neither in creatures, nor in the things of this world, and the Lord will do the rest." So it was that she obtained everyone's serene effort in the commitment to personal formation and in carrying out the activity in the workroom and oratory. These "educative works for the girls" were now the heart of their activity, and the means of sanctification for each of them.

The state of soul of the people of Mornese showed no visible transformations. Rather, it seemed that the coldness would settle into perpetual ice. Yet, here and there, slow, quiet signs of "melting" could be discerned. A few began to see that life at Borgoalto "went forward simply," and that the new institute was not the product of an ephemeral enthusiasm. The girls who frequented the workroom and those who were in the Sunday oratory were unconscious advertisements. Through them, many houses heard the real story about how they lived with the Daughters. The girls themselves were living "information" when they helped their mothers with needlework, which they learned at the workroom (and some even knew how to cut materials), or when they taught their brothers and sisters a new song they had learned.

If a few families had withdrawn their daughters from the workroom, feeling that they would be pressured into becoming sisters, the girls who stayed could also tell other stories when they got home, for example, those about new faces. Every now and then, new postulants arrived, usually sent by Don Bosco. However, he did leave complete freedom to the vicar. Some eventually stayed and entered the congregation and others did not. The sooner one got to know their characters, the better it was. (Even the novice Clara Spagliardi left after a few months.)

As the number of postulants grew, so did the problem with food. Then too, there was the pressing need to instruct them because not all knew how to read and write. The teacher, Sr. Angela Jandet, set up sort of an elementary course for these young people. The vicar, Sr. Mary, joined them, becoming a student among the students. She was already thirty-five years old, and had known how to read since she was a young girl. Now she wanted to learn to write, even though her hands, used to hard work, became "slow and stubborn" with a pen, as the *Cronistoria* tells us. Seated there, trying and making mistakes, receiving corrections from the teacher, she was not afraid of ruining her "image" and authority before the others, who were canonically her subjects. Her great capacity of simplifying things helped her find a quick, sure solution: what is most important for a superior is that she give good example. Seated there with pen in hand, she actually taught humility to the other students, to the teacher and to those who already knew how to write.

(From September 1872 she regulated herself in the same way for the weekly conference to the community. It was her job as vicar, but she also wanted the sisters to speak. A century later, these meetings open to the ideas of all would be highly recommended in the industrial world as a valued managerial tool: brainstorming.)

Because Sr. Jandet was the only teacher among the sisters, a second, Candida Salvini, was accepted in the role of lay teacher, with a small stipend. Sr. Mary entrusted the students to her, and later the postulants, until 1874, when the first two Sisters of Mary Help of Christians obtained their teaching diploma.

Corinna Arrigotti also gave music lessons. All in the house had wept much for her a few days after her vestition. An unexpected letter had arrived from her father who called her home to Tonco, a town in Monferrato. All were afraid that they would never see her again. She didn't want to go, and even Fr. Pestarino and the bishop of Asti were called upon, but you couldn't say no to a father. She left in tears, dressed in secular garb, accompanied by Felicita Mazzarello. Even Mary Mazzarello felt like crying, but she was the vicar, and so she invited all to pray. She also told them to stop complaining— enough with tears. They were to work and be cheerful because you could not be in God's presence with a pessimistic attitude.

A few days later, Corinna returned in triumph. She had convinced her father with two decisive arguments: her dexterity as a pianist had increased, and the assurance that her staying at Mornese would be of no expense to him. It really hadn't been necessary to become so desperate when she left.

At the end of 1872 a new arrival came from Turin, but she was not a postulant. Twenty-year-old Emilia Mosca had come to teach French and to earn something for her family. She belonged to a once well-to-do family which had become impoverished. (Her grandfather, Carlo Bernardo Mosca was the famous engineer of bridges and roads at the service of the Napoleonic empire. Later, during the 1820's, he built the great bridge which bears his name over the river Dora in Turin. Charles Albert named him senator of the Kingdom in 1848.)

It was a new encounter for Sr. Mary with another type of woman, with other habits, even in religious instruction. Emilia had never seen such poverty. Those little touches of feminine refinement typical of even the most austere communities were lacking. (Rather, they were found here, but were reserved only for the chapel, which they sought to continually embellish.)

Notwithstanding the diversity between them, they immediately understood one another. Guided by Sr. Mary with loving trust, Emilia quickly adapted to the ways of the house, overcoming the obstacles and discomforts of the environment. A dialogue naturally followed and the *Cronistoria* tells us: "The young teacher studied the vicar's reflections well; she knew how to appreciate the generous virtue which she heard and saw around her, even though it was vested in humble garb."

After only a month's sojourn, Emilia Mosca asked to be accepted as a postulant among the Daughters of Mary Help of Christians.

The Sisters of St. Ann

The 19th century saw crowds of Catholics fighting on a variety of fronts, those within, those of school against school, group against group. At the same time, Catholics offered a strong witness of fraternity, but because of their less ostentatious nature, they did not get overly involved in polemics. Here is a document linked to the origins of the Daughters of Mary Help of Christians and taken from the chronicles of the Sisters of St. Ann in Turin: "On the last Sunday of the month of January (1873) we listened to a sermon by Rev. Father John Bosco, founder and superior of the Salesian Congregation. He had come to ask our venerated Mother General for the cooperation of our institute for the foundation of the Daughters of Mary Help of Christians, which was dependent upon him. This was a propitious occasion to render to others that charity which we had received during the beginnings of our existence, and so, our beloved Mother General, with the consent of her council, acceded to the request and sent to Mornese, the cradle of the new institute, Reverend Sr. Frances, her secretary and second general assistant, giving her as her companion in this important mission our good Sr. Angela."

Enrichetta Dominici, Mother General of the Sisters of St. Ann, was forty-four-years-old and Mary Mazzarello was thirty-six. They were two country girls, one born at Carmagnola (Turin) and the other at Mornese. They had reached the religious life by different ways and were two examples of its dynamism: from a condition of being anonymous and submissive they rose to leadership; from a severely circumscribed reality—the sullen limits of the fields, the vineyards, the garden, the limits of status and language—they went to a total openness of horizons, to a freedom of protagonists in the world.

In 1871 Mother Enrichetta had sent a group of sisters to teach the children of Chieri, near Turin, and another little group to open a mission in India, in the apostolic vicariate of Hyderabad (Don Bosco helped this expedition). Sr. Mary Mazzarello, instead, in the midst of the poverty of Mornese, did not yet foresee anything. But in her turn, she prepared herself for a daring future by that precept which she taught and followed: *be always in God's presence,* the God who walks with his people and does not allow us to get lost on the long journey.

The two Sisters of St. Ann, Francesca Garelli and Angela Alloa, arrived at Mornese during Lent and remained there until September, except for a brief return to Turin for Easter.

Like true sisters, they showed the others what to do. The little family of Mornese received the Sisters of St. Ann with an authentic joy for learning and with refreshing sincerity in confessing themselves to be inexperienced and clumsy. One sister worked with the sisters, the other with the postulants and aspirants. Francesca and Angela were called upon to give direction with regard to formative activity and administration, on the way of praying, and of dealing which those who came to visit. The little natives of Mornese continued to ask questions; there was a whole lifetime to refine, a great need of rationality in this little spontaneous universe. They also learned how to "put in order the clothing of the girls, how to mark the articles of clothing, how to place the children in the dormitory, the dining room, the chapel, on walks, how to deal with the relatives of the children, how to regulate themselves in their correspondence, etc."[2]

Sr. Francesca and Sr. Angela also learned something. They were moved by the joyful humility of all, beginning with Mary Mazzarello, the vicar, the superior, who was the first to say that she was ignorant. There is a Franciscan perfume in making oneself humble with the most beautiful smile, while for many humility means wrapping oneself in misery and being downtrodden. In her there was not the least impediment to making herself small, like the student who receives instruction and later seeks to put it into practice diligently, drawing from it only joy.

At the end of their service, Sr. Francesca and Sr. Angela pointed out certain excesses which they noted in the practice of poverty. For example, they pointed out the poverty of the diet of these women and girls, even the most delicate, and how much fasting they imposed upon themselves, beginning from the vicar. They also noted some formal insufficiencies in manifesting discipline even exteriorly, which were like rough edges to be smoothed. But over and above any experience and expression, the remembrance of Mary Mazzarello, teacher of humility, remained in them.

But there were also peals from other bells. One, for example, suggested to Don Bosco that he put an end to all that was happening at Mornese, because those women and girls would never succeed at anything. This suggestion came from Andrea Scotton, bishop and archpriest at Breganze, near Vicenza. He was one of the three famous Scotton brothers, all priests and fiery preachers. In July-August he preached the retreat to the Daughters of Mary Help of Christians and found them lacking: "Too little instructed, ignorant of so many things, they will not succeed. You, dear Don Bosco, should have no further thought of them."

"Fine, fine, we'll see." This was Don Bosco's answer to the illustrious preacher. And he continued to send girls to Mary Mazzarello. Every now and then he would send a few beds, sheets and straw mattresses—for those who would come.

The second vestition took place on August 5, 1873 in the chapel of the Daughters. This time the novices and sisters appeared in chapel with large, black bonnets on their heads. The bishop of Acqui was the celebrant again. Don Bosco had arrived a few days earlier, but had to leave. This time Petronilla's niece Rosina Mazzarello, Maria Grosso and Corinna Arrigotti, who had overcome her father's opposition at the last moment, pronounced their triennial vows, becoming "professed sisters." The vicar followed the ceremony as though she herself was making her vows; these three sisters were the result of her special work. They had been formed by her example, words and silences. They were formed by the cheerfulness learned at her school.

Emilia Mosca was among the nine postulants who donned the habit of the novices. There was an eighteen-year-old girl from Rosignano Monferrato, Enrichetta Sorbone. Like many others, she showed that Bishop Scotton may have been a well-trained preacher, but a poor prophet.

Not only this, but her religious adventure could begin thanks to Don Bosco who had granted a mysterious exception; and thanks to Sr. Mary Mazzarello, who had made four of them. The priest and the sister may not have observed the rule, but neither did they go against it; they developed it. For this reason the family of sisters dressed in brown—the early habit—would explode upon the world, even if now the great house of the school did not even have an entry for visitors, as Bishop Scotton complained.

Enrichetta Sorbone's story is quickly told. She was sup-posed to have studied to become a teacher, but then her mother died and she was dedicated to raising her two brothers and four sisters, all younger than herself. Having heard people in Rosignano speak of Don Bosco and call him a saint, she wanted to see him up close. In May 1873, he visited Borgo San Martino, in Monferrato, and she got there by traveling four hours by foot from Rosignano. When she was able to draw close to him, he immediately said to her: "You will go to Mornese," without knowing who she was, without first inform-ing himself, violating every ecclesiastical rule. He asked this information of her later, learning that her dream was to study. "You will study at Mornese." He spoke of the future matter-of-factly, with complete security.

A few weeks later, Enrichetta left for Mornese, accompa-nied by her bewildered father. It was June 6, 1873. The Daugh-ters of Mary Help of Christians and the two Sisters of St. Ann welcomed them. Knowing that Enrichetta's vocation was for teaching, the vicar, Mary Mazzarello, put her to work with twenty students for her first trial. Later she became aware of the problem of the four little sisters left at home, two of whom were very young. They were with their father and brothers, but they needed a mother's care. The two Sisters of St. Ann of-fered to take in the little ones and to care for them at the institute in Turin without charge.

However, Mary Mazzarello intervened. Regulations or not, postulant or not, "the little ones must stay with you," she told Enrichetta, the only one who could be a mother to them. She added: "We're ready to take the bread from our own mouths so they don't lack for anything. Then we'll have the older girls come." She spoke like a mother, and even a father. Listening to her, we see ourselves before a new and special law, a right which goes above certain venerated prescriptions, one which cancels out the old idea of separation between religious and the family, almost denying it according to a certain misplaced fervor. Flour and eggs, vegetables and firewood arrived at Borgoalto from families. Mother Mazzarello brought out the principles and the teachings which a family could give. From the time she was a young girl she had seen her father and mother, uncle and aunt accept two orphaned nieces as their own children. This was the spirit which she impressed on her community of Mary Help of Christians.

The two little girls came to Mornese, and later, the other two also arrived. Their story concludes with the five Sorbone sisters, Enrichetta, Angiolina, Carolina, Marietta and Angelica all becoming Daughters of Mary Help of Christians.

Chapter Five

Mary Mazzarello kept insisting: "When will you send us a Mother General? We need someone to guide us; we can't go on like this." In February 1847, one of Fr. Pestarino's relatives noted that the institute of the Daughters of Mary Help of Christians at Mornese had thirteen professed sisters, eight novices, eight postulants and seventeen students.

The "boarders," as Fr. Pestarino called them, were not future sisters. They were students, coming for the most part from Mornese and the surrounding area. They lived at the large house of Borgoalto (frequently called "the school") and attended the girls' elementary school recently started by the Daughters of Mary Help of Christians. There were two groups living side by side: the community of sisters, novices and postulants, and the school which came about as a result of their initiative, the center of their commitment to "do for girls what the Salesians were doing for boys."

It was still the very early days, and they lacked everything: organization, teachers, students. Don Bosco provided teachers, sending them from Turin. He also started a careful campaign in order to have more students. On October 1, 1873, the newspaper, *Unità Cattolica,* spoke of "a good institute for girls," founded at Mornese, "a healthy village in the diocese of Acqui," by Don Bosco during "the past year" (1872). The paper continued that his scope was to accept and educate in a Christian manner "those girls who, due to financial straits, could not enter other houses for a ladylike education." During the first year the school had already borne good fruit, and "this was solemnly testified to by professors from Turin who had gone to Mornese at the beginning of this month to interview the students." The institute was open even during vacation time, and the monthly fee was twenty lire or "one marengo."

Don Bosco also distributed to the Piedmontese clergy a more detailed circular with an explanation of the program, which intended to give "moral and scientific teaching in such a way that nothing was lacking for a young person from an honest, Christian family."

To this scope "the teaching took in the four elementary classes, a complete course of Italian, calligraphy, arithmetic, metric system, bookkeeping and domestic economy. Declamation and a special exercise in writing letters also made up part of the teaching. Lessons were also given in drawing, French and piano, but only by request and at additional expense to the relatives of the students." Domestic work was taught in theory and in practice. It consisted in "making clothing proper to the condition of the students, knitting, making stockings, blouses, weaving, mending, needlework, lacemaking and all the ordinary work of an honest family." Furthermore, students over twelve years of age "took turns serving in the dining room and helping in kitchen and garden work, insofar as it was reconcilable with their other duties." Religious teaching was imparted, using as a text "the catechism and Bible history with reflections and practical applications."

The students ate separately, with food adapted to their age and which was very different from that of the religious. "In the morning they had bread, coffee and milk, or fruit. At dinner, they had as much bread and soup as they wanted, and a second course with wine. At snack time they ate bread. At supper, they again ate as much bread and soup as they wanted, with a second course of fruit and wine. Those who desired better fare could have it through an opportune agreement with the superior." Finally, the school also offered lessons in "good manners."

This was fine. But the more Don Bosco showed himself to be pleased with these beginnings at Mornese, the more Mary Mazzarello insisted: that which was a motive of complacency for others, was a daily cross for her, precisely because the number of religious was increasing and because school was being taught, so it was urgent that they have someone who knew how to direct, guide and form as soon as possible. "I need it, too," she added.

It seemed that she would finally be satisfied. During October 1873 an upper class woman, a lawyer's widow, arrived from Turin. Maria Blengini had been sent by Don Bosco. Was she to be the new superior? No one either affirmed or denied it, so the vicar believed it. Then, too, this woman had the demeanor and correct way of speaking for a religious house. She showed a good experience of community life, much tact and much attention to persons and things. Thus, without anyone saying it, in a natural manner, the Daughters placed themselves at her orders, loved her counsels and sought to be useful to her in everything. However, she came with her own maid.

She was also treated differently at table, but she saw how the others were eating—poorly and meagerly. Yet, this was still not enough for some of the sisters. Some were inflicting special privations on themselves, voluntarily renouncing a part of their poor meal, after the example of Mother Vicar. How long could they endure this harshness?

It goes without saying that Maria Blengini was sincere in seeking the good of all. She was right to fear that such a sacrificed life would weaken their energies. Yet, she could not understand the primary substance of those denials, which were primary and perennial because young people like to try themselves and to face challenges. They would always like them, even though they would change according to the times and ways. At the time of Mary Domenica Mazzarello one of the most familiar fields of trial was that of nourishment. It was there that she and others took their risk—willpower against appetite and more often against real hunger. There each controlled the authenticity of her choice for a poor life, and the strengthening of her character, the capacity not to cave in.

Hard work was joined to scant food, and then all became clear for Maria Blengini. These women and girls were dragging themselves ahead badly and were headed for worse, because their way of living was harmful for piety. According to her judgment, for example, they prayed little because they had too much to do and this was not the way sisters should act. Neither were they religious in their way of speaking, moving or casual acting. It was as though they were in the threshing room, or the vineyard, or the pasture with the sheep.

This woman had a right intention to change things for the better, according to her view and the experience of other religious families. She admired them very much and was particularly impressed by Mary Mazzarello's stature, shown through a cordial humility. She would make gracious recommendations here and there, but in the meantime, she wrote to Don Bosco. Then, in the heart of the winter of 1873-74, she went back to Turin for a visit and spoke directly with Don Bosco, telling him everything.

Don Bosco clarified the fact that this was exactly how the Daughters of Mary Help of Christians were to be. It was what he wanted. On this point they definitely did not agree. Maria

Blengini, cordially thanked, as she should have been, would not return to Mornese.

There are a few things that Mary Mazzarello would not know completely, during these months when she insisted on having a Mother General. One was the drama which Don Bosco was living in Rome during the first months of 1874. It was a long, busy and tormenting sojourn to follow and push the last documents of the Salesian Society toward definite recognition, and the definitive approval of his constitutions after a minute exam, word for word, disposition by disposition. This would signify the confirmation of the Salesians as an institution in the whole Church, dependent only on the Holy See and governed only by its own superiors. The long, heavy exam was dramatic for Don Bosco, because it was aggravated and damaged by his bitter conflict with Lorenzo Gastaldo, archbishop of Turin. They just could not come to an understanding of one another.

In this climate, four cardinals named by Pius IX had to give their decisive word on the constitutions. They had to hear the opinion of numerous bishops other than that of Turin, and not all were favorable toward Don Bosco.

Completely ignorant of Vatican procedures, Mary Mazzarello and her companions understood, however, that something important was at stake in Rome, because Don Bosco wrote to them: "We must double our supplications before God's throne." He wrote a detailed program of prayer, adoration, reading and fasting for three days during the month of March.

The second thing which the vicar did not know were these words which Don Bosco had spoken of her: "Mary Mazzarello has special gifts from God. Her limited instruction is abundantly supplemented by her virtue, prudence, spirit of discernment and her gift of governing based on goodness, charity and an unshakable faith in the Lord."

He said this to Fr. John Cagliero, who was returning from a visit to Mornese in the capacity of director general and who was Don Bosco's lieutenant (Fr. Pestarino was the local director of the Daughters). During that visit he had listened to all, sisters and novices, also bringing up the question of food. Madame Blengini was not completely wrong on this point, and they could give coffee and milk every day to those who were less strong.... Mary Mazzarello was not against this (in fact, every now and then she would order someone to eat more, and would see to it that they did), but for the moment, the Daughters preferred to continue in their usual manner: polenta, bread soup and boiled dried chestnuts, which in this area were already a delicacy.

At the moment when he was leaving Mornese, Cagliero was once again questioned in public by Mary Mazzarello and one can guess what the topic was. The vicar felt it her duty to insist clearly: this is an institute born to teach, to spread instruction, and it cannot be governed by an ignorant woman. Fr. Cagliero was asked and begged to obtain the nomination of a Mother General who had all the necessary qualifications. This was even more urgent now that the school had obtained substantial recognition from the civil authorities. In December 1873 the scholastic delegate sent from Castelletto d'Orba, by order of the superintendent of schools in the province of Alessandria, answered a request from the teacher Emilia Mosca, communicating that: "There is no prohibition on the part of the provincial scholastic authorities that she keeps open in Mornese the above mentioned house of studies." Here Emilia Mosca was acting in the capacity of the directress of the elementary courses.

In going to the school Cagliero told the novices and postulants that if in the meantime they wanted to call Mary Mazzarello "Mother Vicar" it was all right. "And if by chance you happen to call her even 'Mother,' go right ahead!" He had no further problems. He understood that for the religious, and even for the people of Mornese, "Maìn of the Valponasca" was the logical, natural, "born" superior. But Mary would not let go, and she dogged him with a letter which has not been conserved, but which the *Cronistoria* reports as her "first attempt at epistolary correspondence": "This letter, without many words, will tell you if I am adapted to the office of superior. You will be able to judge from this writing which I am actually ashamed to send to you. My instruction, my penmanship is like chicken scratch; the mistakes in spelling and grammar are those more of an ignorant peasant.... Tell Don Bosco that I am not even capable of directing myself, much less others."[1]

All Whispered Her Name

1874 was a year of mourning in Mornese. On January 29, Sr. Maria Poggio died, the cook of the community and one of the first "professed." In March, the drama of Sr. Corinna Arrigotti began.

It was a very painful story. Her father had arrived at Mornese in a fury to take her home. He took it as an outrage to his person that she had become a sister. He was her father, and he had to be obeyed, Fr. Pestarino told Sr. Corinna. She had to remove the habit of the Daughters of Mary Help of Christians, set aside her bonnet.... Bareheaded, her badly cut hair looked awful, and a novice quickly cut off her own long braid to give it to the disheartened girl. She refused to give in on one point—when they told her that she could be released from her vows. Her response was no, she would be faithful to her promise no matter what happened.

Once at home, the family tried in every way to persuade her to forget Mornese. Her father tried, with his hard character, as did other relatives, but all without success. Sr. Corinna would not speak and would not go out. She cared for her grandfather (and later persuaded him to receive the sacraments before he died). It was a bitter battle, which she finally won. Without reconciliation, her father allowed her to return to Mornese, and she once more dressed in the habit, but her physical strength had been affected. She wanted to return to her music, but could not; she was overtaken by an invincible fatigue. She no longer had any life. Sr. Corinna had come back only to die among her companions.

Before her, Fr. Pestarino died on May 15, at 57 years of age. He had been the director and confessor of the Daughters, the man who had spent his inheritance and himself for Mornese, who had allowed himself to be accused in the place of others, who had first discovered in Mary Mazzarello the beginning of her call. He was seized by an apoplectic attack while he was at the Daughters' house reading a letter. He suffered five hours of agony before the end came.

It was a grave blow for the young community. Don Bosco immediately sought to give them a new director, Fr. Joseph Cagliero, cousin of Fr. Pestarino and director of the school at Varazze. By May 23, he was already in Mornese at his task. He arrived just in time to assist Sr. Corinna during her last days. She used her last strength to ask that her father be advised of her death, to tell him that she forgave him, but he did not respond to the communication from Mornese. She died on June 5, toward evening, and the girls of the village had to sing her funeral Mass because the Daughters and the students did not have the strength to do so. A note in the *Cronistoria* about this death gives us a brief glimpse into the life of the community at its beginnings: "In her died the first music teacher, and the first to do some accounting and registration in the institute."[2]

Things went along more or less like this. When Fr. Pestarino died, they also found on his desk a letter from Don Bosco which requested from the Daughters of Mary Help of

Christians at least partial payment of their debt with the Salesian mother house.

Don Bosco thought little about these things. For him it was important, very important to have won the final battle in Rome. On April 3, 1874, his constitutions were finally approved, thanks to the personal intervention of Pius IX. The approval also included in some way the Daughters of Mary Help of Christians. Their institute, from the time of Fr. Pestarino, had known the founder, and had been inserted into the Salesian Congregation. "Inserted" is not a term of the curia; it was Don Bosco's invention, and for this reason the Daughters had no need for gradual approval on the part of the Holy See. As long as possible, he had remained absolutely quiet with Rome in dealing with the question of the girls. There was not a word on the first two vestitions of the sisters; it was enough for him that he had the approval of the bishop of Acqui.

There was not a word after, until the moment in which he could no longer keep quiet, since he had to ask Rome for a "yes" on the constitutions. Only then did he tell them something, and even then, it was the least possible. Peter Stella tells us about his method of proceeding: "In 1874 he presented the institute of the Daughters of Mary Help of Christians to Rome. After having given an account of the Salesian Society, he noted that it had an "appendix at Mornese," that is, a House of Mary Help of Christians approved by the bishop of Acqui with the aim of "doing for poor girls that which the Salesians did for boys."[3]

In this way he had ingeniously placed within the institutions of the Church even the women's group. As soon as possible, he went to Mornese to speed up their preparation. This was during June 1874 and was one of the longest visits. He celebrated the three month anniversary Mass in memory of Fr. Pestarino, then each day, as the *Cronistoria* notes, "He heard confessions, spoke individually, visited the house. He had a good word for each of the students. He found many of them, and saw they were good and very close to the sisters. He observed the playground where the games, songs and playing, and the harmony between girls and sisters assured him that his aim for the institute was being realized.... He visited the work-room and the school, and approved, comforted, consoled and encouraged them."[4]

Then he announced the first piece of news. A few sisters would go to Borgo San Martino near Casale, where the Salesian school which had been opened at Mirabello Monferrato had been transferred. Their task was to be very practical: to cook and do the laundry. It was a small step in all senses, but it opened a new movement in history. Not one of them would ever have thought of leaving Mornese; they would have lived there forever. They never imagined a life outside of those hills, without the Roverno river, the vineyards and the chestnut trees. Fr. Cagliero spoke of the example of the bees and their necessary swarming here and there. Mornese would always be the nest, but it would also be a springboard; the future of the Daughters of Mary Help of Christians would lead them to other horizons.

There was a second fundamental, long-awaited piece of news: now the Mother Superior and her council, at that time called the chapter, would be nominated. It was the first step toward the future, and it was carried out with a ceremony started by Fr. Pestarino. A crucifix was placed between two lit candles on a table; a hymn to the Holy Spirit was sung and then the voting was carried out. Since not all knew how to write, Don Bosco himself functioned as scrutineer. Each sister would go to whisper in his ear the name of the person whom she chose, and he would write it down. All whispered the same name to Don Bosco: Mary Domenica Mazzarello. All except she. She was, therefore, elected by a unanimous vote, and became for all and forever, the superior, the Mother. She accepted, because all wanted it and clearly so did Don Bosco. "They know how little I am worth," she commented in a low voice with a humility which did not dramatize anything. They had given her a task; she would do whatever she could.

Petronilla was then elected vicar; Giovanna Ferrettino, treasurer; Felicina Mazzarello assistant; and Maria Grosso mistress of novices. The directive body of the Daughters of Mary Help of Christians was formed; Don Bosco could return to Valdocco. A few days later two religious in brown habits appeared. They were Sr. Emilia Mosca and Sr. Rosalia Pestarino, who had stopped at the oratory before going to the Sisters of St. Ann where they would receive hospitality. They were to prepare themselves for their teaching license, and would do so in two phases, because during the summer exam all would go well, except for mathematics.

On August 16, Mother Mazzarello, for the first time after her election, received a new postulant. Her name was Catherine Daghero, and she came from Cumiana, in the province of Turin. Her cousin Rosa was already at Mornese. In this way in the birthplace of the Daughters of Mary Help of Christians, the newly elected Mother Superior and the one who would be called to succeed her were already present.

But this does not only belong to the inscrutable future. It was also part of the inconceivable present, because Catherine Daghero had no intention of becoming a Daughter of Mary Help of Christians. She said so very clearly, and had no intention of even unpacking. Newly elected, Mother Mazzarello had murmured, "They know what I am worth." But she was mistaken. This Catherine Daghero with her prickliness for Mornese had come to mysteriously be the test case, to show all that in reality they actually did not know how much Mary Mazzarello was worth.

The First to Return Home

The rhythms of the year at Mornese had become regular; a tradition was being established. Once more, at the end of the summer of 1874 the spiritual exercises were held, dedicated primarily to the Daughters of Mary Help of Christians, but open to the "ladies" who sustained the Salesian activity in Piedmont and beyond. The others who participated were young teachers and dedicated girls, from whom there came numerous vocations for the institute every year. At the conclusion, on August 29, the vestitions were held: two sisters pronounced their triennial vows and four postulants received the habit of the novices.

That year saw many funerals. A few days after the death of Fr. Pestarino, the student Emilia Chiara died, a niece of Madame Blengini. On September 5, it was Fr. Joseph Cagliero's turn. The local director of the Daughters had been at Mornese for a only a short time.

He had been unwell when he came from Varazze and had not been able to regain his health. At the beginning of October Don Bosco sent the new director, Fr. Giacomo Costamagna. On October 8, the little group destined for Borgo San Martino left Mornese guided by the new Local Superior, Sr. Felicina Mazzarello, Mary Domenica's sister. She was accompanied by Sr. Felicina Arecco, Sr. Angiolina Deambrogio and Sr. Carlotta Pestarino. Fr. John Cagliero had spelled out their work in greater detail: kitchen and laundry for the boarders, but also a workroom for the girls of the village, and naturally, the festive oratory—all of the typical works, the unmistakable distinguishing features of Salesian identity. It was clear that four sisters would not be enough to do all this, and soon reinforcements were sent.

Meanwhile, Don Bosco was thinking about other kinds of expeditions. On New Year's Day, 1873, he confided to those around him: "If I were to express all that now passes through my mind, I would describe to you a great number of oratories spread throughout this land, in France, Spain, Africa, America and in many other places where our brothers would work untiringly in Jesus' vineyard. This is now simply my idea, but I think that we may affirm that it is something historical." On another occasion, he said that he had already received about fifty invitations for missionary expeditions abroad. He never stopped studying the perspectives of evangelization through books and atlases. Even his famous "dreams" frequently went back to the theme of evangelization of non-Christians.

Among those who would need missionaries for Christians was the archbishop of Buenos Aires. The priests of his diocese were too few for the natives of that place and for the immigrants living there.

The departures from Italy grew in number, even though it was not yet the impressive and dramatic flow of persons who would leave by the end of the century. During the first three months of 1874, from Genoa alone about 6000 Italians left for Argentina. One has to see how they and other emigrants left. The President of the Council, Giovanni Lanza, spoke of it in a circular letter in 1873, emphasizing the need to keep those departing from the tricks and theft of those recruiting laborers. They were frequently in league with money changers and hotel keepers in the port cities, who wanted to strip the emigrants of everything before they set foot on the ship. The circular also points out some bureaucratic means to somewhat discourage emigration, especially for young men of military age. Finally, the great agricultural interests militated against emigration, because it saw fewer numbers of hired hands, tenants and sharecroppers, people impoverished by the taxes, especially those on flour. Some people left with bitter songs: "Pick up that stone, throw away that bread, pay the miller, cruel villain; throw away your work gloves, fieldhands and farmers, we're going to America!"

Italy was approaching the exhausting finishing line of the State's balance of payments for its foreign debts. King Victor Emanuel II was approaching his twenty-fifth year as sovereign, a date to be celebrated, especially considering how his reign started, with Piedmont conquered and occupied in part, Genoa in revolt, the Chamber in tumult in Turin.... Yet, it seemed that no one was content with this Italian unity, neither those who had constructed it nor those who feared it. It seemed as though all was hopeless, too poor, ordinary, stripped of heroic deeds and courage. At the beginning of the year, the *Almanacco Reppublicano* printed the poem, "Forward, Forward!" by Giosuè Carducci: "O People of Italy, old, indolent Titan, cowardly, I say to your face, and you cry out to me 'Bravo!'"

To the council, Francesco Crispi, in the name of the Democratic Left, hoped for the renewal of the parliamentary class; it was necessary that the Senate be elective, and that they could be deputies at twenty-five years of age and senators at thirty. "This is new blood...which I want introduced into the political body, so that a virginal, more lively action, which comes from youthful years and is lacking in the second age, will once more give Parliament that strength and vigor which we seek today."

These mourners exaggerated a bit. Savings "to the bone" did not stop them from going ahead with much needed projects, and one of these concerned upper Monferrato, with some advantage even for Mornese.

On September 27, 1874, the Savona-Acqui section opened the railway line from Savona to Turin, among senators, deputies and mayors who had all come together in an Acqui decorated with flags, with a musical band, and a dinner for 300 people organized by Mr. Carozzi, impresario of the Baths. It was another good link between these territories and Liguria.

In October 1874, at 37 years of age, Mother Mazzarello finally had the opportunity to ride on a train. Her first stop was

Borgo San Martino, where she brought the novice Agnes Ricci to reinforce the little community of four Daughters. Her journey continued toward Turin, together with Emilia Mosca and Rosalia Pestarino, who were going to take the make-up exam in mathematics.

So many things happened to her for the first time: going to Turin to visit the Sisters of St. Ann at the motherhouse, and above all, going down to Valdocco to see the schools, the oratory, the workroom, that universe of young people, and finally, the imposing sanctuary of Mary Help of Christians, which she had heard described so many times. She heard about how this place had been a squalid field, inhabited by misery and evil, until Don Bosco arrived. She heard how the site of the grandiose sanctuary was still a poor pasture just a few years ago, until one day Don Bosco pointed it out to his boys with the prophecy: "You will see, here we will build a great church with a high cupola...." Now, in fact, the gold plated statue of Mary Help of Christians shone from on high, just as Don Bosco had said.

When her visits were over, this was also her first "return to the motherhouse" with Emilia and Rosalia, who had both received their teaching diploma. She came back with candy from the Sisters of St. Ann and with the medals sent to the Daughters by Don Bosco, whose prodigious works she had seen with her own eyes.

On December 13, with Fr. John Cagliero present, they had another vestition. Among the seven novices who took the habit was Catherine Daghero, the reluctant native of Cumiana, who had not even wanted to bring her trunk to her room, because she didn't like anything about Mornese and the institute.

Sr. Petronilla and Sr. Maria Grosso would have happily sent her home, because while she had consented to stay in the institute for a while, she never opened herself and never gave a cordial gesture; she lived like an exile. Even Fr. Costamagna and Fr. Cagliero had expressed their perplexity to Mother Mazzarello, but she who also saw everything (and perhaps who alone saw beyond) never tired of repeating: "I have told you time and again, this young woman must stay here because she is called to do great good in the institute."

Now there she was in the chapel. The *Cronistoria* tells us that once she put on the habit "Catherine regained that light of serenity in her eyes which she had had when doubts and per- plexities did not torture her thoughts."

Mother had been sweet yet firm with Catherine. She did not lighten her burdens to convince her to stay; she did not camouflage the discipline. She was ready, instead, to impress on her mind an idea: you are capable of doing all that we do; we want you to succeed, because you have the gifts.

Her simple conversations were woven through with trust, but they were, above all, authenticated in her way of being mother and sister. One doesn't have to listen to a discourse, even a sharp one, but seeing facts is different, and Catherine saw many of them. She found herself near Mother Mazzarello in chapel, during the morning Mass. She saw that she was tranquil and serene, even though she knew that she had been fasting when she washed the clothes at the Roverno at two or three o'clock in the morning. She discovered her in the vine- yard working like a laborer, or in the kitchen helping the cook or leading the donkey laden with the clothes to be washed. At a certain point the sisters had begun to insist: "A Mother Gen- eral should not do certain tasks, especially when people could see her; dignity must be shown, especially to those who don't understand...." In those cases there was almost always a silent, efficacious smile, the smile of Mother General, a sign of the perfect joy experienced precisely when she bent herself to "inferior" tasks, seeing the surprise and compassion in so many stunned eyes.

Catherine's behavior during the early days must have

embittered many. For example, once, stubborn and decided, she wanted to write to her family in Cumiana to come and get her, that she couldn't take it any longer. Mother Mazzarello probably didn't forbid her, but asked only that she not write immediately, that she should wait a bit. However, she knew also from her *Imitation of Christ* that the real problem was not acting only on Catherine: "If you do not see yourself as you would want to be, could it be possible that you are reducing yourself, and others, to your own behavior? We want others to be perfect, but without doing away with our own defects."[5] Mary Mazzarello worked much on herself to keep Catherine Daghero as her daughter.

Coffee and Milk at Breakfast

Mother Superior, Mother General, fine. But she still did not have a little room, even a tiny one, which could serve as her office. In order to speak with her, you had to look for her in the workroom with the others. She had talks even when she was sewing and mending. The *Cronistoria* tells us: "Since she did not yet have a room for her own use, she continued to speak from her place of work, to those who needed a good word."[6]

To the others, she herself would go to give a good word, looking for them one by one. From the beginning of 1875, she exchanged a new greeting with them: "Live Jesus!" to which they would respond: "Always in our hearts!" The usage, typical of various communities of friars, had been introduced by Fr. Costamagna, after the example of St. Francis de Sales, and Mother Mazzarello was quick to make it her own.

From Don Bosco she had already taken the invention of the "good night," the brief, evening talk to the whole community. At times, it was given by the director (Fr. Pestarino) and at times by herself, in a simple, affectionate manner. It was a custom which was always pleasing. Fr. Pestarino had already remarked to Don Bosco: "Even the little people, knowing that there would be a 'good night,' did not want to go to sleep without hearing the director address some words to them."

On March 15, 1875, another one of the first professed sisters died, Rosa Mazzarello, who had also been one of the Daughters of the Immaculate. She was from a well-to-do family but had always lived the poor life of the community joyfully, far from the habits of her own previous life, enduring rooms which were freezing in winter (she wrote letters in the evening after work with hands numbed with cold) and with little food throughout the year.

Wasn't it time to finally change something in regard to food? This death once more brought up the question, but the Daughters still said no. They chose the hard way in a letter to Don Bosco, signed by all.

Seen in the light of the 20th century, this behavior seems to be excessive, almost inflicting discomfort without reason, something close to fanaticism. But these discomforts were those which the majority of country folk endured, even those of the sisters, whose relatives would now and then send eggs, flour, chestnuts and wood to the institute. Mother Mary Domenica and the sisters, obeying the vow of poverty in such a severe way, also wanted to remain in solidarity with those who lived a poor life without having made vows, but who because they had so little, lacked almost everything. They felt that they would betray their parents, brothers and sisters if they took on another type of life, "going to live well," as they said.

When he received this letter, Don Bosco praised the austere determination of the Daughters, but judged it necessary that from now on there should be breakfast for all, with coffee and milk. On this point, Mother Mazzarello chased away every doubt; Father wanted it this way, and so it would be. (Keep in mind, however, that which they called "coffee" was usually a mixture of barley and other toasted grains. Sometimes a guest, upon tasting it, would murmur "Poor daughters!" and this tells us everything about its particular taste!)

One of the signers of the letter to Don Bosco, Sr. Teresina Mazzarello, had extreme need of a little coffee and milk, and one day, speaking with her mother, happened to mention it. Her mother then sent one of her cows to the school for Teresina and her sisters. "My dear mother's cow," she wrote much later on, "served us well until Mother Superior had the money to buy one for the community. What a celebration it was to see it come into the playground! It had wreaths of flowers, and passed in the midst of the sisters and the girls, who welcomed it with cheers and applause as though it were a great personage!"[7]

Mother Mazzarello had planned that entry, making it an occasion of great joy. The money had come to the institute with the arrival of a group of postulants from Sondrio, sent by a priest friend of Don Bosco, Fr. Luigi Guanella, future founder of the Servants of Charity and of the Daughters of Holy Mary of Divine Providence. Each postulant brought a contribution, and so they could purchase a milk cow for 220 lire. According to the Piedmontese custom for bovine trade, they paid with eleven "marenghi," each equal to twenty lire.

Money problems were always very difficult due to the small number of boarders they took in. At the end of 1875, they had only twenty-five boarders, even though Don Bosco sought with great insistence to make the institute known far and wide. Here we must say that the little village of Mornese, as much as Mother Mazzarello and the other veterans loved it, had little to offer as a center of attraction for scholars. Isolation continued to render it far even when it had a railway, and throughout Piedmont itself some people ignored its existence.

As we have said, the boarders were asked to pay a fee of twenty lire a month (after a few years it would rise to twenty-five). It was quite a small sum in comparison to that of other religious institutes. This was because the Salesians had chosen to work for the poor. Another reason they had so little cash was because Mother Mary Mazzarello, in the face of certain situations, unhesitatingly gave deep reductions in fees. From those who could pay, she always asked for what was just. But rather than send a beggar away hungry, she would give him her own portion of soup. Therefore, she would not allow a child to be deprived of instruction and Christian formation, or deny her the possibility of learning a trade because of inability to pay the tuition. Faithful to all the rules and always obedient, in this case she knew how to set aside the dispositions and customs of her authority.

A letter written in 1874 by Sr. Elisa Roncallo to an uncle about the acceptance of his daughter, Santina, shows us this in action. "I spoke with our Mother Superior to see if you could have a discount for Santina's education, and our good Mother told me that for now you could pay only eighteen lire instead of twenty, and later on we would see if it could be less. Truthfully, it would be very good if you would send her to be educated here because she would be a well educated, wise little lady."[8]

Few students could pay the entire fee, also because many were orphans. We may assume that there was an average payment of between five and fifteen lire. This generosity was dearly paid for, because naturally they could not ask the students to make the same sacrifices asked of the sisters. They had to be well fed and surrounded by a minimum of external decorum. "It was the objective of the institution also to offer the students a dignified, serene environment, in accord with social conveniences." Here the girls were placed in a condition of growing culturally, of developing their capacity of maturation in rapport with others, and of contact with their peers and with the solicitous educators of their integral formation.[9]

Another succinct precept of the rule showed all of Mother Mazzarello's attention for the poverty of the families of many sisters. It was a point established in the meetings of the superiors in 1878 and regarded the gifts which they and the directors received for their feast days. The gift giving habit was widespread, and they decided to put an end to it: "Gifts of any type are not to be given." It would be enough, instead to dedicate to the guest of honor, "a letter of good wishes and a few songs," because the sisters "could not possess and those who do not possess, cannot give presents." Neither were they to ask money from relatives for this reason. Relatives of religious, though they at times agree, are not happy being taxed in this way.

The First for America

The meetings of the superiors during those first years when the Daughters of Mary Help of Christians threw themselves into the work of forming themselves and others, of teaching and learning, must have been interesting. It was not the time to precisely measure the tempo of the sisters' accurate formation or of their teaching activity. Mother Mazzarello, transforming herself into a student, learned to write, and molded the destiny for every Daughter of Mary Help of Christians of that early hour. You could not say to the rough, unlettered girls of the times: "Wait, we have to prepare ourselves, we need a few years." They had to begin right away, with the risk of failing, with all the misadventures of inexperience.

Who knows how many stories were told in those gatherings, and how they learned. There was the feminine reality on one side (especially of good peasant women, but not only this), and there were the principles of Don Bosco's pedagogy to be translated into the feminine aspect. Later on in life the pioneers recalled the "spirit of Mornese." This expression bears in itself much patient and joyful sacrifice, and at the same time, a tenacious and courageous experimentation, so creative and imaginative in the face of problems with little or no hinterland of techniques or procedure, with the continual necessity of inventing, and the anxiety for doing so quickly.

The needs of those times were not to raise pioneers, exceptions, leaders who already existed, expressed naturally, by the aristocratic elite and middle class. The times needed others, as Don Bosco taught: the primary need for today and tomorrow is to call the poor to instruction and spiritual formation. These were the men and women from whom the founder sent forth the Daughters of Mary Help of Christians. Even the woman who remained a peasant must grow and receive culture, betterment of professional capacity, religious education. Remaining in ignorance was no longer acceptable.

This drama was given a stronger representation by an old friend of Don Bosco and Fr. Frassinetti, Bishop Gaetano Alimonda, future archbishop of Turin and at the moment prevost of the metropolis of Genoa. In one of his conferences in church in 1874, before a large crowd, he described the undertaking of women who had become "freethinkers" in the town of Paris: "They go up into the pulpit in church and announce God's decline. Fearless after having done such a bold act, they come down and run through the streets, seeking, looking for others...and for what? There comes to mind a word not found in our dictionaries, one which I have never before spoken. The free thinkers become bearers of combustibles. With bottles in hand they throw the killer liquid at foundations, pour it over factories and public monuments; they cry out death to the rich, to soldiers.... Paris is burning, and among the flames of the incendiary, the socialist, the sad daughter of free thought exults...."[10]

The Daughters of Mary Help of Christians (at least a good number of them), knew of Gaetano Alimonda. He was one of the Genoese priests whom Fr. Pestarino, when young, visited often in Liguria. Perhaps they would not function well in this tragic scene, accustomed as they were to a very different, simple way of facing problems. They were aware of how urgent it was to "educate young girls in a Christian manner," as the anguished bishop recommended. They were dedicated to "Mary Help of Christians," which, in their tradition, could be understood as "Mary who lends a hand." It was a vision which we could understand to be operative, a stimulus to trust, a touch of supernatural support to the stamp of cheerfulness which accompanied their work, in prayer, in victories and in defeat.

They received fundamental direction from Don Bosco for their educational activity, and they applied it in the concrete reality of Mornese, sustained by the local director Fr. Costamagna, the future bishop, who dedicated himself full time to the institute during the very important years from 1874-1877.

He was not a sweet-natured person. He had a brusque frankness which at times did not even spare the Mother General. She took even his public corrections with perfect serenity, because they showed how to accept criticism and how to obey. Those which could have been bitter moments for her, before all, were actually lessons. Every sister, novice and postulant could learn humility without reading about it; it was enough that they kept their eyes fixed on Mother Mazzarello. To those who could "read" her, she was the best text for the Daughters.

Fr. Costamagna gave a specific impetus to the institute, taking upon himself the general instruction of the sisters. They arrived as postulants and girls who possessed great qualities, but at times they were completely illiterate, and they all had to make a cultural leap.

Meanwhile, Fr. Costamagna worked for the preparation of the didactic training of the future teachers. The institute, after having been "ready made" in Turin, now began to form itself in the house. Another initiative of the director was the preparation of animators for the local festive oratory and for others which would be opened elsewhere. As Maccono wrote: "He did not occupy himself only with spiritual and scholastic direction, but as a poet and musician, composed songs and taught them to the students, postulants, novices and sisters, so they could later teach them to the children of the festive oratories, as the Salesians did with the boys, according to the spirit of Don Bosco."[11]

Communicating from a Distance

The family of Mornese was engrossed in the two vestitions of 1875. In August, after the usual spiritual exercises, there were fourteen new sisters and fifteen new novices. Furthermore, for the first time the ceremony of the perpetual vows was solemnly celebrated in Don Bosco's presence. The vows were pronounced by thirteen Daughters, led by Mary Mazzarello with her sister Felicina and Petronilla. The others were Teresa Pampuro, Giovanna Ferrettino, Caterina Mazzarello, Maria Grosso, Assunta Gaino, Virginia Magone, Enrichetta Sorbone, Rosina Mazzarello, Emilia Mosca and Teresina Mazzarello. It was the "senate" of the congregation.

On December 12, before Fr. Michael Rua, fifteen other postulants took the religious habit and six new sisters pronounced their triennial vows.

Between these two moments there was another great notice, that of the first missionary expedition to leave from Valdocco. Destination? Argentina. The archbishop of Buenos Aires, Federico Aneyros, had officially asked Don Bosco to help in evangelization (the Patagonia which all at Valdocco dreamed of), but also in the spiritual assistance for many Italians; more than 3,000 lived in the capital alone.

The first group sent beyond the Atlantic was made up of six priests and four lay brothers, including an administrator, a master carpenter, a shoemaker (who was also the cook) and a music teacher, the Salesian seal on a missionary undertaking. Fr. John Cagliero was the natural leader, because of his gift for guidance and carrying out plans, and for the solidity of his theological preparation (a degree from the University of Turin). Upon greeting them in the crowded basilica of Mary Help of Christians, Don Bosco told them that the scope of every mission is primarily the announcement of the Gospel to the non-Christians, and that this was the reason for their going to Patagonia. "But I remind you most insistently," he continued, "of the painful situation of many Italian families, many of whom lived dispersed in those cities and villages and throughout the countryside. Parents and children, little instructed in the language and customs of the place, far from schools and church, do not go to religious functions, or if they do, they understand nothing.... You will find a great number of children, and also adults who live in the most deplorable ignorance."

Leaving Genoa on November 14, 1875, the ten arrived in Buenos Aires a month later. At Mornese, sisters, novices, postulants, students and teachers gathered around a map of the world and ran their fingers across the great blue expanse of the Atlantic Ocean, trying to follow the route of the ship *Savoia,* which carried the expedition.

"When will the Daughters of Mary Help of Christians go to America?" This was the question found in the first letter of Mother Mazzarello to Fr. Cagliero in the missions. She had dictated it to the teacher Rosalia Pestarino during Christmas time in installments, and mailed it on December 29. The little peasant from Mornese would never have thought that she would one day be corresponding with the other part of the world, where even the seasons of the year were the opposite. This fact struck her and she spoke of it to Fr. Cagliero, the one time peasant lad from Castelnuovo d'Asti, who was now the head of the first missionary expedition to America.

"You tell us that it does not seem strange to you to celebrate the feast of Christmas and begin the New Year during the summer! I don't think that these feasts can be so beautiful during this season, right? The snow which covers our fields, and the silence which reigns everywhere give a clarity to the child God in a stable, all alone, trembling with cold. However, with all this, if God would want some of us to celebrate the birth of the Baby Jesus in that far away land called America, we would go willingly."[12]

The letter went on to tell about the latest events in the institute, which were not always happy: personal crises, those who couldn't adapt, impatient outbursts....

For example, in April of 1875, a singular personage arrived from Turin, sixty-three-year-old Angela Bacchialoni. The *Cronistoria* tells us: "Don Bosco could not refuse her attempt to try the life, because of his friendship with her brother, a noted professor and benefactor." Distinguished and cultured, refined in manner, Angela found herself to be the oldest person in the institute; she could have been Fr. Costamagna's mother. Frankly, because of her age, she could not be enthusiastic about the tenor of life at Mornese, and certain customs which were a bit too rustic in her eyes. Still, because of age and her "worldly ways," it seemed more just that she criticize this or that usage, with the usual dual result: afflicting the community and baiting someone to agitation. In this case it was the sisters Felicina and Maria Arecco, sister and novice, who had already murmured about their discontent.

Because of these three, things were not going well. This is the way that Mother wrote the news in a letter to Fr. Cagliero: "A few days after the vestitions, we had the devestitions. Sr. Angela Bacchialoni was the first to leave on December 14 for Turin, accompanied by Fr. Rua. On Tuesday, on the 21st of the same month, Sr. Maria Arecco set aside the holy habit and returned home; Sr. Felicina is still here, but before the end of the year she will go with her sister and then to Cottolengo, if they accept them."[13] Further on in the letter, continued after the feastday, she also gave news of this departure, and then of the illnesses in the institute, besides a disturbing note of her own: "I had become deaf, so much so that no matter how close I got to the altar, I couldn't hear anything of the sermon on the child Jesus. I was in such pain about the loss of this consolation, that I begged Fr. Director to give me a blessing. As soon as I had received it, I was freed from the discomfort and could hear all the sermons. Help me to thank the child Jesus."[14] We cannot conclude without another sign of her familiar candid and affectionate interest in everything that was going on across the ocean. "While I write, you will probably be asleep, since here it is already past 10 PM. The students hearing this laugh, and want me to write something for them, also. First of all, there are twenty-five of them, good beyond belief, that is, what they should be, and I, too, recommend them to your prayers, promising that they will not forget you in theirs.... Be good enough to send us Spanish books, so we can study and be ready at the first call. I would like to send you some of the cool weather, which we have in abundance, but not being able to do so, we will wait until you send us some warmth with your guardian angel, like that which the child Jesus spreads."[15]

We would wish to tell all of Mary Mazzarello's stories in her own words. After years of recollected isolation, the winds of the world entered the institute with the missionary news, and they were welcomed with tranquil joy. The intercontinental perspective was not seen in an upsetting or dramatic way; all was simplified through the filter of Mother Mazzarello. Every grand development entered the stream of things naturally, suggesting playfulness. This woman, and these women

and girls, were serenely conscious of *having to do* unimagin-
able things for all the preceding generations of Mornese; but
she also knew that she *could do* them. She only needed to pray,
observe the rule and maintain cheerfulness, after which all was
possible and all beautiful, either to go to Buenos Aires or to
Borgo San Martino.

In January 1876, Don Bosco sent to the bishop of Acqui
the text of the rule for the Daughters. He had carefully re-
viewed it with the help of Fr. Costamagna during one of his
sojourns at Ovada. A few days later Bishop Sciandra returned
it to him, accompanied by a very precious document for the
founder, his decree in solemn Latin, *probamus et confir-
mamus,* which approved the rule for experimentation, as was
the custom. For Don Bosco this was enough. The bishop's
"yes" covered him, and for the moment he did not have to look
for complications from Rome.

Meanwhile, other bishops were asking him to send the
Daughters of Mary Help of Christians to their dioceses. Bishop
Giovanni Biale of Ventimiglia wanted both the Salesians and
the sisters. The work dealt with creating oratories and schools
near Vallecrosia to reinforce the Catholic work in the face of a
strong Waldensian presence. Bishop Basilio Leto of Biella
asked for sisters for the kitchen and laundry of the seminary.
At Alassio there was need of their work in a Salesian boys'
school and a girls' oratory. At Lu, Monferrato, they were to
take upon themselves a nursery school and workroom for girls.
Finally, Bishop Lorenzo Gastaldi, archbishop of Turin, resolved to accept Don Bosco's repeated request and allowed the
Daughters to start a free school for girls at Valdocco, under
various disciplinary conditions. They also had to promise that
"they would make no noise about it in the newspapers."

Five foundations were realized during the first ten
months of 1876. Mother Mazzarello had successfully vested
herself in the garb of an organizer of "teams" to be sent to the

various destinations, with the choice of superiors and instructions for work. She gave succinct notice of this to Fr. Cagliero in a letter of autumn, 1876, and also described the situation at Mornese: "Here we are about sixty between sisters and postulants. I cannot give you a number of the students, because the greater part have not yet returned from vacation. Last year they were twenty-nine; let us hope that this year the number will be greater, but they come slowly because of the distance from the railway."[16]

This letter had a particular importance because chronologically it was the first written in her own hand; the battle for literacy has been completely won. She announced it to Fr. Cagliero: "I set myself to scribble with all the others."

Chapter Six

Word spread—there's a saint at Mornese. She's at Borgoalto, in the school, among the Daughters of Mary Help of Christians and she's going to become one of them. She appeared in the village in the Corpus Christi procession of 1876, blonde, beautiful, dressed like an angel, carrying a cross which seemed to rest lightly on her shoulder. It seemed as though she was doing extraordinary things in the institute, and that she was also a prophet....

It's always a sad fact when a novice or sister puts aside the habit and returns home, but she can honestly draw to a close a personal choice which was not for her. During these times, for example, Mother Mazzarello saw Sr. Jandet leave. Things had come to a point where the only solution was her departure, but certain arrivals were also a scourge. For example, when certain persons presented themselves with an astonishing exterior devotion, renown for prodigies, with the pose of being sent from heaven...these people caused more disaster than those who left.

At Mornese there was a budding disaster with the appearance of this "saint," a vivacious, blonde girl named Agostina Simbeni. She had come from Rome, and an aura of mystery surrounded her family. She had been sent by Don Bosco who had never met her; she had been recommended by someone of importance from Rome. With her appearance, the most disagreeable trial began for Mother Mazzarello and the sisters.

Agostina overdid it immediately, as Ferdinand Maccono tells us, after having heard more personal remembrances in the testimonies which he collected: "She was accepted as a postulant and immediately drew the attention of all. She showed an extraordinary fervor, and went for days without eating; at times we would see her rise off the ground as though she were in ecstasy. She foretold the future, or announced things which were happening elsewhere which no one could humanly know; she revealed matters of conscience of the sisters and the students, who affirmed that these were true. She seemed, in short, to have contact with invisible beings."[1]

We can imagine the great marvel of sisters and postulants before this girl with such polite ways, who spoke an Italian so different from theirs, and dressed in such a ladylike manner. Even the times were propitious for attention toward a figure so privileged by special gifts and powers. For years and decades people had breathed a climate of the decisive, last battle between good and evil. On the one side, the adversaries of the Church loudly announced near, definitive ruin; they spoke of the "ruins of the Vatican," upon which there would arise immortal monuments to free thought. On the other side, some of the faithful at times expected supernatural interventions in defense of good and those who were good. In 1846 the Marian apparitions of La Salette occurred, and twelve years later, those of Lourdes. In both cases the bearers of the invitation to prayer, penance and the continual struggle against blasphemy or the profanation of holy days were ordinary young people: Melanie Calvat, Maximin Girard, Bernadette Soubirous....

Then why not Agostina Simbeni? She further claimed to be in contact with a supernatural being called "the child." Some thought that Agostina was Our Lady's messenger. In her name she asked—and imposed—special acts of devotion, and improvised gatherings in the chapel during the night. Fr. Costamagna sometimes seemed to believe in her. Sisters and novices were divided between fascination and disbelief. Mother Mazzarello practiced her methods also with Agostina, and this consisted in not contradicting her for the moment, and meanwhile observing, examining, discerning the most suitable way of intervening. At the beginning, she cordially believed everything, always, and did not deny Agostina.

But then she heard a warning, a sign, the first alarm within herself. Watching her during recreation, Mother saw that Agostina did not play, laugh or make noise with the others. The *Cronistoria* tells us: "She preferred to walk with someone and repeat words full of unction and fervent enthusiasm, but Mother was not too pleased with this, and she watched carefully, while she recommended to the sisters that they remain united and enjoy Salesian-style recreations."[2]

Then there was another sign. Even with all of her "saintly" attitudes, her flowing prayers and noisy penances, the children were *afraid* of Agostina. There was something about her glance which frightened them. This does not happen with saints.

Because of her apprehension for the extraordinary, Mother warned Agostina that if she went on this way, she would have to leave. She got to the point, in fact, of flying into a public rage, claiming to have seen this or that other person in purgatory. Because she wanted to become a novice, she promised to change, and for some time she did, but the sisters' chapter did not trust her, and voted against her vestition. She was to return home.

She left, but after one day was back at Mornese. Don Bosco suggested that they try her in humility and obedience and the story repeated itself. At first she showed impeccable conduct, then fell into the usual excesses, leaving the community confused and divided. Some believed in Agostina, in whatever she said or did, and others feared the worst if she were not sent away.

This, however, was not easy. Meanwhile, Fr. Costamagna agreed to let her make vestition (but he soon changed his mind). Some religious already seemed completely dependent on her. Mother Mazzarello decided that Agostina was to return to Rome.

Here the *Cronistoria* notes with surprise that two sisters had accompanied her to Serravalle Scrivia, and had put her on the train for Sampierdarena where some Salesians were waiting to set her on her way to Rome. All was in order. However, on returning to Mornese, the sisters found a happy Agostina. "My little child brought me back here, because before I leave, many others must go."

Don Bosco saw her briefly at Borgo San Martino and told Mother Mazzarello to send her home. She was once more placed on the train, and once more reappeared at Mornese. Finally, two men accompanied her to Sampierdarena, and the departure took place, without a return.

Mary Mazzarello wrote to Fr. Cagliero on July 8, 1876: "...not finding any solution, upon Don Bosco's orders, we sent her to make some miracles in Rome. Come soon, and we'll tell you all of the particulars of this comedy."[3]

She must have suffered very much. But she never let her perception of the reality, in her scant inclination for the "extraordinary," escape her lips. And she did not allow herself to be dominated by ugly memories. In the same letter to Cagliero, she makes a point on the situation of the Daughters halfway through 1876: "There are thirty postulants, about ten novices, thirty-six professed sisters and thirty students."

This meant that even the Daughters of Mary Help of

Christians could go to the missions beyond the At.
ginning with Mother, they were ready to leave as the
of all. "Now listen to what I have to say: Keep a place
in America, understand? I really mean it. It's true that I'i.
good for much, but I do know how to make polenta, and 1
know how to keep after the laundry so that we don't use to
much soap, and if you like, I could learn to cook a little. In
short, I will do everything in my power to make everyone
happy as long as you let me go."[4]

During the first months of 1876, the institute suffered
hard blows. On February 9, Sr. Maria Grosso died. She was
only twenty-one and had been called Mother Mistress by the
novices. She had been the child from Santo Stefano Parodi
who had held Mother Mazzarello's hand. Don Bosco had
prophesied: "One day she will become mistress of novices,"
and this happened when she was nineteen years old. She grew
up healthy, had a beautiful voice and was full of energy. Perhaps she wanted to afflict herself with too many privations in
the matter of food; whatever it was, she, too, was struck with
tuberculosis, and she was not the last. The "subtle evil" during
this era was a little known, unconquerable evil.

In the First Line in Turin

Now Don Bosco found new leaders. March 1876 saw two
important events: the birth of the newspaper, the *Corriere
della sera* in Milan, and in the capital the political event which
would pass into history as the fall of the right wing, that
parliamentary section which had governed during the first fifteen years of the Kingdom of Italy, continuing the politics of
Cavour. It had finally brought a balanced budget to Italy.

It was a great victory, but was immediately followed by a
fall. After having been able to announce the reaching of a
historic finish line, the government presided over by Marco

Minghetti found itself in a minority in the Chamber on March 16, regarding a question of little importance, and quit two days later. The leftists took power, with Agostino Depretis as head of the government, and with Francesco Crispi—number one man of the leftists—destined to become president of the Chamber and later Minister of the Interior. Don Bosco knew the man; he had met him in Turin when he was a refugee from the Kingdom of the Two Sicilies and was so poor that he was not even eating regularly.

For the Daughters of Mary Help of Christians, however, the memorable event of March 1876 was their visit to Turin. On the 29th, seven religious left from Mornese, among them Elisa Roncallo, superior, and Catherine Daghero, vicar. They were on their way to Turin to start the first institute for girls near the oratory of Valdocco. As we have seen, Archbishop Gastaldi had finally authorized this initiative, and Don Bosco had hurried to buy a house for the sisters. They had a double task: to care for the laundry of the Salesians and the boys, but primarily to start a workroom, a catechetical school, an oratory for children and girls of the area, and a free school, as many families had requested from Don Bosco.

In May, Mother General went to Turin to personally view the work of the new foundation, during those difficult months of settling in. The "domestic" work in the laundry was quickly on its way; the Daughters were experts in this. The educational work among the children and girls was more complex and had other rhythms. During this time Don Bosco was out looking for his boys, those "rogues" and "scoundrels." He was often seen with them...gathering them was easy for him, but the sisters could not act in the same way. Then, too, the archbishop had warned: "Don't be too evident."

For the inhabitants of the area, the Daughters were a completely unexpected novelty, which in part corresponded to the expectations of many families, but on the other hand remained

mysterious. The beginning of the educationa,
house dedicated to St. Angela Merici, having Fr. .
as spiritual director, could not start immediately. F,.
they had to get to know one another, and at times kno
begins with the wondering glance of a girl who had see, a
sister on her doorstep. This was a great novelty. Then there
would be a little conversation, a casual invitation. The first
guests appeared in the afternoon and evening when the sisters
had recreation. (We must repeat that in the male and female
Salesian world, recreation is not optional, but prescribed. The
1878 general meeting of the superiors would establish: "Recreation must be lively and cheerful."[5] A sister during recreation
is a sister who is serving effectively, like a sentinel at her post.
Mother Mazzarello did not only assist at the games and noise,
but took active part and drew others along with her.)

Later, referring to Mornese, Mother said: "Now there are
a good number of girls. They go where they want, especially
during the recreations at noon and in the evening. They go to
speak with the sisters and to greet them before going to work,
telling them of their own events."[6]

Going to Turin was a great step, not only because they
were in contact with the heart of the Salesian world and with
Don Bosco, but also because they placed themselves in
harmony with a major principle of the founder's strategy: to
throw themselves into the midst of the city. The greater the
city, the more possibility for Salesian activity. John Bosco, a
country boy, never denied or forgot it. He wanted to see it
progress and move toward the future. He wrote his first popular textbooks to help them to master the metric system, decimal
system and to teach new techniques of winemaking. He was
well aware, however, of the real battles being fought in the
city, even those of faith. The city was the first line, and he was
not one to turn back.

Son of the fields, he did not share the poetic vision of

farming which was in style among the upper classes during this era, or at least on the part of some of those who were afraid of the city. They feared it because it was the cradle of that industry which also had gotten involved in social questions, in the world of the worker who was becoming aware of himself, preaching revolution. That industry, in short, incited fear.

As Federico Chabod wrote: "From the state of soul of the conservatives there flowed the celebration of agriculture as the great moral educator, from the mother earth of familiar and civic virtues, the only real security for tranquil and regular progress.... And the younger generations, already moving easily toward the machine, should not forget the fact that the older people (and not only they) would remain gripped in the secular ideals of life. Nature led man to God; the shop rendered him an atheist. It was not by chance that the great extollers of farming desired a renewed religious fervor for all, where nature and God, along with work for the moral education of the people, were joined with one sole feeling."[7]

Don Bosco had not studied the works of Marx and the other revolutionary theorists, but neither did he fear the shop, nor did he consider it to be an enemy of the faith. On the contrary, he started workshops even at Valdocco—the great professional schools, with the latest machines, to transform wild immigrant boys from the countryside into workers and specialists, leaders and guides, even at work.

So it was that the same impulse captured Mary Mazzarello. She was a native of Mornese from head to toe, but was tranquilly leaning toward the future, in all directions, even the most remote. "Oh, what a pleasure it would be if the Lord truly gives us this grace of calling us to America! If we would do nothing more than win one soul for him, it would be worth all our sacrifices."

She wrote this to Fr. Cagliero, in her own hand, on December 27, 1876. In the letter she refers to the opening of new houses, now that the Daughters of Mary Help of Christians were presently in seven locations in Piedmont and Liguria: Mornese, Borgo San Martino, Bordighera, Turin, Biella, Lu Monferrato and Alassio.

But she insisted on going to America, indicating the names of seven sisters who were already well prepared. Her own name was among them, and she added a cheerful self-caricature to the proposal: "I have many white hairs; luckily the bonnet covers them. Those who want to frighten me tell me that in America there are also natives who eat Christians, but I'm not afraid, because I am so dried up that certainly they wouldn't want me! Call us quickly. If you write to us telling us when we must leave, we will prepare something beautiful to bring along with us. One more thing, though, you'll have to send us the money for our trip because we don't have any-thing."[8] However, they did manage to pay their entire debt with the Salesians at Valdocco—20,000 lire.

Sunday Wisdom

They paid their debts, helped the institute to grow and opened new houses, thanks to the harsh sobriety of their lives and the spirit of sacrifice which had become common, even ordinary, without heroic scenes. Here and there in the institute we read the warning posed by Fr. Costamagna: "Every reli-gious must be a copy of the holy rule." Two of the living copies were Sr. Anna Succetti and Sr. Paulina Guala. Assigned to heavy work because of their physical strength, they joyfully accepted the effort as a means of growth, always asking more of themselves. Sometimes they could be found working side by side with Mother Mazzarello. She continually praised both of them before everyone for their dedication.

They were two examples of creatures who gave them-selves so that the community might live. They died just a few days apart, Sr. Anna on March 24, 1877 and Sr. Paulina on April 9.

Struck by this tragedy, Don Bosco entrusted a message for the sisters to the Salesian, Fr. Carlo Ghivarello, sent to Mornese a few days later to hear confessions. "Use every possible means to impede the more common maladies; remember, once professed, your health no longer belongs to you, but to the congregation, and you must therefore care for it as the possession of all, being careful not to waste it by imprudence or melancholy."[9]

Mother Mazzarello was very attentive to this, perhaps because of the habit gained as a young girl when she cared for her younger brothers and sisters. She would observe, then intervene, at times anticipating a request for help. With the more timid postulants, for example, she would point out the nurse so that they would know whom they should go to in case of need. Frequently, she herself acted as nurse, even for the disagreeable tasks, so as not to disturb a sister. During the cold winter nights of Mornese, before going to rest, she would quietly walk through the dormitories to make sure that all were well covered.

Then there was the matter of food. She kept in force the general rule of austerity, and was the first to respect it, even beyond the prescriptions. (One day the sisters saw her staggering as though she were unwell, but it was only due to hunger. She was instructed to eat, but they had to borrow some bread because the pantry was empty. Every now and then they were forced to change suppliers because they couldn't always pay on time.)

She was respectful of the rule; however, she also kept her eye on individual cases of need and immediately intervened, at times even having food brought at night to those who needed it. Or she would order a sister to take a walk and a snack. Or she would give secret instructions to the cook to add meat to someone's plate. In the depositions of the canonical process a number of testimonies revealed secret episodes of her quiet, almost conspiratorial maternal acts. They were like the "little flowers" of Mornese, guarded like living relics for years and decades by the recipients of her generosity.

Sometimes her quick assistance took the form of example. "Frequently she was afflicted with toothaches, earaches, deafness and other ailments, but we never heard a word of complaint from her. We saw her working as quickly as she always did, or going around the house with a serene face and a smiling greeting."[10]

An elderly sister recalls an episode when she was a child and had frostbitten feet. They were so painful that she couldn't take off her shoes, and so she went to bed with them on. "Mother, passing through the dormitory before rising time and not seeing the shoes on the floor, understood what had happened. She questioned me, and then with a charity and affection that was truly maternal, she washed my feet with warm water and bandaged them. When she had finished, she brought me to the chapel, set me on a chair near the altar rail and said: 'Sit here and don't even get up for the elevation. Jesus will be just as pleased with you.'"[11]

Now events were no longer centered only in Mornese, and so a season of movement began for Mother Mazzarello. She often had to visit the houses of Piedmont and Liguria, stopping at each for a few days to see how things were going, to listen, to solve big problems and to nip little ones in the bud.

She would have been pleased with shorter stops, a simple passing through, so as to cause as little disturbance as possible. She had another reason: she was hesitant to show herself around so much (to priests, bishops, authorities) because she feared harming the prestige of the Daughters by appearing as Mother General here and there, being so little instructed, so devoid of the "ways of the world."

What happened instead was that priests, bishops and

various personages found themselves in an embarrassing admiration before her humility and the everyday wisdom of her words and gestures. She would pass the night on a chair so as not to deprive a sister of her bed, or she would be found carrying a bunch of twigs for a fire to warm her travel companions. She would go around the stores, even in Rome, to buy supper for her sisters. Again, still in Rome, they would find her with her aching head wrapped in an ordinary scarf, because she had given her shawl to someone who was colder than herself. She did all of this with the greatest simplicity, not worrying about the anxiety of "What will they say?" or "How will I look?" or "No one has ever seen a Mother General who...."

There is something sovereign in this, her indifference to what we would today call "image." It was necessary to be humble, to keep after this Mother who, finding difficult words in a book would ask public clarification from a little girl, and then explain: "You know, I am not very well instructed...."

For her, the model of humility was the one who was above all sovereigns and ruled over kings, putting down the powerful, dispersing the proud.... Practicing a great humility, therefore, was simply imitating God who came down to the human level, to the sinner, becoming a candidate for a terrible torment.

Supremely sure of all this she—who at times could show uncertainty or preoccupation over a point of instruction or etiquette—always had a ready answer to any objection to her behavior, with the serene certainty that she communicated to her daughters: "This is the way, the only way, and here I can really ask you to follow me."

Leaving to visit the sisters at Biella, she took with her Sr. Emilia Mosca and Sr. Magdalen Martini, saying that in this way she would not make the institute look bad "with a superior like me." The visit became, as Don Bosco said, a brief living together which permitted her to speak with, explain to, and confide in all. She did this at Biella, and shortly after, at Borgo San Martino. It was also this way at Alassio, where Mother found the sisters still in mourning for the death of Sr. Catherine Mazzarello, one of the very first sisters, who, as a young girl played the concertina for the carnival dances at the Maccagno house. After suffering from erysipelas (an acute infectious skin disease), Catherine seemed cured and had left the infirmary. Instead, she died suddenly, after an attack of coughing.

In 1877 a group of Daughters of Mary Help of Christians received their teaching diploma. Six new teachers qualified as elementary school teachers: Carolina Sorbone and her sister Angiolina, Catherine Daghero and her sister Rosina, Giovanna Borgna and the postulant Angiolina Buzzetti. This time they had not taken the exams in Turin, but in Mondovì. Here the Dominican Giovanni Tommaso Ghilardi was bishop from 1842-73. He was a native of Casalgrasso (Cuneo) and had been a blacksmith until nineteen years of age. Dedicated to catechesis and the instruction of the people, he founded a monastery of Dominicans in his episcopal city. Near the monastery a school for adult women had also taken life, and also a normal school, approved by all and recognized for the formation of teachers.

The vocation of the Daughters for school began and they were led to prepare themselves under the direction of Emilia Mosca. There was a strong need for sisters who had been rigorously prepared, with all titles prescribed by law, to respond to the growing demand for instruction and the call from many sectors for them to begin schools.

That's not all. In July 1877, the Coppino Law on obligatory and free elementary instruction excluded programs for the teaching of catechism. Teachers would teach the rights and responsibilities of citizens. Parents could request religious instruction from the municipality on the basis of the preceding legislation, and in that case, the mayors would have to provide for it. This, however, frequently depended on the political color of the individual city administrations. The catechism could be taught as a simple elective only outside the school schedule and in a different place from the schools, which were forbidden to priests.

The leftists had come into power with a highly proclaimed program which extended the right to vote to a greater number of Italians, beyond the eternal two percent. Someone had even spoken of universal suffrage. However, in February 1877, Baron Nicotera, Minister of the Interior, told the Chamber that the government was intent on opening up the right to vote, but not right away; it would happen later at an "opportune" time. The chronicles tell of "smiles from the extreme left" at this point, at the indication of the sandbagging of this project. The "extremists," however, didn't pay any attention to them.

Both right-wingers and leftists thought in the same manner about the expansion of the right to vote, even though their language was a little different. It was wonderful, a very wonderful thing, but not just yet. It was necessary to wait, to put it off, because the people wouldn't even know how to make good use of their vote; they were too immature.

"Certainly, that refrain about the people's immaturity would be played over and over again; the populace was the hope of the future, the future resources of the country, but it was necessary to let these seeds grow naturally, not to wear them out and ruin them by entrusting to them social offices which they were not yet capable of handling. The fatal transition from the social to the political field inspired an aversion not only to universal suffrage, baptized in a loud voice by conservative Italians as by their French teachers, in the great delirium of the century, but also only to an enlargement of suffrage which would remain within certain restricted limits."[12]

In the first elections managed by the left, November

1876, 2.2% of the Italians had the right to vote for a total of 621,000 electors, but only 358,000 had voted. The Depretis government had obtained an imposing majority of seats. Therefore, there was no urgency to have more people vote. Only in 1882 would there be a modest increase. It rose from 2.2% to 6.9% of the people. Hesitating and timid in matters of civil rights, the government was ready for even more marked anticlerical politics. So it was that the issue of the school became a fiery first line in the Church-State battle.

A Headache and Happiness

On Pentecost 1877, the Daughters of Mary Help of Christians dressed in the new habit which was "less black" as many had hoped. Though the black remained, it was lightened by the white of the bonnet and wimple. Seeing it worn for the first time by an anxious Catherine Daghero in Turin, Don Bosco approved it in his own way: "Well, it's not that bad. You can try it."

But in 1877, there was something else beside the habit. The isolated position of Mornese had been spoken of for many reasons. For one, even with the train, the trip to Turin took three days. In the little village, they could not find the necessary items for the institute; everything had to come from the outside and there were delays, difficulties and additional expenses. The families of the students also experienced serious inconveniences. The increased number of postulants caused problems of space in the school, with the inconvenience of new expenses for later expansion.

Finally, there was the negative, dramatic fact of the climate. That "too thin air," those rigid winters and all those deaths of young women and girls.... With the sisters, Mother had always been reserved about her anguish for this mourning, but she told the founder everything. "She had spoken with Don

Bosco who, like a true father, had taken everything to heart and looked for a place in which the climate was milder and closer to some railway station, so that there would be less need to transport food, clothing, work and all that was necessary for the house and school.... He also wanted them to have a central location so that they could more easily have commissions for work, and in this way both the students who would later return to their families and the sisters who would be destined to other houses would be rendered more able in various types of feminine work."[13]

He was lucky in his search. In Nizza Monferrato there was a convent of Our Lady of Grace with a church attached. It had belonged to the Capuchins, and in 1855 the government had confiscated it in virtue of the "revolutionary laws." At first it was given to the local municipality, and was later bought by the Wine Makers' Society of Savigliano who had turned it into a warehouse. In 1877 the wine producers once again put it up for sale, and Don Bosco bought it for 30,000 lire (paid in two installments) by a contract which was drawn up in October 1877 by the notary Tommaso Miretti of Savigliano.

From October 26, 1867 to December 1876, the State had completed the sale of 119,525 lots of ecclesiastical goods which had been confiscated, taking in more than 516 million lire. At Nizza Monferrato the property of Our Lady of Grace would now have a new journey, once again welcoming a religious community.

The confiscation of monasteries and churches, of woodlands and countryside, struck ecclesiastical institutions. But the government didn't stop there. The Depretis government, as resolute in this field as it was prudent in others, at the end of 1876 took upon itself an initiative which could be very serious and transformed it into a law "against the abuses of the clergy." It was a provision "which was not only limited to striking down ecclesiastical patrimonies, destroying generalates and houses, suppressing institutes of assistance, closing seminaries and other educational institutes, but it also gradually suffocated the very possibility of contact and communication of pastors with their faithful, and appealed to the State and to the duties of citizens to paralyze and stop the apostolic mission of the priest, to keep him from transmitting to his 'flock' the orders or prohibitions of the pontiff, under threat of grave personal sanctions. Almost at the end of his long reign, Pius IX protested with all the vigor of his eloquence and all the fire of his disdain...."[14]

The Chamber approved the proposal, but the Senate rejected it in May, after a difficult nine-day discussion in a hall which had never been so crowded.

It is important to see to whom Pius IX pronounced these severe discourses. Certainly, there were cardinals and the pastors of Rome, but it was principally before a group of pilgrims who had come to honor him on his fiftieth anniversary as bishop. They arrived from the whole world, unexpected, and almost transformed the face of Rome, as the newspapers commented. It was a great sign for all, if they wanted to understand it; both for those who had celebrated the taking of Rome and for those who had cried over it. It showed that the loss of the pontifical kingdom had not diminished the prestige and influence of the Holy Father. To the Catholics of the world—who could be clearly seen on this occasion—the life and death of a Papal State with borders, soldiers and customs officers did not seem to be a decisive question. The pope was something more than a king or president.

The jubilee of Pius IX was celebrated even in the male and female Salesian world. Don Bosco had decreed special prayers, and then, on June 17, the "external celebration" took place at Mornese. At night the school building was illumined, fireworks were set off and an air balloon was launched. Those who thought that this world was beaten by the honorable

Depretis were truly mistaken. "We are afflicted believers, but we are always cheerful." These words of St. Paul to the Christians of Corinth also applied to the sisters of Mornese, because added to the jubilee of the pontiff, they rejoiced over a series of important local facts: even the Daughters of Mary Help of Christians would be going to America.

The first concrete sign was the arrival at Valdocco of the archbishop of Buenos Aires, Leone Federico Aneyros. He, too, had crossed the Atlantic for the jubilee celebration of Pius IX. He was accompanied to Turin by Monsignor Pietro Ceccarelli, pastor of San Nicolas de los Arroyos, a little city about four hours distant from the Argentinean capital.

Their coming confirmed in person the news which had arrived by mail. The two Salesian expeditions (in 1875 with ten missionaries and 1876 with another twenty-three) had, until now, undertaken three activities: the oratory at Buenos Aires, the offices of the church of *Mater Misericordiae,* and the direction of the parish in a suburb of Boca. At San Nicolas, they had a boarding school, day school and festive oratory, and they also served the hospital. Finally, at Montevideo, in Uruguay, they directed the Collegio Pio of Villa Colón.

The first arrivals thought they would immediately go to San Nicolas to begin their work, but the archbishop kept them in the capital to care for the Italians, those of whom Don Bosco had spoken. Thousands of young people, children and adults, all "no one's children," were strangers in Argentina, and officially unknown to Italy. They faced misery, ignorance and exploitation by people taking advantage of them. In 1875 fanatics had burned the Jesuit school, and many erroneously accused the Italians of the deed. Fr. Cagliero organized the regular religious services in the church *Mater Misericordiae,* the parish *de los Italianos,* which had begun to fill up with people anxious to listen to him and to Fr. Baccino who spoke both Italian and Spanish, thus making the archbishop very happy. He forbade them to set foot in the rebellious and miserable alleys of Boca, where he himself had never gone, and where, by his order, priests did not go.

Fr. Cagliero had gone there immediately, once, and then again, even ready for insults (as a young man in Turin he had been one of Don Bosco's bodyguards) and nothing had happened. He had established a bit of friendship among the throngs of wild boys. "Fine," responded the archbishop when he found out, "then I will give you that parish where we have never been able to celebrate Mass regularly." So it was in that place, where not even an Argentinean military chaplain had succeeded, the first Salesian pastor, Fr. Bodrato, took over.

With the help of an Argentinean lawyer, Fr. Cagliero rented a house in another section of Buenos Aires, near the parish of the Immaculate Conception. He began the first Salesian school of arts and trades in the New World. In April 1877 he started with workrooms for tailors, shoemakers, carpenters and bookbinders. The Patagonian project had not been abandoned, but it was first necessary to work in Buenos Aires.

Extraordinary days were being lived at Mornese during August and September of 1877. Along with the Salesian Fr. Giovanni Bonetti, Monsignor Pietro Ceccarelli, the pastor from Argentina, came to preach the spiritual exercises. He was interested in the fact that the Daughters were learning Spanish, and was immediately assaulted by all, asking: "When will we go?" "Who will go?" He gave only one answer: "Certainly, the Daughters are necessary and much awaited in America, but you must wait for the arrival of Fr. Cagliero, who will be coming for the general chapter of the Salesians at Lanzo to learn of the first departure." Don Bosco would decide with him.

In the meantime, other departures took place. One was for Lanzo, where the sisters went to serve the Salesian school and also to assist with the extraordinary needs of the chapter. Another was for Nice by the Sea, in France. This was the first time the Daughters had left their native soil. Here, on Saturday, September 1, at the same time as the Lanzo group, the little group in France began their work alongside an already established Salesian work, the school and oratory called the *Patronage*. It had been opened in 1875 and dedicated to St. Peter in honor of the local bishop, Giovanni Pietro Sola of Carmagnola (Turin), an old friend of Don Bosco. Here, in addition to the usual work for the boys' school, the Daughters promoted the festive oratory for girls.

Mother Mazzarello, though bothered by headaches, was tranquil and happy, without being overly effusive. She had made her first trip to a few of the Daughters' houses, and had reported to Don Bosco. She had worked for the expeditions to Lanzo and Nice, and she now allowed herself to be caught up, like the others, in the winds from America. She had only one response to the incessant questions about when and who would go—"Let's wait for Fr. Cagliero...."

Meanwhile, in the cheerfulness of recreation she continued to sow her teaching in a low-key manner. "The Daughters of Mary Help of Christians must not take on too many devotions, but must be fervent in all they do."[15] Today it was at Mornese, tomorrow it would be in America and everywhere. Then, on September 3, unexpectedly, the news came from Valdocco: Fr. Cagliero had arrived!

Sisters on the Atlantic

Now, finally, decisions were made about the departure and selection of personnel. Don Bosco planned it and made the necessary working decisions with his alter ego who had come from America. Don Bosco had already been informed by mail of the field of work and evaluation of priorities. The situation of so many Italian immigrants had already been noted before the departure, but the facts, once seen, had been found to be more serious and desolating. Some didn't even know what the sign of the cross was; they did not go to Mass on Sunday because one day was the same as any other for them. Furthermore, the archbishop of Buenos Aires wanted the Salesians to establish themselves in the capital. The missionary undertaking in Patagonia was still the grand objective, but it brought environmental difficulties, and met with obstacles and even political risks. This did not matter. Fr. Cagliero, great leader and great realist, had already written to Don Bosco in March 1877: "I say it again, that with regard to Patagonia, we must not run with the speed of light, neither are we to go by steamer, because the Salesians are not yet ready for this undertaking. First we have to enter the cenacle and with holy patience resign ourselves to invoke and await the *strength and light* of the Holy Spirit.... Definitely, it would be convenient for us to proceed with *zeal and laborious activity toward this goal,* but not to make too much noise, so as not to make these people expect from us, so recently arrived, the conquest of a land which we do not know and of which we are completely ignorant, even of the language."[16]

On September 8, Don Bosco had already communicated to Mornese the first decisions: the new Salesian expedition for America would be made up of eighteen men between priests and coadjutors, and six Daughters of Mary Help of Christians, destined for the diocese of Montevideo, in Uruguay, chosen from among those who had made a written petition.

Fr. Cagliero had selected Fr. Giacomo Costamagna to head the expedition and, therefore, he had to leave the direction of the institute at Mornese. His successor would be Fr. Giovanni Battista Lemoyne, who was presently director of the school at Lanzo.

The second decision was the names of those who would go. Sr. Angela Vallese of Lu Monferrato would be superior of the little community; Sr. Giovanna Borgna would be returning to her native land, since she had been born in Buenos Aires; Sr. Angela Cassulo of Castelletto d'Orba; Sr. Teresa Gedda of Pecco (Turin); and two from Mornese, Sr. Angela De Negri and Sr. Teresa Mazzarello Baroni.

Before the departure, those leaving were to go to Rome for an audience with Pius IX. But only two of the Daughters went (Angela Vallese and Giovanna Borgna) because funds were lacking. Still suffering pains in her head, Mother Mazzarello accompanied them. But she was still apprehensive for a reason which the collective memory of the Daughters will always cherish with love and pride, and which the *Cronistoria* relates in this way: "Mother Mazzarello said to Fr. Cagliero: 'Father Director, don't you think that in going to Rome I will make others lose their esteem for the institute? The Holy Father will expect to see in the Mother General an instructed, educated sister, and instead he will find before himself a poor, ignorant person.' Fr. Cagliero smiled as only he could, and told her to go just the same. Then he turned to the two sisters and others who were present, including Fr. Costamagna and Fr. Paul Albera, director of the house and said in a low voice: 'Let's learn the lesson.'"[17]

The hand of Pius IX rested on Mary Domenica's head, on that of Angela Vallese and of Giovanna Borgna. The eighty-five-year-old pope, who had just a few months of life left to him, thus took his leave of a future saint; the future visitor of the Patagonia and of Tierra del Fuego, remembered as the "heroine of charity"; and the sister born in Argentina who was destined to establish a rare missionary record: sixty-eight years of service.

Pius IX was impressed by the number of Salesians leaving for America which Fr. Cagliero presented to him. "Where does Don Bosco find all these people?" Cagliero responded that this was the job of divine providence.

(The papal audience of November, 1877 about the expedition for America took place during a bitter moment in the rapport between the pope and the founder of the Salesians. The latter, at only sixty-two years of age, was seriously worn out, yet he had made two trips to Rome in 1877, meeting with the pope. Coming again for a third time in December, he asked for an audience over and over again, but it was in vain. It seemed that a few of his letters to Pius IX had never reached their destination. A wall had been erected between the two, who would never meet again.)

The meeting place of those departing was the Salesian school of Sampierdarena. Don Bosco had come, and for the first time blessed the sisters whose destination was America. Fr. Cagliero, who would remain in Italy as Director General of the Daughters, was there; he had brought the missionaries a picture of Mary Help of Christians.

The departure took place from Genoa on November 14, on the *Savoia,* which they reached by a small boat. Having boarded the ship, Mother inspected the sisters' cabins, knelt with them and received Don Bosco's blessing. Finally, "she embraced her daughters one by one, addressing a word to each of them, with an accent of indescribable tenderness. Then she left quickly, with the two sisters who had accompanied her to the waiting boat. Don Bosco also went with them."[18] The first field of labor for the Daughters of Mary Help of Christians was Villa Colón, (Columbus' city) a short distance from Montevideo, destined eventually to become part of it. During that time, it was a very small center, in part only a plan, for which the early pioneers of 1868 had given their lives, and which later had passed on to the company which built the aqueduct of Montevideo, welcoming many laborers. The development, however, was greatly contrasted by Uruguayan political events (seven presidents in twelve years, 1868-80). The aqueduct society was dissolved in 1875, liquidating its properties in the area. It had offered to Fr. Cagliero the gift of the church of St. Rose of Lima, with the adjoining building, built for a school. The only condition was that they would have a school there.

The gift was accepted by Fr. Cagliero, Fr. Tornatis and the carpenter, Scavini, who had arrived from Buenos Aires to put the abandoned edifice in order. In December 1876, the group of Salesians sent from Italy landed. "When they arrived, they found the city plan newly drawn up, but it would shortly rise and grow in the sight of all. All of the wide, long, straight ways would lead to the outskirts of the school, formed by various groups of buildings.... The interior walls of both the church and the house were only plaster and whitewash; there were no ornaments or furniture of any kind."[19]

As soon as they could open the school, the students arrived in large numbers, confirming the great need for the institution which Don Bosco had named "Collegio Pio di Villa Colón" in honor of Pius IX.

For the time being, the Daughters of Mary Help of Christians were called to start the girls' school, workrooms and oratory. Don Bosco wanted the work of human and Christian advancement to be extended to the girls as soon as possible. The six sisters found a place near the boys' school, in a house donated by the Jackson family, one of the most noted in Montevideo.

Before this troubled yet beautiful year of 1877 drew to a close, Mother Mazzarello took advantage of a Christmas letter to reach out, in her quiet, determined way. Now it was necessary to think of the future. The recipient of the letter was Fr. Giovanni Battista Lemoyne, new director at Mornese.

Mother offered her wishes: "...poorly expressed, but sincere and heartfelt," promising all the collaboration possible, and then formulating a request: "I ask you, dear Father, not to spare me anything. Use me as you believe best, correct me without any regard. In short, treat me as a father treats his firstborn daughter."[20]

Who are the firstborn children in the countryside, male or female? She knew very well. They are those who must grow up faster, being the first to help their parents. At the Valponasca, as the firstborn, she was sent early into the vineyards, with the hired hands. Then, the firstborn are responsible for younger brothers and sisters, they are the guardians, the loving teachers.

Mary Mazzarello was fully aware of her duty as Mother. At the same time, she had also arrived at the clear discernment of the only way of being more and more a mother: "If I always give good example to my sisters, things will always go well."[21]

Chapter Seven

In the space of a few winter weeks, 1878 would see all of Rome changed; there was a new king and a new pope. Umberto I took the place of Victor Emanuel II; Leo XIII took that of Pius IX. All told, the facts linking the two deaths and successions showed that the Kingdom of Italy was solid, as was the papacy, and that the loss of the Papal State was a benefit for the universal Church. Victor Emanuel died of pneumonia at fifty-eight years of age on January 9, after having received the last rites from the head chaplain of the Quirinale, Monsignor Anzino. The funeral was held on January 19.

A few weeks later the Pope also died. Pius IX expired at eighty-six years of age on the afternoon of February 7. Since a great crowd went to pay their respects at St. Peter's, the necessary arrangements in the public line led to a collaboration between the Vatican and Italian forces responsible for order. There was the immediate problem of the conclave for the election of a successor. Where would it be held? One group of cardinals even suggested that it be in Malta, but common sense prevailed and it was decided that the gathering take place in

Rome. In 1870 Don Bosco has already told Pius IX: "The sentinel, the angel of Israel, will remain at his post." Even the Italian government, anticlerical as it was, saw the need for everything to proceed in an orderly manner, according to the rules. The conclave went ahead well, and on February 20, the new pope was elected. It was Gioacchino Pecci, who would be called Leo XIII.

Don Bosco had seen Pius IX for the last time in the immobility of death, in St. Peter's between candles and mourning vestments. He even interceded between Vatican and government authorities, speaking with Francesco Crispi, Minister of the Interior. In March he had his first papal audience with Leo XIII. From Rome, he informed the Daughters of Mary Help of Christians about events at the Vatican.

Also from Rome during that time, he decided that Mary Mazzarello, accompanied by a few Salesian priests, should visit the convent of Nizza Monferrato. It was necessary to have an idea about the repairs and major adjustments needed so as to be able to begin in time for the scholastic year, 1878-1879. This was the first step of Mother Mazzarello on a necessary, but painful journey. She was to imitate Abraham, abandoning her native home, leaving Mornese for all the aforementioned reasons, for the development of the institute.

Fr. Giacomo Costamagna, who had also dreamed of America and had thrown himself into the study of Spanish, from beyond the Atlantic would remember the years of Mornese as the happiest of his life. "That house was holy, among other reasons, because it had at its head a saint, Mother Mazzarello."[1]

Mornese was unforgettable, and would never be reduced to a mere enthusiastic memory. It was already a definitive patrimony of the Daughters of Mary Help of Christians who were there and for those who would follow. At Mornese, after the time of the first development, they realized that it was necessary to move toward Nizza Monferrato, for reasons which Mother saw confirmed from the time of her first visit: everything was more accessible; it was easier to acquire necessities and more convenient for making connections; the locale was better adapted to a greater number of postulants and students.

Visiting the building, she spoke with Sr. Enrichetta Sorbone, assistant of the students. She had wanted her to come along so that she would be distracted from an inconvenience which was making her suffer. At the end of 1877, Don Bosco had sent two girls to Mornese from a well-to-do family in Turin which had suffered financial reverses. (A third little girl would stay at Valdocco with the sisters.) They were Emma and Oliva Ferrero. The first was a beautiful, cultured eighteen-year-old who acted as though she were an exile, isolating herself from prayer, entertainment and even meals. At times she was sullen and insolent, trapped in her past, capable of losing herself in the contemplation of her trunks of finery and ornaments from bygone days. She was not an Agostina Simbeni, filled with wild transports and restless mysticism, but rather one who refused the present, especially the present of poverty and dedication which was being lived at Mornese. Sr. Enrichetta Sorbone looked after her with all her intelligence and good will, understanding and amiability, being careful not to embitter her, preoccupying herself more with her than with the others.

This was too much, said Mother Mazzarello. "Emma's case" shows how she was an educator with the educators. It was a pedagogy which placed the preventive method in a feminine light, enriched by her own original contributions. Meanwhile, there was no praiseworthy commitment of recovery, no preoccupation for the cases of specific seriousness which could justify personal indulgence, the preferring of one person more than the others. There was a need for equity even in

one's preoccupation. Then, too, since the behavior of an educator toward a person always has good or less good effects on
the whole, Sr. Enrichetta's attention toward Emma sowed
seeds of envy and ill will. Mother frankly reproached the sister, even in public. To cheer her up, she took her as a companion on some trips and visits, during which Sr. Emilia Mosca
looked after Emma.

Mother's humility lay in never allowing herself and not
permitting others to deviate from the general principles of
discipline. It lay in being tranquilly firm with regard to whatever happened. She was defined by many as being strong, yet
prudent. Cardinal John Cagliero wrote: "Though she was very
loving toward her daughters, when necessary she was firm and
resolute in wanting them to correct their faults. She did not
avoid correcting them when she saw them unwilling to listen
to her exhortations."

"She did not hesitate...." But one of her resources was the
capacity of obtaining the collaboration of the person to be
corrected. She seemed to say, more by gesture than with
words, "Help me to make you better; let's create this master-
piece together." A witness at the process of her canonization
defined her in this way: "When she corrected, her aspect was
rather strong, but her sweetness immediately appeared, so
much so that the sister corrected was consoled."[2] She did not
shorten the journey by even a millimeter, but she offered tremendous support and comfort until the finishing line. She did
not fail to give a merited reproach—"what she wanted, she
wanted" said another witness—but she never denied the frater-
nal word, the gesture of esteem immediately after. She wanted
her daughters to be capable of clearly examining themselves
and rectifying their journey with the joy of one who has found
the right way.

"Keep them always happy," she wrote to Sr. Angela
Vallese, superior at Villa Colón, condensing the formative

direction in a few lines. "Always correct them with charity, but do not overlook any defect. A defect which is corrected immediately becomes nothing, but one which is allowed to take root is difficult to uproot later on."

Therefore, defects were not to be tolerated. Yet neither were they to frighten or be overestimated, she writes in the same letter. It was necessary to remain cheerful, not as a static happy condition, but as a weapon. "Be cheerful; don't be so afraid of your defects if you cannot correct them all at once, but do so little by little, with the good will of fighting them, never making peace with them whenever the Lord chooses to allow you to recognize them. You do your part to correct them and you will see that sooner or later you will have conquered them all."[3]

The sisters of the expedition to Montevideo had to undergo a few days of quarantine before disembarking, because the ship had stopped in Rio de Janeiro which was infested with yellow fever. (This was also done in Italy when ships arrived from Brazil.) For the first two months the sisters received hospitality in the convent of the Visitation Sisters. Finally, on February 19, they took possession of their own house, and began a free school and an oratory. Now they needed to receive reinforcements from Italy in the person of other Daughters. In the meantime, Laura Rodriguez, one of the girls who attended the oratory, had become a postulant. Laura was from an important family of Villa Colón and would be the first American sister of the first American house of the Daughters of Mary Help of Christians. This was the first of the 400 houses which the sisters would gradually establish in the New World.

Sr. Laura was also the first Daughter whom Mother Mazzarello would not know personally. She sent her a letter after her vestition, emphasizing that she was to become "a great saint, so that many American girls would be able to follow her example." With a constant realism she continued, observing that she did not think it necessary to recommend obedience, humility and love of work: "It has only been a few short months since you made vestition, therefore you are still full of fervor. I recommend only that you never allow the flame of this fervor which the Lord has lit in your heart to go out. Remember that one thing alone is necessary—the salvation of your soul. Yet, it is not enough for us religious to save our souls, we must become saints, and make other souls who expect our help saints through our good works."

How were these good works to be carried out? There was another brief counsel from the Mazzarello handbook, written with the usual firm starting point: *"Always be cheerful;* have great confidence in your superiors, never hiding anything from them; keep your heart open; always obey them in all simplicity and you will never be mistaken."[4]

France Calls

The Italian houses moved ahead in the poverty which Mother watched over vigilantly. At some rare times it happened that she noted small digressions in the austerity (very small, for example, that of having a few breadsticks at table) and she would immediately intervene to "take away the defect while it was still small." More often it happened that she was seen to be moved by the privations and sacrifices of the Daughters, which even threatened their health because of too much work. Accompanied by Sr. Enrichetta Sorbone, in January she arrived at the houses of Alassio and Bordighera, leaving her companion in the latter, because she really needed a break after dealing with Emma's problems. She went on alone to Nice by the Sea, where the Daughters could not house two more persons at the same time. Having reached the place, she saw that there was not even an extra bed, and that one of the

Daughters would have had to give up hers. She would have done so willingly, but this was not acceptable. The sister who worked all day needed her rest, and Mother said that she herself could very well spend the night in a chair, resting her head on a table. In the morning she was fresh and tranquil, and those sisters needed no treatises and sermons to understand the meaning of poverty.

From France, the bishop of Fréjus and Tolone had indicated to Don Bosco that there were two orphanages in his diocese (one at Navarre and another at Saint Cyr-sur-Mer) which had been started after a cholera epidemic by a priest, Fr. Jacques Vincent, who could no longer continue. Other priests who had gone to Navarre were also in difficulties, not being able to form a stable organization. In 1878 Mother Mazzarello and Mother Emilia Mosca, at Don Bosco's invitation, went to visit the two institutions, and found two disasters: there were vast fields to set up a good agricultural school, but crumbling buildings, filth everywhere and there, in the midst of it, were the orphans. Here we don't have the profile for a foundation, but one of first aid, a life raft.

Under the guidance of Fr. Ronchail, director of the Salesian *Patronage* of Nice by the Sea, everything was worked out, especially at the institute La Navarre. Two Daughters of Mary Help of Christians took over its direction in October 1878.

At Saint-Cyr, instead, more time was needed. After a new on-the-spot investigation carried out together with Don Bosco and Mother Mazzarello, three Daughters were established there in April 1880. They had to live there together with the elderly founder, Fr. Vincent, along with a group of his volunteers who had run the orphanage for years. It was a new and trying experience for the Italian religious, who were used to even a bitter poverty, but in their own homes, on their own. Between the weariness and the need to exercise diplomacy, it was a difficult trial. Mother Mazzarello, however, indicated

without hesitation who was to assume the new responsibility—
Sr. Catherine Daghero, then superior of the house of Turin
where the sisters did not look upon her transfer with a kindly
eye. Mother, however, consoled them with a prophetic phrase:
"For now you will lose Sr. Catherine, but you will have her
back in another capacity."

At Mornese there was another change, and it was called
Emma Ferrero. She was becoming another person, but without
pious scenes or racket. She became another person, regaining
her smile, and this was the first sign of good news. During the
time of recreation, "she would run and jump with her companions and with Sr. Enrichetta, without losing herself in the
contemplation of the little idols in her trunk. She even began to
make acts of humility in the presence of her companions."[5] She
was also very active and quick to take part in activities, serenely weaving at the loom. It was a real change, precisely
because of this sign of serenity.

It goes without saying that her father had entrusted her
and her sisters to Don Bosco only for their studies, since he
was not able to send them to expensive institutes in Turin.
Emma's goal was that of receiving a teaching diploma, and her
recent change had also made of her a good Christian who was
an assiduous recipient of Holy Communion. At the moment,
there was nothing more.

This was during the time when the Daughters of Mary
Help of Christians were opening a new house in Chieri, an
important Piedmontese center. However, they faced some difficulties, so that at the beginning they limited themselves to
starting, as in other places, an oratory for girls and a workroom
for young people. The superior of the new institution was
Felicina Mazzarello, Mother's sister, and the work began on
June 22, 1878. At the end of the month, Mary Mazzarello
stopped in to visit the new house, and when she returned to
Mornese, a small bonfire was burning in the courtyard. During

recreation time, with calm and determination, Emma had set fire to the contents of the famous trunk. She was healed of her past ills, and had decided on her future course: she would become a Daughter of Mary Help of Christians. Her vestition took place on August 20, 1878. From that moment on, Sr. Emma "was studious of the holy rule, exact in observing it, especially taking care not to lose a moment of time, to observe silence and to keep herself in God's presence. The peace of her heart was reflected on her face, and her beauty seemed to have taken on something celestial."[6]

Two years were enough for her to take her place in the history of the Daughters, with her succession of conquests through renunciation, with the joy which flooded her in prayer and work, with her old vivacity intact and visible at all times during her day, in the serenity of the equilibrium which she had reached. In February 1880 she was struck with an unexpected, violent pulmonary hemorrhage, a sad sign of hemoptysis. Emma understood that she was at the end and still spread serenity around herself: "If I live, I live for Jesus; if I die, I die for him." Her voice echoed the exhortation of Paul, apostle to the Romans, "Not one of us lives or dies for self." She died on March 1, 1880, after having received the last rites from Fr. Cagliero.

Let us go back to 1878. During August the usual general meetings of the superiors were held, but this time they had many irons in the fire. In close connection with the now proximate transfer to Nizza Monferrato, the decisions tended to better coordinate the educational activity of the institute. Even mainly logistical choices were to move in this direction. Poverty, which the superiors affirmed, should be rendered "lovable," and be shown in order and neatness in every environment. As a particular attention to the families of the educators, "the reception room for outsiders should be set up in such a way that social conventions are not neglected."

Then there were directives about their specific function: "The Superior General should send as many Daughters as are capable to study; the others should perfect themselves in needlework, knitting, embroidery, design, in such a way that they, too, could become teachers for the respective works." As Mother Mazzarello always said, whether the work be intellectual or manual, it should be carried out with all one's strength. She further emphasized this by saying that every Daughter, without exception, must be ready to "do anything which the superior thought best to command." But be careful: "True humility consists not in carrying out the lowest tasks, but rather in fulfilling that which obedience commands, with a heart ready to renounce even these if a new order should come."

After these formative premises, they further discussed the need for music and song, which were no longer merely an extra, but "a need." They established as a condition for acceptance that the postulants should know how to read and write fluently.

Finally, they focused on Nizza Monferrato. The transfer would take place in steps; therefore for a certain time Mornese would continue to function (and with a special passion, with a greater love) despite a reduced number of personnel. However, it was necessary to begin as soon as possible, since they had already waited so long. On Easter Sunday in 1878, another young person died at Mornese. It was the novice Teresa Guiot, from Fenestrelle. The funeral was held on the following Tuesday morning, very early, also so as to not make too evident to the people of Mornese, as the *Cronistoria* frankly notes, "the frequency of these passings in the school."[7]

The climate of Nizza was something completely different, noted the local physician, Doctor Sannazzaro, following the request of Don Bosco and the scholastic authorities for authorization to open the school. The doctor stated: "Having frequently visited the convent entitled, Our Lady of Grace, now become a house of education, at a distance of about 250 meters from the city, I declare that because of its beautiful location at the foot of a hill and to the south, and the healthfulness of the environment, erected in a safe, dry place, ventilated on all sides, made up of rooms, corridors and airy, wide atriums, this place is very adapted for an educational institute."[8]

In the New House

On to Nizza, then! On September 16, 1878, the first sisters set foot in the new location: Enrichetta Sorbone, Giovanna Ferrettino, Ermelinda Rossi, Maria Fiorito and Teresa Moretta. They still had much to do to bring everything up to par. Laborers worked at the restorations and the four sisters went to perfect the work with cleanliness and improvements, especially in the locales destined to the "School of Our Lady of Grace" as it would be called according to the desire of Don Bosco, acceding to a name very dear to the people of Nizza. After a week, Mother Petronilla Mazzarello, who would be the temporary superior, arrived to help, bringing with her Sr. Elisa Roncallo. They had traveled by train from Genoa to Turin, and then from Turin to Nizza. During the first stretch Don Bosco had spoken at length with them and the two sisters had received many instructions and counsels for this beginning.

The work proceeded well; the date for the inauguration and entrance into the work would be met, especially in view of Petronilla and Elisa's help. However, they were still preoccupied. Don Bosco had given them the task of visiting Countess Balbo, who, along with her husband, was a great benefactor of the work. Naturally, even this task would be taken care of, but a preoccupied Mother Petronilla had questioned the founder, "What do you do on a visit to a countess?"

The meeting went very well, and help from the Balbo house was not lacking, even for manpower. So everything was ready for the solemn blessing celebrated by Fr. Cagliero with Mother Mazzarello present, on Saturday, September 27. On Monday the 29th, the first postulant from Nizza arrived. She was Maria Terzano, daughter of the expert-accountant of the place, who had helped a great deal with the legalities for the acquisition and restorations of the ex-convent.

On September 31, the first group of students arrived from Mornese and school began. (The authorization would be granted a few months later.) During the second week of November, Fr. Lemoyne arrived with three sisters and two more students. So it was that the religious community (but not all of them) and the students began their new life. At this time Mornese was still the motherhouse, and in November three sisters left from there to open a new foundation at Quargnento, in Alessandrino, with a nursery school, workroom and oratory.

Mother Mazzarello also returned to Mornese at the end of November. As usual, the feast of the Immaculate was celebrated with a few professions of perpetual and temporary vows. In the name of Don Bosco, Fr. Cagliero was also present at these ceremonies which would be celebrated here for the last time with the impassioned fervor of a moment of farewell. These were intense moments, with waves of memory, but the future called.

"Thanks to the goodness of our heavenly Father, the institute of the Daughters of Mary Help of Christians, of which we are fortunate members, has had a happy development. In the space of a few months, we have been able to open a good number of houses in Piedmont, Liguria, France and even in the far regions of America...." This is what we read in a sixty-four page booklet entitled "Rules and Constitutions for the Institute of the Daughters of Mary Help of Christians, Associated with the Salesian Society." Don Bosco had it printed, explaining that the manuscript text was enough while the institute was concentrated in Mornese, "But now that, because of divine providence, the houses have multiplied and the sisters have gone there, this was no longer sufficient." The printed rule would now accompany every sister, wherever she went, to "exercise herself in Christian virtue before anything else," and to then dedicate herself to the good of her neighbor. "It will be their special care to assume the direction of schools, orphanages, nursery schools, festive oratories and even to open workrooms for the benefit of the poorest children in cities, villages and foreign missions. Where necessary, they may also accept the direction of hospitals and other similar charitable offices."

The cities and villages were in Italy and abroad. It was precisely from abroad, from far away America, that a rather urgent request would arrive: more sisters were needed; the first six were not enough for so much work.

Mother Mazzarello was quick to send another ten, formed and prepared under her direction and with the strength of her example. She lived what the rule said.

The work of the sisters in America was asked for not only at Villa Colón in Montevideo, but also in Argentina, by churches and other institutes in favor of *los Italianos,* and for another undertaking which moved forward among many difficulties: the advance toward the south of Argentina, the march to Patagonia. This time three Salesians left with the ten Daughters of Mary Help of Christians. One of the sisters was Sr. Magdalen Martini, who went to be the "provincial," that is, superior of all the Daughters in America. Mother Mazzarello explained the situation concisely: "I'm sending her to you to direct you in your work." It was a "clear, very clear" conversation in the manner of Bernardine of Siena.

There had been a bit of a battle with Sr. Martini, because this sister "had a treasury of virtue, but hated every appointment and was excessively timid."[9]

Others wondered why Mother had chosen her. How could such a person command, especially in that first American frontier of which Fr. Cagliero had told so many turbulent events and adventures? But Mother knew that Sr. Magdalen Martini was "fit to command," as they say in military language. She had watched her with a tranquil eye which never seemed to scrutinize, but which saw everything. She knew and had discovered the necessary gifts in the depth of her character. Sr. Magdalen Martini had the qualities of a leader; it would have been a sin not to use these talents. The *Cronistoria* seriously mentions the work which Mother Mazzarello carried out in this timid sister: "She sought to help her to love her new duties."

What were these duties? Becoming a provincial does not mean obtaining a grade or a position. It means receiving an order for a service. Humility does not enter here, because as Mother Mazzarello would frequently repeat, humility does not consist in merely desiring only modest tasks and responsibilities; it means serenely accepting even the highest functions, the places of authority.

So it was that, because of the tranquil conversations, even during recreation among the noise of the youngest children, Sr. Sr. Magdalen Martini was instructed as a guide of her sisters. She received from Mother Mazzarello the primary directive under all the heavens: "She never stopped," says the *Cronistoria,* "recommending vigilance for a good spirit."[10]

The other sisters who left for America were Emilia Borgna, who would meet her sister, Giovanna, in America, Filomena Balduzzi, Vittoria Cantù, Caterina Fino, Maria Magdaleine, Virginia Magone, Giacinta Olivieri, Domenica Roletti and Giuseppina Vergniaud.

Traditionally the departing missionaries (or one of the delegation) would go to Rome to receive the blessing of the pontiff. This time, however, the greeting of Leo XIII would arrive via telegram. They had no money for the journey to

Rome; they had scraped the bottom of the barrel to obtain what was indispensable for the missionary journey.

They had farewell celebrations at Mornese, with the certainty that these would not be the last. Then the ten missionaries left for Genoa. The *Cronistoria* has a page rich with the simple grace of the *Flowers of St. Francis.* It describes the departure from the poor, isolated, uncomfortable but much loved little village. To get to a train, they had to brave the night for hours and hours in the midst of snow and mud. For transport they had only a rustic farm wagon.

The first sisters had discreetly boarded the cart, but the others.... The wet footstool froze immediately, and the others had to be careful not to slip and fall to the ground before they could seat themselves on the rough four-wheeled cart, which was high and pulled by horses and mules. It was so bumpy that some preferred to walk, even to try to warm themselves. But they could not make their way on the icy road. They also had to pass the Albedosa river which, while not deep, was wide and rocky. It was so dark that they were forced to conquer the same difficulties they had in formerly climbing onto the cart."[11]

When they had reached the station of Serravalle Scrivia, they found Mother Mazzarello already there holding the tickets for Genoa. She had taken a shortcut.

The Salesian school of Sampierdarena housed the missionary expedition for the last night before their departure. A weary Don Bosco had also arrived, and while not yet very old (he was about sixty-four), he seemed oppressed by an invincible tiredness; his vision, heart, the poor circulation which made his legs swell painfully, and that conflict with the archbishop of Turin which also had poor echoes in Rome. He was there for the leave taking, but did not feel up to going to the port. He said good-bye to those departing from the school.

It was the first day of 1879. The group boarded the ship *South America* along with Mother Mazzarello, who had prepared letters for the superior of Villa Colón, Sr. Angela Vallese; for the Uruguayan sister, Laura Rodriguez; and for Sr. Giovanna Borgna, whose sister Emilia would give her the message in the New World.

Sr. Emilia was not given much hope by many. She was an excellent religious, but her health was so poor and she was so emotional. Wasn't it a risk to send her to the front lines? In fact, during the last greeting, Sr. Emilia paled, became faint, and Mother Mazzarello grasped hold of her. The scene seemed to confirm the most fearful prognosis.

But Mother did not waver. She helped Sr. Emilia to gain control of herself, tranquilly left the ship and did not change a comma in her heart of what she had said of her fragile Daughter: "Emilia will work more than you think, and she will do much good." The *South America* left at 4:30 PM. on that New Year's Day, carrying Sr. Emilia Borgna, destined to work and "do good" year after year, and decade after decade, until she would see Mother Mazzarello on the way to the altar.

Mother Leaves Mornese

The chronicles could never fully describe the thoughts of Mary Mazzarello because her world was history. She was a woman with a long, tranquil memory, accustomed to relegating the momentary, even the dramatic, to the second place that is its due in the broad succession of generations. Living—as she wanted and knew how—always in Dante's view of God, "to whom all times are present," she had a natural and vigorous sense of the connections and accords of the times, of the weave between past and future. For the rest, the future was her profession, not as a prophet or fortune teller, but as a builder; it was up to her to discover the woman present in the girls, to discern the existence and direction of a vocation, to see in today's gestures the premises of successes and failures.

It was this contemporariness of vision—past and future—which kept her serene while those Daughters whom she would never see again sailed away. In the boat which brought them back to land after the departure, in saying good-bye to other groups sent to open new houses, far and wide, she already considered the future. She already saw those women beyond the Atlantic or the Belbo river, at the head of a youthful work to be enriched by culture, education, self-awareness, self-sufficiency. Faced with this vision she did not cry; she gave thanks. "He who is powerful has done great things for me, and holy is his name."

In the meantime, Don Bosco insisted that she leave Mornese and he was right. The majority of the sisters and postulants were at Nizza Monferrato, and the school with the students was also there. The regular inhabitants of the "Collegio" (in Mornese) were a few sisters, some of whom were ill, and others who did the work of the house; a few postulants; and a little group of children accepted without tuition. It was a type of hospice. Everything called for an official transfer of the headquarters to Nizza.

Mother also knew this, and on February 4, she said good-bye to the last few people remaining at Mornese. Then she went to Nizza, her definitive headquarters, the new mother-house of the Daughters of Mary Help of Christians.

Nizza had the convenience of the city, along with the great open spaces of the institute where it was so marvelous for sisters and girls to be able to run as the owners of the house. From Nizza one could reach Turin or Genoa in a few short hours, traveling at the speed of the world.... Nizza, however, was not Mornese, where every stone spoke to "Maìn of the Valponasca," where her generous family remained. Those who had followed the first chapters of her adventure were there; these people were both enthusiastic and suspicious, quick to criticize but also to help; these people had their suspicions and their trust, as well as sentiments of pride for what their friends of long ago had built. Now those people were aware that something was ending on February 4, 1879, as Mary Mazzarello walked down from the heights of the "Collegio" and moved toward the new house.

Meanwhile, from America news reached them of the happy arrival of the ten sisters, who were now divided between Uruguay and Argentina. In the first of the two countries they were about to open another house at *Las Piedras,* still in the diocese of Montevideo, beginning a school and an oratory. From 1879, there had been a school at Almagro (Buenos Aires), Argentina, with a day school, boarding school and oratory. There was also a school with an oratory in the turbulent suburb of Boca. At the beginning of 1880, they took their first step toward the South, to Carmen de Patagones, in the diocese of La Plata, establishing an educational center with an oratory.

Still on the theme of Latin America, it is now time to look at an important document. It was a letter-report to Don Bosco on the activity of the missionaries, written by the "too timid" Sr. Magdalen Martini, whom Mother Mazzarello wanted as provincial. After having described the initiatives in preparation, the letter continues: "Thank God we are all in good health and we are also content and cheerful; on the contrary, I can tell you that we are very happy at being destined for these missions, much more so since we have the fortune, as in Italy, to be directed by our reverend Salesian superiors, who truly have every care and solicitude for us. Our sisters and missionary companions in the nearby Republic (Uruguay) have much to do with the girls. As for us, our greatest occupation for now is taking care of the linen of the school. But we are working to soon open a school for the many girls of this section, and their Argentinean, Spanish and Italian parents also want this. Now we have only to correspond to this great grace which we have received from God, that of being chosen, from among so many who desired it, and sent to these faraway lands to save so many poor young women from the fangs of rapacious wolves."[12] This "timid" person was the leader whom Mother knew her to be.

Mother Mazzarello had her base camp at Nizza, but she frequently traveled from one house to another. She did this for a reason which is forgotten in the recounting of the foundations, institutes and schools: poverty. There was a numerical poverty of personnel, and a chronic one of means. This meant heavy fatigue for those who were failing, the incessant problems—and discouragement for those who do not look on high—of providing another bed, using a worn-out garment, paying debts, seeking orders for the workroom, and at the same time presenting a good image to outsiders. Unknown to the students and families, this could bring very difficult sacrifices and bitter renunciations for the sisters. When arriving for a visit, it was necessary to share sacrifices and work, to encourage, to lighten the burdens at least for a day.

Not being able to go to America in person, she sent letters, which were frequently dictated or written over a period of time, one part in Nizza, another at Turin, and the conclusion in a completely different place. A typical example was the long letter written to Sr. Angela Vallese and all the Daughters at Villa Colón in April 1879.[13] It is full of illuminating flashes on the events of the institute and the interiority of one who took occasions for teaching from any event. At times, however, it has brief allusions to life's daily problems. Dedicating a few lines to each sister, Mother Mazzarello arrived at Sr. De Negri, asking her if she had already learned French well, and she immediately added a note from on high: "In studying the languages of this world, study also the language of the soul with God. He will teach you the science of becoming a saint, which is the one true science." Then, suddenly, "Your parents are

well, and they gave me a salami to send to you, but since you
are so far away, I thought of keeping it for you. You'll thank
them, won't you? Write to them soon." It would be well not to
forget that in the midst of the development and success, the
arrival of a salami was an event, and a rare one at that.

In the same letter she confided to her Daughters of
America her pain at having to leave Mornese, but she did so
with a touch of singular elegance: "You probably know already that I am no longer at Mornese, but here in Nizza." That
was that. This painful transfer had a lesson: "As long as we are
in this world, we must make sacrifices willingly and cheerfully. The Lord will take note of everything and in his own
time will give us a beautiful reward."

It had even become easier for the postulants to reach
Nizza. In June 1879 a girl from Lucca named Carmelinda
Dianda entered. In her city they were saying: "Those sisters in
Nizza, in Piedmont, have a saint for a superior." As soon as she
arrived, she heard Mother ask her "Carmelinda, are you cheer-
ful?" The first recommendation followed: "Always be cheerful."

Naturally, this was wonderful. It was a relief for those
who usually arrived full of fervor and also of fear. But it was
also fairly logical and usual to open the way with a smile for
the newly arrived, to free them from burdens. On this point
only the pedagogy of joy is announced. But Carmelinda later
understood that Mother Mazzarello's attitude was not merely
one of expedient courtesy. Upon receiving letters from home,
the girl sometimes cried. Then Mother Mazzarello appeared
before her and spoke seriously: "Your heart is still too attached
to Lucca. If you act this way, I won't give you any more
letters." Carmelinda didn't bother too much about these words,
and had even forgotten them, but Mother Mazzarello had not.
Two days later she reappeared and said: "I told you that you
were still too attached to Lucca, and I've come to ask pardon. I
should not have spoken like that." Now Carmelinda saw how

real cheerfulness worked. For two days Mother had scolded herself for those words, then she had come to ask pardon of Carmelinda, to give her the joy of having respected her feelings; "Now I know that Mother is truly a saint."

Papa Mazzarello Dies

Even she, Mary Mazzarello, had her heart attached to Mornese, the little village which had been her birthplace, and which had seen her early childhood and her growth in the family. On September 22, she was called there, because her father was very ill. She had to be at his side to the very end. The *Cronistoria* tells us: "She could not have been more of a daughter and more of a religious."

Joseph Mazzarello was her father and first educator in the faith. It was he who had responded to that unexpected question from his little girl: "Papa, what did God do before he created the world?" It was he who had formed her by his example: how to receive Holy Communion even outside of Easter time, when very few dared and those who did were regarded as strange people. Now it was she who stood at his bedside and pronounced words of faith, in a certain sense "officiating" at his passage with the prayers which the Church recited for the agonizing. As soon as her father breathed his last, she reminded everyone of the doctrine of the last things with a specific invitation: "Let us kneel and pray; this is the moment of judgment." She herself composed the body and then carried out two acts of the ancient patriarch, described by Maccono: "She remembered one by one all the benefits received, and especially the good example and Christian, virile education which he had given. She took care of the family interests without allowing unpleasantries to arise."[14]

In the newspapers and in many cities of Italy people were heatedly speaking of Bosnia-Herzegovina. These two regions of the Balkans, already under Turkish domination, had now passed into "administration" by the Austrian empire, to impede their being taken over (or at least influenced in a political-military way) by Czarist Russia. In 1878 an important international congress had been held in Berlin to straighten up Europe and the vicinity after the Russian victory in the brief war against the Turks. Almost every country had obtained something, from Cyprus (England) to Tunis (France). But Italy received nothing because the Prime Minister, Benedetto Cairoli, spoke of "clean hands," that is, "let's not get involved in foreign affairs."

He could have been right, but no one told him so. They accused him of ineptitude and almost of betrayal. Then, on November 17, in Naples a Lucan cook named Giovanni Passanante attempted to assassinate King Umberto I who was riding in a carriage, and wounded Cairoli in the leg. In this complex climate, the Italian political world made its own examination of conscience. While some mourned because new territories had not been conquered, one member of parliament (the Honorable Toscano) said: "Sirs, with five million hectares of land which are laying untitled, the Italian citizen is abandoning the sweet climate of his country to go and die of yellow fever on Rio de la Plata, or black vomit (smallpox) in Brazil and in the republic of Argentina. Sirs, it is time that we should blush to the roots of our hair for this state of affairs."

From there, the countries of the yellow fever and smallpox, messages arrived at Nizza, succinct bulletins about daily work, accompanied by very scant information on personal health problems. From Uruguay Sr. Virginia Magone asked before anything else why Mother Mazzarello did not go to visit the Daughters in America. She insisted a great deal, then she confided: "Do you want me to tell you something? I think I will die soon, because I have a cough which I can't shake off and which torments me. So, if you don't come soon, I'm afraid that I will never see you again...." [15] She went on to describe her own imperfections and failings, praising the other sisters: "They're humble, obedient, very charitable and sweet, and I'm the opposite." She excused her terrible handwriting: "Today I have a fever, and therefore, I can only write from bed, if I am to write at all.... If I cannot write later on, I want to wish you a happy feast day, happy end and beginning of the year...." This was Sr. Virginia's last letter to Mother.

Sr. Angela Vallese, superior of Villa Colón, was disturbed about the house of Las Piedras because there were many difficulties, even due to the lack of preparation of a few sisters; she spoke frankly to Mother about it, and the latter acted quickly, inviting her to write more often. "Don't think that your letters bother me.... Write often, and write long, long letters...." [16]

She wrote about the problems: "I'm sorry that the new house of Las Piedras has difficulties. However, you must not be afraid; persuade yourself that there will always be defects; you must correct and remedy all that you can, but calmly, and allow all to rest in the Lord's hands." Naturally, she said that it was necessary to intervene, and not let things go on. "Correct, advise always, but be compassionate in your heart, and use charity with all. You see, you must study the characters so as to know how to take them and to have success; you must inspire confidence." So it was that in a tranquil style of prose from Monferrato she gave the rule for being a good leader: never seem so, do not feel the office, but look within the character, earn trust.

She could have said to Sr. Vallese: "But didn't you think of how I would have done things, and how I still do them, how many games I join in on the playground to 'study the characters,' and how I don't worry about appearances when I have to say 'I made a mistake' before everyone?"

Another lesson in good government can be found in this

letter: never to substitute herself for the local superiors, but on the contrary, to respect their authority. "When you do not know how to act, turn to Sr. Magdalen (Martini) and do all that she tells you; then be tranquil." For all, finally, she recalled the decisive importance of working on one's own personal and communitarian formation. "You tell me that there is much work, and I am very pleased, because work is the father of virtue. When you work, whims disappear and one is always cheerful. While I recommend that you work, I also recommend that you care for your health and that all work without ambition and only to please Jesus."

In a successive letter to Sr. Vallese, she explains how the spirit of the Lord can be assumed by practicing neighborly charity. "That humble, patient spirit, full of charity, but of that charity which is proper to Jesus, who never gave up suffering so much for us...." Taking on this spirit with joy protected herself from offending anyone and taught her to give relief and comfort. "Be cheerful, right?...and always cheerful. Never become offended, never; on the contrary, as soon as you are aware that someone needs some comfort, extend it quickly and console one another...."[17]

With her Piedmontese expressions, Mother translated the impassioned warning of St. Paul to the Christians of Ephesus: "Do not let the sun go down upon your anger...."

Chapter Eight

They had no money and the pantry was empty. Mary Mazzarello spoke of it rarely and only in passing, but the hardships continued both at Nizza and Mornese. Assistance increased, but the needs were ever greater. The 150 members (postulants, novices and sisters) frequently suffered privation so that none of the students would suffer. The "spirit of Mornese" had truly been transplanted to the shores of the Belbo, even during what could have been moments of desperation, if she had not been there to illumine and explain them.

It was wonderful to see her face these food crises by arranging for an unscheduled chestnut roast. Upon having understood that during the "St. Martin's summer" of 1879 there was nothing for supper, she improvised a countryside outing for all to a sanctuary and its surroundings. Gathering the chestnuts of the season, the outing with its visit to the shrine church was enriched by an unexpected picnic. So it was that upon returning home, it was natural to go to bed without even thinking about supper.

At other times, instead, Mother briefly explained the situation to the community, presenting the inevitable fasting not as a disgrace, but as a moment in a providential plan which touched each and every one. So it was that the supper of dry bread and watered down soup became an enrichment, not a punishment.

The experts in sanctity would be startled that those who were inexpert would dare to say that this Mary Domenica Mazzarello was a saint who was not very "penitential." In reading her writings and discourses, we do not continually come up against sin, its anguish and its punishment. Her words and especially her behavior inspired others to prevent sin: avoid the occasions; act sensibly to get away from the danger; use the arms of prayer, next to which she tenaciously placed that of work.

We do not find in her teaching dark warnings about damnation, or that technique of fear which had bothered her from the time she was a child, hearing pessimistic thunder in the church of Mornese. That word "sin" was rarely found in her conversation, which was usually fraught with incessant stanzas of the hymn of joy. We also find great reference to "merits" and "works," two continual elements in the urging toward a world which was to be encountered on its own terms, without fear or flight, a world to raise up and enrich.

In the exhortations to Laura Rodriguez, her first Daughter of America, Mother does not mention sin or evil. She speaks instead of "making herself a great saint" and of sanctifying others with our "good works." Her entire correspondence is shot through with the invitation of making herself "saintly and rich in merit," because "merits never fade." Further on she writes: "At the point of death we will have only our works; what is important is the good which has been done"; "You are in a position where you can gain many merits;" "Do all that you can, and you will see that all will go well." She showed tremendous support for a Daughter with great simplicity: "There is no need to cry to show a good heart," and yet neither should we prostrate ourselves because of our mediocrity: "We are miserable and cannot be perfect; therefore, let us be humble, have confidence and be joyful."

From America, insistent invitations arrived for her to cross the Atlantic. The sisters wanted her among them to visit with them. They felt the need of having her see them at their work, among so many novelties, with her unassuming imagination in the face of the unforeseen, inventing solutions which others would find hazardous or unbecoming, and which she knew how to impose with a disarming question: *"Am* I doing something wrong?"

Long after her death, another sister remembered the need and joy of being together with these words: "During the time when I was together with Mother Mazzarello, I never heard her speak of hell." From America a few innocently asked for her photo (this was probably toward the end of 1879) and she said that she wanted to please them as soon as she had a picture, but she didn't worry about it too much. "You want my picture, right? I'd be happy to send it to you but I don't have one yet. Ferrero finally said that he had never taken the picture, because no superior had given the order to do so. If he does, I'll send it with the first sisters who go to America."[1]

From America there came pleasing confirmation on the work undertaken by the Daughters in the ill-famed quarter of Buenos Aires. "The day before yesterday," wrote Fr. Costamagna to Don Bosco, "our sisters arrived at the new house of La Boca in good spirits. Up until now they have not encountered any opposition, because divine providence has permitted that the four or five Masonic sects which exist there are arguing among themselves...they're like lions without claws, and do not have the strength to attack us."[2]

However, problems arose at Rome because of the Daughters. The Congregation of Bishops and Regulars was absolutely not in accord with that which Don Bosco had said of the

Daughters of Mary Help of Christians, presenting them as being "associated" to the Salesian Society. The institute had consisted only of the community of Mornese at the time of Pope Pius IX. Now, instead, the cardinals of the Roman Congregation maintained that they could not approve the existence of a female institute which was dependent on one that was male, and they personally told Don Bosco: "You want to introduce a contrary maxim which this Congregation must reprove."

Don Bosco defended himself, noting that at the moment of the approval of the constitutions of the male Salesian society it was agreed that the examination of the case of the female institute would take place at another time. He also informed them that the sisters already had their own Superior General. For the moment, the problem remained undecided, but was aggravated by the Daughters' opening an oratory for girls in Chieri. The initiative, authorized and started in agreement, saw the birth of a bitter dissension between the pastor of the duomo of Chieri and the Salesian Giovanni Bonetti, spiritual director of the Daughters. It occasioned severe intervention on the part of Archbishop Gastaldi and polemics in the newspapers, along with anonymous libel.

A conflict already existed between the Salesians and the Curia, and now the battle became very difficult. It was embittered by misplaced zeal—unfortunate is a better word—of those who supported Don Bosco or the archbishop, with their offensive and defamatory publications against one or the other. These articles were sown throughout various anticlerical newspapers with the support of some ex-priests. Lorenzo Gastaldi sent an official report against Don Bosco to the Vatican which was also answered in the same way, until Leo XIII intervened conclusively, imposing a formal reconciliation. Meanwhile, the Founder of the Salesians lived under a terrible threat, even though it was never carried out: the prohibition of hearing confessions.

The news of the events little by little reached Mother, who kept everything inside herself. She did not want others to carry this cross; the Daughters were to be protected against every reason for discouragement because of these events. In the *Cronistoria* itself, at times so rich in particulars on less important facts, the drama is summarized in barely four lines, but four lines full of bitterness and apprehension: "The sisters don't know, but Mother is aware of a few serious thoughts which Don Bosco has because of certain requests from Rome about the relationships between the two Salesian families. The situation is still difficult; only divine intervention can help to overcome every obstacle."[3]

In the house of Nizza Monferrato, the immediate preoccupation was with cases of smallpox already present in the city, as elsewhere in Piedmont and which, naturally, were always very dangerous where large numbers of people live together. No deaths were registered. Ferdinand Maccono speaks of "two religious and three students" struck by the illness, but later cured. The *Cronistoria* refers to "some sisters and students afflicted only by chicken pox." There were no fatal cases, although it was said, according to the *Cronistoria,* "even among us there were deaths for the epidemic, and the victims were buried in our home."

Given the climate, we're not amazed at these rumors. During this time people hungered after stories of secrets and death. In Europe, the fame of *The Mysteries of Paris* of Eugene Sue continued and the magazines were sold in the countryside together with needles, thread and buttons. For a few years now, the successful sales of the books of Caroline Invernizio had marched forward; in 1877 she published *Rina, Angel of the Alps,* followed by other bloodthirsty tales: *Buried Alive, The Kiss of a Corpse, The Body in the Trunk, The Accusing Corpse....*

Now, with the leaders suffering physical exhaustion, the

decisive moment of the great battles had arrived. At sixty-five years of age Don Bosco was almost blind in his right eye, had to wear elastic stockings and suffered fevers accompanied by migraine headaches. Maria Mazzarello, just forty-three, had frequent pains in her head and hip, and suffered temporary loss of hearing. She had lost almost all her teeth and her body had worn thin.

Even under these conditions, each of the two continued their battle. In 1879 Don Bosco had completed a trip to France, succeeding in creating a network of new friends and supporters of the Salesian works, and he had decided to visit them every year. He did this also in 1880, accompanied by Fr. Cagliero. They went to Saint-Cyr where the arrival of the Daughters was imminent, and also to La Navarre where they were already working. Wherever he went, his presence was a public event.

At the beginning of 1880 Mother realized a dream: to place in the chapel of Our Lady of Grace, the sisters' church, the images of the *Via Crucis,* and to obtain from the bishop permission to observe there the "pious exercise," traveling in prayer the "stations" of Jesus' journey toward Calvary. It was necessary to have the written authorization of Bishop Sciandra of Acqui. She worked to obtain it, later treating it as a real victory.

In fact, it was. *The Way of the Cross* was one of her most vital, frequent meditations. The meaning of all of their sacrificed, impoverished life, of being at times derided or embattled, lay in mirroring the poverty and the complete sacrifice of Jesus for love of humanity. The victory lay in arriving at the height of identification, as far as possible, for human beings. Mother taught this "going back to Jesus" with an inventive gesture which she impressed forever on the character of her family: indicating the figure of Jesus on the cross which all the sisters wore, she would point to him and say, "He is here," then turning the cross over would continue, "and we are here...."

That was all, nothing more. It was a doctrine in a few syllables. They were two little gestures to express and motivate her incessant exhortation to cheerfulness as a permanent and operative condition: be cheerful and make all around you cheerful. "He is here; we are here." This was certainly a condition which did not exempt from suffering, even unjust suffering, because Jesus suffered and so must all who would follow him. It was a continual battle, and even a continual victory because they were imitating him who had conquered death.

Farewell to Mornese

Finally, after that first brief announcement, more news came from Patagonia. With the completion of the first missionary expedition of Salesians guided by Fr. Fagnano, a second expedition arrived at Rio Negro and started the mission of Carmen de Patagones. The newspaper *L'America del Sud* of Buenos Aires reported: "The missionaries were joined this time by the worthy sisters of Don Bosco, true heroines of charity working under the title of Daughters of Mary Help of Christians. With these outstanding collaborators, the mission cannot help but bear copious fruits of eternal salvation for the native tribes. This is the first time that the known world will see sisters in those remote southern lands, and these, with their sweet manners and with a proverbial charity will contribute much toward the conversion of the Indians."

At the end of January, the superior of the mission in Patagonia, Fr. Joseph Fagnano, reported: "We have begun a chapel where we teach catechism and preach, while the Daughters have opened a type of school for the girls, according to the possibilities of the place. The climate of this region of Patagonia," he added, "is healthful, the waters of the river good. The heat, however, is suffocating, and there are clouds of voracious mosquitos." The Daughters were Sr. Angela

Vallese, Sr. Giovanna Borgna, Sr. Angela Cassulo and Sr. Caterina Fino. The sisters were the first to have arrived in the place described by John Bosco after having seen it in a dream.

"Oh, how far you are from me, my poor daughters, but be brave, we are very close in our hearts.... You are always the first in my prayers."[4] These were Mother's words written to the four pioneers, in a letter addressed to the farthest place her words had ever traveled. "I hear that you are very content to be there, and that you already have a student and twelve girls who come to you and that on feastdays you are working well with the girls who come for catechism...." These are the words of a woman overcome with emotion, a happy Mary Mazzarello. She wrote as she spoke, moving from one to another, with an amiable blend of recommendations and playfulness: "Sr. Angela Cassulo, are you cheerful? Your sister is well and sends you her best wishes. She's very good. Pray for her and for me. Courage. And you, Sr. Giovanna, are you already a saint? Are you working miracles? Are you praying for me? Be cheerful, hear! Your sister (Giacinta) is beginning to be good and is well. Be brave and always humble; have confidence in your superior and help all. Sr. Caterina, are you cheerful, humble, obedient? Always confide in your superior and be cheerful. Never have any 'whims,' right, Sr. Caterina? Sr. Angelina, keep some grapes for me, because soon I will be coming to eat them...."

Other Italian localities wanted the Daughters. At Cascinette, in the diocese of Ivrea, there had been requests for a nursery school and oratory. At Catania, the Duchess of Carcaci called them to direct an already existing oratory, and also in the spring of 1880 the work of the Daughters began at Saint-Cyr.

Actually, activity and hunger both began, because there the situation was even worse. The food (whatever there was), was harvested from the fields, and for the rest, the sisters had to ask for alms, a situation which the Daughters had been spared until now. They also experienced new humiliations, as when a Salesian priest came to visit and they trembled with the fear that he would stay for lunch.

Sr. Alessandrina Hughes arrived from Saint-Cyr for the spiritual exercises of 1880, and during the time of recreation Mother invited her to tell the sisters about the hardships in the house. That splendid figure of a superior, Sr. Catherine Daghero, stood out among the sisters. When she had finished her account, some sisters had tears in their eyes, and Mother commented: "I wanted you to hear these things so that you would realize that virtue does not consist in being good when everything is going according to plan, but especially when we are suffering want or things are not going well; affection toward the superiors is not manifested by words, but in deeds, like those of Sr. Catherine who suffers and prays, suffers and keeps silent, suffers and smiles."[5]

Then a house was closed—and what a house—Mornese! On April 12, 1880, Mary Mazzarello herself went to take away the last residents there: five sisters, three of whom were ill. It was necessary to empty the house, to close and sell it. This was difficult but proved useful. From the sale (the buyer was the Marquis d'Oria) they would gain enough to pay for the whole Nizza Monferrato complex.

With a last glance at the playground which had been silent for so long, Mother left the "Collegio" for the last time, that very place which had cost them so much struggle. They left in a carriage, not for her comfort, but for Sr. Ortensia Negrini, who had been paralyzed for four years and who also suffered from asthma. She would live only a few weeks more. She was placed in the carriage in Mother Mazzarello's arms, and she remained there for the whole trip, like a child to be rocked. Yet the struggle was so great that she arrived at Nizza "unrecognizable," as the *Cronistoria* tells us.

A few sisters wanted to write something in memory of the house of Mornese, and one of the earliest sisters, Rosalia Pestarino, recalled the last day in this way: "Abandon- ed...squalid in its misery! Poor Mornese! Our poor hearts grieve at leaving a place so dear and adapted to us, for its solitude, saintly counsels and thoughts, disdain for the world and so ready for the ascent toward perfection!"

(But this detachment was not permanent. Mary Mazzarello and the early companions of her adventure did not know that this house, much, much later, would once more return to the Daughters of Mary Help of Christians; and it would be their house even at the end of the second Christian millennium.)

Among the things which did end, however, was not only Mornese with its memories. In the summer of 1880 Mary Mazzarello received the participants of the usual spiritual exer- cises with a different soul. Soon after the retreat, the general chapter was to meet for the renewal of the assignments, and she wanted to step down. Reasoned out according to her style, she told her two reasons to many of the sisters: one was her health, which was becoming worse and worse, even because of the loss of hearing in her left ear. They needed a more vigorous Mother General because the houses were growing in number, necessitating more frequent trips and visits. The second reason was that the number of sisters was growing, and along with them so was the cultural level, so the superior should have a suitable preparation. "Speaking to the gathering of retreatants, with tears in her eyes she recommended that they pray, pray...because as had been said over and over again, she no longer felt that she should be Superior General...."[7]

She also indicated those who could be her successor: Sr. Magdalen Martini, for example, who was in America, and if they did not want to have her return, there was Sr. Catherine Daghero.

"You need instructed superiors," she insisted. She added that in substance it would be better to change those at the head regularly now, at the time when the constitutions were to be renewed, rather than to have to do so perhaps in an emergency in a year or so.... We read in the *Cronistoria:* "Truly, Mother is fading before our very eyes and—extraordinarily—sometimes she even leaves the sister-retreatants during the recreation with Mother Emilia, Mother Enrichetta and Mother Daghero, who had come from Saint-Cyr. The unifying center was not lacking, and perhaps Mother thought that in this way the other superiors could be better known and appreciated by the sisters."[8]

This fact of the recreation tacitly confided to others was a strong indication, even more than a discourse would be. It was "relinquishing the command," a calling to others to guide.

Yet, she was reconfirmed in office. When the retreat ended, the second general chapter, reunited in the church of Our Lady of Grace, read the unanimous vote for Superior General. Sr. Catherine Daghero was elected vicar; Sr. Giovanna Ferrettino, treasurer; Sr. Emilia Mosca, first assistant; Sr. Enrichetta Sorbone, second assistant.

Emilia, Enrichetta, Catherine.... She had seen them arrive at Mornese in years long gone, one with her providential baggage of culture in a time of much simplicity, the other with the compassionate story of her sisters, and the third, with the sullenness of the first days, with trunks always ready to return home to Cumiana. She had helped them to form themselves in so many conversations and recreations, and above all by an infinity of examples. Now she had the joy of seeing that each of them could succeed her, since each of them knew how to be "Mother" for all.

As for Petronilla Mazzarello, with this election, she was no longer part of the council and no longer had any office. Yet she was there, smiling in the midst of the sisters, rejoicing for the re-election of Mother Mazzarello, and for herself, happy to finally be just one of many sisters. She would accept the obedience of going to Alassio, but not certainly as a recompense or a "right." It was merely another service which she would render to the institute, content as always to be able to help. Petronilla's beginning as an "ex" in the light of authentic humility was stupendous, but at the same time, she must have felt that she was somewhat alone. This election ended a confraternity which had sprouted in the early days of the workroom and in the Maccagno house, with Petronilla's character which gave Fr. Pestarino so much to do, with the domestic problems with her sisters-in-law, the hunger both of them shared, the tears shed together for the misunderstandings and detachments, with the joy of those first children to be cared for, of those first Sundays full of voices and song.

Send Me Good News

Therefore, they wanted to re-elect Mary Mazzarello as Mother. From Turin Don Bosco quickly confirmed the election, and she humbly accepted. Of course, she would use all her strength, but in the meantime, she felt it necessary to make essential preparations for a not too distant future. There was Sr. Catherine Daghero, of the new generation who was doing stupendous things. Not only was she much loved at Saint-Cyr, but was proficient in two languages. However, she now had to go back to Nizza because Mother Mazzarello did not want her far from the center, especially now that new houses were being opened and the trips were also multiplying. Therefore, Sr. Catherine was to come to Nizza, and Sr. Santina Piscioli would go to Saint-Cyr as superior. For a while, Sr. Catherine would stay to help her get settled.

But the other sisters were not happy with the change, and in the little, very poor French house a disagreeable, uncomfortable situation arose, which forced Mother to intervene quickly but amiably. "I need something from you," she wrote to those Daughters. "I want you to allow my vicar Sr. Catherine to come here. Now I hope that you have all gained confidence with your superior Sr. Santina. She's very good.... Why don't you want to confide in her?"[9]

Then she goes to the heart of the problem, lamenting the serious dangers of certain coldness in community. It is true that the affection which they bore for Sr. Catherine would make her leaving bitter, but the bitterness should not fall upon the one who was taking her place. This is a frequent problem in common life: at times some want to "punish" a successor for the virtues of the one who had preceded her, because of the displeasure of those who have seen her leave.

Mother spoke of the harm produced by certain states of soul: "We live badly and want the poor superior to live badly." Then she passes on to an exhortation: "There is the duty of humility which adds much to reciprocal love; there are vows which were solemnly pronounced and must be honored each day and hour. And there is for all the same perspective: 'Time passes, and we could find ourselves at the point of death with empty hands;' therefore, it is necessary to take courage, practicing virtue 'only for Jesus, and for no other reason'; which, in the end are all stories which we place in our heads." On this point, as on others during her teaching, we see a flash of irresistible simplicity in a few words which clarify everything: "A daughter who really loves Jesus gets along with everyone." That is the proof; it is there that we face ourselves. Then, all at once, the letter becomes very affectionate with a last clear, but good-natured request: "Send me good news quickly. Remember, I want you to be happy. Woe to you if you become idle dreamers," that is, if you abandon yourselves to brooding and moodiness.

The crisis of Saint-Cyr was not the only one she had to face. At times, amid the recounting of foundations, growth and missionary enthusiasm, we forget that this was all happening in a very young religious family, with only a few years of life (and Mary Mazzarello was doing all this in nine years of religious life.) In short, mistakes were made, not only at Saint-Cyr but also at Borgo San Martino, the first little house founded by the Daughters when they left Mornese. Sr. Felicina Mazzarello, sister of Mother General and greatly loved by all, was superior here. But in 1880 it was decided to send her to Sicily to open and direct a school for girls at Bronte.

First of all, the sisters of San Martino tried to keep Sr. Felicina until the end of the year. Then, on the day of her departure, they hung around for hours as though they were "dazed" even though they already had a new superior in the person of Sr. Margherita Rasino. "No one took care of the kitchen, and when dinner time came, the fire was not yet lit. And this with a whole school waiting!"[10] They responded with tears and laments to every invitation and disposition of Sr. Rasino, who finally, in tears, abandoned the house and took refuge at Nizza, while those who remained elected their own superior to lead them.

"Whining" news arrived at Nizza, but no response came. Mother Mazzarello kept quiet and awaited the right moment, leaving them alone to think about the whole story. When she finally appeared at Borgo San Martino, it was to install a new, real superior, Sr. Catherine Ricca whom she brought with her, and who had been nominated by the chapter. Then she left without further comment. She allowed another brief experimental period to pass and finally returned in official form. She presented Sr. Catherine in the proper manner and carried out the visit to the house as though nothing had happened. No one was reprimanded and no one dared to bring up the case. She had resolved all without dedicating even one word to the specific argument. Even the sister who was elected superior (seemingly by herself) during the time of disorientation, was elegant and redeeming: "Kid stuff, kid stuff! Rest easy, it won't happen again! That which was done is behind us."

Now we see Mary Mazzarello at work even with the superiors, especially with those who hold an important place. There was Sr. Pierina Marassi, for example, nominated in March 1880 as superior of the Daughters who worked in Turin, right under the eyes of Don Bosco—and of Bishop Gastaldi.

Mother knew her well, this sister from Alassio, and she had already spoken to her of her new task. Still, she sent her a letter with greetings for the sisters in Turin and a series of recommendations which were usually given in these situations: "It is up to you to give good example, to see to it that the Daughters observe the holy rule.... See to it that there are no jealousies. You must give good example to all so that none may say: 'She likes that one better...she talks to her, sympathizes with her more...etc.'"[11] With reference to the Salesian superiors, she recommended attention to their counsels and prompt collaboration, even at the cost of self love, and avoidance of comparisons of competence. As for the defects of the sisters, the formula was always the same, in two words: *be aware,* that is, don't ignore them or pretend they don't exist; *be compassionate,* because we all make mistakes.

But even here, amid maxims of solid, habitual good government we find a quick illumination: "Freely do all which charity requires of you." This is how you guide a person, an entire life—charity, a charity which does not admit deviations, limitations, obstacles. Whoever does whatever is required of her, need not fear anyone on the face of the earth.

There was another very delicate work: the postulants, those who came to become sisters and who needed to be observed, deciphering words and gestures, guessing thoughts, to ascertain authentic vocations. This had been her task from the very beginning, and now she limited herself to following the sisters who had the direct responsibility for it. She also trained Sr. Giuseppina Pacotto in this work, and she explained, for example, that the half hour of recreation at mid-morning was not merely an interval, an "exemption from the law." No, the half hour of chatting was an order, or in her own language: "It is a concession of the rule, to be respected like any other point." It had a very important function: "During this time we come to know a postulant better than at any other, because it seems that she is not under the vigilance of the assistant, and we must make use of this.... Don't trust those who are always around you, hanging on to your apron strings."[12]

Perhaps Mother Mazzarello did not know one of the episodes in Don Bosco's life. One day, while visiting a non-Salesian Institute in Rome, he was astonished and then scandalized because of the silence of the great number of boys. He warned the directors: "You'll never discover their characters this way." A boy who moves, sings, shouts, runs, fights, is an open book, revealing all of himself. In some way, he is confessing himself. There is no other way to distinguish the frank, open person from the hypocrite, the authentic from the false except by allowing them to express themselves.

She may not have known of the episode, but she did know how to put it into practice. It comes easily to us to add: "Thanks also to her broad experience." Rather, we should say that Mary Domenica Mazzarello's experience was all too brief. Not only did she have to constitute herself as a religious and as a mother, but she had to do so quickly, in the midst of poverty, illness, of a moving lack of preparation on a good part of her first sisters. "Mother General" was a beautiful title, but we have to see what it really meant and what problems came along with calling oneself by this title during certain winters at Mornese when illness and hunger struck, and the shopkeepers of Gavi or Ovada were waiting to be paid.

"I Will Not See the End of the Year"

In a letter of July 9, 1880, she wrote to the Daughters at Villa Colón and Las Piedras: "You want to know when I will come to visit you. I would like to leave immediately, but until I am sent, I can't go. Don Bosco and Fr. Cagliero have promised that they'll let me go, but I don't know when...."[13]

On that same day, she wrote to the girls of the Oratory at Las Piedras: "I really want to come to visit; pray, and if it is God's will, I'll come; otherwise we'll meet in paradise and that will be so much better."[14]

We read in a letter of December 20, 1880, to the Daughters of Carmen de Patagones: "How I long to see you! But we must both sacrifice this satisfaction because I don't think they'll ever give me such a permission."[15]

In these letters we see a dream come to birth and disappear. Certainly, Mary Mazzarello did not thirst for adventure in far off lands, but felt an infinite tenderness for those Daughters who had crossed the ocean. To see them she would have been ready to do the same.

But she could not. The "superiors," that is, Don Bosco and later even Fr. Cagliero, did not want her to take that journey which would have been fatal for her. They saw how she was struggling with her ordinary work because of her weak health. Then her hearing problems caused her continual embarrassment. It happened even when Don Bosco arrived at Nizza Monferrato in August 1880. While accompanying him on a visit of the institute, it happened that she could not understand his words: "Look, Father, besides all the rest I have told you as a reason why I should be removed as superior general, I have also become almost deaf." Don Bosco replied: "Better still; that way you will not hear useless words."

So she had to forget about America. She had so much to do in looking after the new house, and that commitment in

France which was giving so many problems. Then news from America arrived which must have hit her hard: it was about a Daughter whom she would never see again. Sr. Virginia Magone had died on September 25 in Carmen de Patagones. It was she who had written in May, inviting Mother to come to America: "I feel that I will die soon...and if you don't come quickly, I fear I will never see you again."

Neither sooner, nor later. At this point she was resigned to the fact that she would never see her Daughters in America on earth. She had to look more attentively for a few sisters to be considered for the new expedition which had been announced several times, others whom to bid farewell aboard ship, others whom she would never see again.

During Mary Mazzarello's last summer, Nizza Monferrato had the novelty of hosting an African girl (perhaps from Sudan), a vivacious, beautiful twenty-year-old. She was an ex-slave, freed along with many others by Bishop Daniel Comboni, the missionary in Sudan and magnificent fighter against the slave traders. He was a friend of the unbeliever Romolo Gessi and also his nurse; a friend of the Englishman General Gordon, the famous "Pasha Gordon," governor of Khartoum; he was also Don Bosco's friend. The latter was the first to know about his plan for the regeneration of Africa "by Africans." Comboni sent or accompanied to Italy a certain number of these young Africans so they could study, and he entrusted them to religious institutes. This girl spoke a little Italian and told fascinating and terrifying stories of the desert and the Nile, of crocodiles and slave traders. She was not a Christian, and Mother Mazzarello recommended to the postulants and students that they "treat her kindly according to charity." In December, the girl was baptized by Fr. Cagliero, taking the name Maria, and at Christmas time, she made her First Holy Communion, towering over the smallest student with a pleased air.

Christmas, 1880. The doctors told Mother that she had to rest more. But from eyewitnesses we hear that she was busy with her usual activities, which were not only those of her office. On the contrary, this superior general did not even have a true and proper office. She would never have one. For reading and writing it was enough for her to have a little corner of a desk; for sleeping it was the same; she needed only a wooden drawer wrapped in a cloth for a pillow. Her habit, while always orderly, could be distinguished only for its poverty, and an outsider could easily mistake her for someone assigned to the ordinary maintenance of the house. When she was not speaking with the Daughters or praying, this superior general was caring for the garden according to the seasons, lending a hand in the laundry, cleaning vegetables in the kitchen or "tidying the most humble places," as the *Cronistoria* tells us.

The end of 1880 came, and with it her traditional "conference" to all the professed sisters at Nizza. She was not yet forty-four years of age, but she could look at the past of the community as a faraway time. She compared the harshness of then to the relative comfort of today; more postulants, a few with a small dowry; more students, who, for the greater part, paid tuition. Now there was for all something which in the past no one could even imagine: "We have everything, in addition to bread and soup, our full meal and a little fruit besides; we have a beautiful house and a beautiful church; we are opening a good number of houses and almost always without a great preoccupation for the necessities of life."

All this was very beautiful. "But what is the use of all this if we were, because of it, to lose our good spirit and diminish our fervor?"

She certainly did not love rigor and suffering for itself, but feared that weakness would insinuate itself: "For goodness sake, sisters, for goodness sake!" She would join her hands, and cry, and look at them pleadingly: "Let us not allow ourselves to be won over by the danger of ease and well-being; let us continue to live united in charity, in fervor and in the true spirit of poverty which was our greatest glory during the time of Mornese...."

She looked toward the future, toward the end of her last year. "This house is large, yet we will continue to build here. We are already many, but more will come, many postulants and even young ladies, even the wealthier ones! The houses will multiply—and how! But let us remember that we have made a vow of poverty, that we must all consider ourselves poor and that each of us must go forward in the spirit of poverty if we want to become saints. If there are those who do not want to do so, worse for them and what a disgrace for the whole Congregation."[16]

In the brief evening talks to the sisters, the "good nights" of Salesian tradition, she loved to return insistently to these themes, linking them to a now proximate event: a new missionary expedition for America, which would also involve ten Daughters of Mary Help of Christians. Mother would make the selection in accord with Don Bosco and Fr. Cagliero. This time, however, a sister in whom she did not have any confidence was included in the list. She had asked that the sister be excluded, but was told that her fears were excessive and the sister was sent just the same. Within a year the sister reappeared in Europe after having abandoned the mission, the congregation and everything else.

Mother proposed to Sr. Josephine Pacotto that she leave for America. Seeing her hesitate, she spoke singular words: "You suffer in seeing that you must leave me.... But even if you were to stay, we would still have to be separated, because I will not finish out this year."

"Go Forward Bravely"

She moved about a little, and had to lie down a little. She frequently kept a heated brick under an armpit to ease the pain in her side due to a pleurisy attack. But she still succeeded in making regular visits to the Daughters of Quargnento and of Lu. During one January evening, at the time of the good night, she returned once more to the past; she spoke of the need of being orderly in everything, even of putting things in their proper places in the house, of internal harmony being evident even in the exterior, and she recalled a moment of happy cooperation among diverse communities. "Let us do as we were taught from the beginning by the good Sisters of St. Ann. Every time we have to go out of our way to put a chair or bench in its place, to pick up a piece of paper from the ground, or the corn leaves which fall from our mattress...let us also say a little prayer, or make an act of love to God or recite a *Requiem*...."

For this expedition, all those leaving for the missions, Salesians and sisters, were together at the basilica of Mary Help of Christians for a crowded departure ceremony. The group was to later take the train bound for Genoa.

During the night spent at Turin, Mother Mazzarello awakened Sr. Josephine Pacotto with an anguished exclama- tion: "Sr. Luigina Arecco has died!" Sr. Luigina was very ill, but was still at Nizza, and Sr. Josephine looked at Mother in amazement. After having uttered those words, Mother Mazzarello became very quiet. When morning came, news arrived from Nizza. Sr. Luigina, that orphan child with a splen- did voice who had been taken in by Mother Mazzarello from the fields of Monferrato, had actually died during the night. She died serenely, after having intoned with what little voice was left to her the *Recordare Jesu Pie* written by Fr. Cagliero.

Mother quickly left for Nizza with Fr. Cagliero for the last farewell to Sr. Luigina. Then she went to Alessandria, where she joined the missionaries aboard the train for Genoa.

As usual, they spent the night at Sampierdarena, and then there were different departures. Mother accompanied four sisters aboard ship: Sr. Ottavia Bussolino, Sr. Anna Brunetti, Sr. Luigina Vallese and Sr. Ernesta Farina.

The ship left during the afternoon of February 2, 1881. A few hours later the *Umberto* weighed anchor, with another seventeen missionaries on board. There were six Daughters: Sr. Giuseppina Pacotto, Sr. Angela Gualfredo, Sr. Caterina Lucca, Sr. Lorenzina Natale, Sr. Giuliana Prevosto and Sr. Teresa Rinaldi. This time Mother did not leave the ship before its departure. She stayed aboard until the port of Marseille. It was her first sea voyage.

It was a very painful trip. She suffered acute seasickness because she already had another illness. At Marseille they had to wait three days for repairs, and meanwhile Don Bosco arrived for the last farewell. It was the first time that Mother cried at the moment of detachment.

She cried for the Daughters who were leaving, who disappeared from her sight. But she was sustained by a reason for serenity. Sr. Magdalen Martini was in America. She was a magnificent provincial, but had very poor health and very few years of life left. Mother knew this, and yet she knew also that the continuity of the mission was assured. On that ship traveling toward Buenos Aires there was also news for Fr. Camisassa: one of the ships crossing the Atlantic carried the person who would one day succeed Sr. Magdalen. She was young and had to be prepared, but she was already on her way. Her name was Sr. Ottavia Bussolino. For all of the sisters, novices and postulants, both present and future, already working in Nizza Monferrato, there was the young, vigorous vicar, the direct successor of Mother Mazzarello, Sr. Catherine Daghero.

Therefore, the essentials were already taken care of. After days of suffering at Marseille, Mother went to her Daughters at La Navarre and later continued toward Saint-Cyr. She would again encounter Don Bosco at Nice by the Sea and would inform him of her illness, but she would not speak of getting better, as she had done at other times. The visit to the sisters of Saint-Cyr was immediately transformed into a stay in bed. It was no longer seasickness, but pleurisy, treated with painful plasters.

Mother patiently followed the directives of the doctors, but she had already understood. The only thing she wanted was to return to Nizza Monferrato. She was helped by a slight improvement, which made those around her think she might recover. She left on March 19th, and on the 28, she was at the institute after a brief stop among her Daughters at Alassio.

She was at home. Even though she was very weak, she was up. They saw her move about with the usual heated brick at her side. She spoke of Don Bosco who was at Rome, of Fr. Cagliero who was traveling through Spain. Shortly afterward, however, she had a relapse. She would never again leave her bed. While in bed, she celebrated her forty-fourth birthday, and had an unexpected and visible betterment. She could move a little and hold a glass, and her face had regained some color.

Fr. Cagliero arrived from Spain. He was at Nizza on May 10 and they had a long conversation. On the point of leaving this life, Mary Domenica still gave an example of the rigorous incarnation of her duty of teacher and co-foundress. There was no special solemnity in the dialogue between that of the peasant of Mornese and the one of Castelnuovo d'Asti, and there was no emphasis of final balances. With a voice that was weakening, but with all her realism, she referred to the state of the congregation. As Fr. Cagliero would state in the canonical process: "She informed me of a few inconveniences, which, according to her special light and her great experience, compromised the religious spirit...and she spoke of several uncertain vocations, so that after her death I would be in a situation to remove these obstacles."

On another occasion Cardinal Cagliero confided to

Ferdinand Maccono: "I confess that if I would have listened, I would have been able to prevent, avert and impede several inconveniences of those early days with reference to the danger of certain vocations in the young institute. That which we did not do then, we did later, with an immense advantage to religious perfection."[17]

Now she was ready. She had done everything possible for the Daughters of Mary Help of Christians. She left 165 sisters, sixty-five novices and twenty-eight houses: nineteen in Italy, three in France and six in America. But by her example, she left the future.

Now she could await death and had the grace to accept it with all lucidity, in her own style. When dawn broke on May 14, 1881, Fr. Cagliero raised his hand, blessing her in Don Bosco's name. She understood and had them fix her pillows. "Prepare me." In all poverty and perfect order, invoking Jesus and Mary, Mother Mazzarello left this earth at 3:45 on a Saturday in May.

The May sun rose early over the Valponasca. Once it was daylight, the peasants spread out over the vineyards for the spring work. The parish church was illumined as usual for the first Mass, and you could see that light from the window of the farmhouse. The footsteps of the early morning faithful recalled those of Mary Mazzarello with Felicina, her cousin Domenica and Petronilla.

It was sunset on the other side of the Atlantic. Sr. Josephine Pacotto was thinking about the last counsels from Mother, on board the *Umberto:* "Be brave, Sr. Josephine. The moment will come in which the cross will seem very heavy, but that will be the time to hold it close to your heart and promise fidelity to the good God."[18]

Sr. Ernesta Farina read over a little slip of paper of "remembrances" which Mother had given to her shortly before she sailed: "Do not get discouraged when you see yourself full of defects, but go to Jesus and Mary confidently and humble yourself without becoming discouraged, then go forward bravely."[19]

Little by little, the news that Mother Mazzarello had died reached all the houses of the Daughters, in Italy and elsewhere. Funeral rites were celebrated and the veterans spoke of her to the young people, just as it always happens. But later, in obedience to the Salesian pedagogy, even during days of grieving memories, the usual time of recreation came; the noise, games and laughter. Joy arrived. It was the spirit of Mary Mazzarello, which rendered her ever present in the midst of youth.

In Today's World

At the death of Saint Mary Domenica Mazzarello the Institute of the Daughters of Mary Help of Christians had only nine years of history; it had already spread to four nations (Italy, France, Uruguay, Argentina), with twenty-eight houses and about 200 members between professed religious and novices.

Today, at little more than one hundred years from the time of her death, the Institute has grown on all continents. The professed sisters number about 17,000 and there are almost 1600 communities. More than eighty nations count on their presence.

Mary Domenica's intuition has been clarified in time and the choices have been defined in a multiplicity of cultural contexts which have been enriched.

The educational commitment, first of all, a fundamental inheritance of Don Bosco, is the heart of the Salesian feminine mission. Every Daughter of Mary Help of Christians knows how to play out her life for God and for young people, seeking to prepare herself in ways ever more adapted to the contemporary world.

For the pedagogical formation of its members, the Institute can count upon the Pontifical Faculty of Science and

Education, the "Auxilium" where, in a particular way the problems of the condition of women are studied under their diverse perspectives. It is the only Pontifical Faculty completely entrusted to women, who commit themselves to an intelligent and intuitive educative research.

The Oratory, an idea which Mary Domenica had even before she met Don Bosco, today has varied manifestations throughout the world . The experience of the origins has been reinterpreted within the socio-cultural contexts and ever changing needs of young people. Human advancement is the first objective in the oratorian activity in the poorest nations, while in industrial contexts the great demand of young people is for free time activities and guidance.

Association with young people, with their questions about life's deepest questions, continues to be the great challenge to education.

With schools, of every kind and class, even today the sisters respond to the need for a systematic education and a critical formation. In many nations, this permits young people, especially of the working classes, to acquire the means of reaching a higher level of culture.

At times, experimenting with new ways within traditional scholastic systems and at times "inventing" structures, the sisters seek, with the support of other professionals and qualified parents, to offer young people the possibility of developing awareness and promoting a more human culture.

Technical schools, different in Italy from those in Africa or Latin America, express Salesian attention to the world of work and to the need which young people have to acquire technical skills for various professions.

Growing unemployment and the need to bring back those boys and girls whom the scholastic system has excluded has encouraged job skills training, to help young people prepare to be artisans, or to work in small industry or service industries.

After the great changes of the 1980's, the fall of ideologies and the opposing blocks, as well as social evolution prompted by the means of social communications in the 1990's the institute has renewed a few options, which, with the passing of years, seem hopeful.

The education of young women is a priority which is carried out in different countries with ever greater means: from the promotion of feminine cooperatives in the missions to the salvaging of the girls on the outskirts of the great cities, who easily fall victim to prostitution; to insertion into the world of work; to the cultural and "support" initiatives so that young people can fight for their own dignity and a development of a feminine culture with a greater awareness.

The inculturation of the charism is another horizon opened during these last few years. In every country of the world in which the Daughters of Mary Help of Christians are present, vocations have sprouted which have rewritten the ideas of the holy founders within the culture. This is being done with attention to the ethnic minorities, to the pastoral needs of native peoples, to the expressions of people who, in various forms and in many ways, respond to the one call of the Lord Jesus.

Within these areas, which allow us to join attention to young people and their education with the evolution of culture and the concrete places in which we build the system of values in society, the Daughters of Mary Help of Christians are still seeking, in an ever deeper way, how to make their Mother live on, in that fidelity and prophecy, which constantly renews them.

The central headquarters of the Institute is:

Daughters of Mary Help of Christians
Via dell'Ateneo Salesiano, 81
00139 Rome Italy
Telephone 87-13-23-10

Notes

Chapter One

1. A. Monti, *La giovinezza di Vittorio Emanuele II* (Mondadori, 1939), p. 80.

2. A. C. Jemolo, *Chiesa e Stato in Italia negli ultimi cento anni* (Einaudi, 1955), p. 90.

3. *Cronistoria* I, p. 32.

4. Maria Esther Posada, ed., *Attuale perchè vera. Contributi su S. Maria Domenica Mazzarello* (Rome: Ed. LAS, 1987), p. 224.

5. *Cronistoria* I, p. 41.

6. F. Maccono, *Santa Maria D. Mazzarello,* vol. I (Turin: Istituto F.M.A., 1960, reprint), p. 53.

7. *Cronistoria* I, p. 65.

8. M. Bendiscioli and A. Gallia, *Documenti di storia contemporanea* (Mursia, 1970), p. 195.

Chapter Two

1. Maria Esther Posada, ed., *Lettere di S. Maria Domenica Mazzarello* (Istituto F.M.A., 1980), p. 103.

2. *Cronistoria* I, p. 53.

3. *Lettere*, 16, 1.

4. *Cronistoria* I, p. 102.

5. *Ibid.,* p. 129.

Chapter Three

1. *Lettere,* 3, 2

2. *Cronistoria* I, p. 162.

3. *Ibid.,* p. 204.

4. *Ibid.,* p. 230.

Chapter Four

1. Jemolo, *Chiesa e Stato,* p. 367.

2. *Cronistoria* II, p. 21.

Chapter Five

1. *Cronistoria* II, p. 76.

2. *Ibid.,* p. 87.

3. P. Stella, *Don Bosco nella storia della religiosità cattolica I: Vita e opere,* Studi storici 3 (Rome: LAS, 1979), p. 204.

4. *Cronistoria* II, p. 89.

5. *The Imitation of Christ,* Book I, Chapter XVI, 2.

6. *Cronistoria* II, p. 118.

7. *Ibid.,* p. 399.

8. P. Cavaglià, *Educazione e cultura per la donna. La Scuola "Nostra Signora delle Grazie" di Nizza Monferrato dalle origini alla riforma Gentile* (1878-1923), (Rome: Il Prisma 10, 1990), p. 98.

9. Cavaglià, *Educazione e cultura,* p. 99.

10. G. Alimonda, *I problemi del XIX secolo,* vol. III (Genoa: 1883), pp. 371-372.

11. Maccono, *Santa Maria D. Mazzarello,* vol. 1, p. 282.

12. *Lettere,* 3, 2.

13. *Ibid.,* 4.

14. *Ibid.,* 7.

15. *Ibid.,* 12.

16. *Ibid.,* 6, 4.

Chapter Six

1. Maccono, *Santa Maria D. Mazzarello,* vol. I, p. 343.

2. *Cronistoria* II, p 189.

3. *Lettere,* 5, 7.

4. *Ibid.,* 11.

5. *Cronistoria* II, p. 429.

6. *Ibid.,* p. 186.

7. F. Chabod, *Storia della politica estera italiana dal 1870 al 1896,* vol. I (Laterza: 1965), p. 413.

8. *Lettere,* 7, 4.

9. *Cronistoria* II, p. 253.

10. *Maccono, Santa Maria D. Mazzarello,* vol. I, p. 388.

11. *Ibid.,* p. 418.

12. F. Chabod, *Storia della politica,* vol. I, p. 398.

13. Maccono, *Santa Maria D. Mazzarello,* vol. II, p. 29.

14. G. Spadolini, *L'opposizione cattolica da Porta Pia al '98* (Le Monnier: 1972), pp. 175-176.

15. *Cronistoria* II, p. 271.

16. P. Scotti, ed., *Missioni salesiane 1875-1975* (LAS, 1977), p. 79.

17. *Cronistoria* II, pp. 282-283.

18. Maccono, *Santa Maria D. Mazzarello,* vol. II, p. 15.

19. G. Cassano, *Il Cardinale Giovanni Cagliero,* vol. I (SEI, 1935), p. 274.

20. *Lettere,* 9, 2.

21. *Ibid.*

Chapter Seven

1. Maccono, *Santa Maria D. Mazzarello,* vol. II, p. 16.

2. *Ibid.,* p. 24.

3. *Lettere,* 14, 4.

4. *Ibid.,* 15, 4.

5. *Cronistoria* II, p. 323.

6. Maccono, *Santa Maria D. Mazzarello,* vol. II, p. 121.

7. *Cronistoria* II, p. 317.

8. Cavaglia, *Educazione e cultura,* p. 131.

9. *Cronistoria* II, p. 367.

10. *Ibid.*

11. *Cronistoria* II, p. 371.

12. *Cronistoria* III, p. 35.

13. *Lettere,* 19.

14. Maccono, *Santa Maria D. Mazzarello,* vol. II, p. 87.

15. *Cronistoria* III, pp. 110ff.

16. *Lettere,* 22, 1.

17. *Ibid.,* p. 111

Chapter Eight

1. *Lettere,* 26, 4.

2. *Cronistoria* III, p. 129.

3. *Ibid.,* p. 140.

4. *Lettere,* 37, 1.

5. *Cronistoria* III, p. 219.

6. *Ibid.,* p. 169.

7. *Ibid.,* p. 234.

8. *Ibid.,* pp. 235-236.

9. *Lettere,* 49, 1.

10. *Cronistoria* III, p. 271.

11. *Lettere,* 35, 2.

12. *Cronistoria* III, p. 250.

13. *Lettere,* 40, 5.

14. *Ibid.,* 44, 4.

15. *Ibid.,* 55, 1.

16. *Cronistoria* III, p. 300.

17. Maccono, *Santa Maria D. Mazzarello,* p. 359.

18. *Cronistoria* III, p. 361.

19. *Ibid.,* p. 325.

 BOOKS & MEDIA

ALASKA
750 West 5th Ave., Anchorage, AK 99501; 907-272-8183

CALIFORNIA
3908 Sepulveda Blvd., Culver City, CA 90230; 310-397-8676
5945 Balboa Ave., San Diego, CA 92111; 619-565-9181
46 Geary Street, San Francisco, CA 94108; 415-781-5180

FLORIDA
145 S.W. 107th Ave., Miami, FL 33174; 305-559-6715

HAWAII
1143 Bishop Street, Honolulu, HI 96813; 808-521-2731

ILLINOIS
172 North Michigan Ave., Chicago, IL 60601; 312-346-4228

LOUISIANA
4403 Veterans Memorial Blvd., Metairie, LA 70006; 504-887-7631

MASSACHUSETTS
50 St. Paul's Ave., Jamaica Plain, Boston, MA 02130; 617-522-8911
Rte. 1, 885 Providence Hwy., Dedham, MA 02026; 617-326-5385

MISSOURI
9804 Watson Rd., St. Louis, MO 63126; 314-965-3512

NEW JERSEY
561 U.S. Route 1, Wick Plaza, Edison, NJ 08817; 908-572-1200

NEW YORK
150 East 52nd Street, New York, NY 10022; 212-754-1110
78 Fort Place, Staten Island, NY 10301; 718-447-5071

OHIO
2105 Ontario Street, Cleveland, OH 44115; 216-621-9427

PENNSYLVANIA
Northeast Shopping Center, 9171-A Roosevelt Blvd., Philadelphia, PA
19114; 215-676-9494

SOUTH CAROLINA
243 King Street, Charleston, SC 29401; 803-577-0175

TENNESSEE
4811 Poplar Ave., Memphis, TN 38117; 901-761-2987

TEXAS
114 Main Plaza, San Antonio, TX 78205; 210-224-8101

VIRGINIA
1025 King Street, Alexandria, VA 22314; 703-549-3806

CANADA
3022 Dufferin Street, Toronto, Ontario, Canada M6B 3T5; 416-781-9131

PENGUIN BOOKS

Miles to go

Pauline O'Regan is already well known to thousands
of readers through her earlier books, among them
A Changing Order, *Community*, *Aunts and Windmills*,
and *There is Hope for a Tree*. Pauline is a Mercy nun
and was the principal of Villa Maria College, Christchurch, for seventeen years. She now works as a
community worker in Christchurch. Her awards
include the Winston Churchill Fellowship (1978),
the CBE (1990) and the DCNZM in 2000.

The woods are lovely, dark and deep
But I have promises to keep
And miles to go before I sleep
And miles to go before I sleep.

Miles to go

A BOOK TO MAKE YOU LAUGH OUT LOUD

Pauline O'Regan

PENGUIN BOOKS

PENGUIN BOOKS

Published by the Penguin Group

Penguin Group (NZ), 67 Apollo Drive, Rosedale

North Shore 0632, New Zealand (a division of Pearson New Zealand Ltd)

Penguin Group (USA) Inc., 375 Hudson Street,

New York, New York 10014, USA

Penguin Group (Canada), 90 Eglinton Avenue East, Suite 700, Toronto,

Ontario, M4P 2Y3, Canada (a division of Pearson Penguin Canada Inc.)

Penguin Books Ltd, 80 Strand, London, WC2R 0RL, England

Penguin Ireland, 25 St Stephen's Green,

Dublin 2, Ireland (a division of Penguin Books Ltd)

Penguin Group (Australia), 250 Camberwell Road, Camberwell,

Victoria 3124, Australia (a division of Pearson Australia Group Pty Ltd)

Penguin Books India Pvt Ltd, 11, Community Centre,

Panchsheel Park, New Delhi – 110 017, India

Penguin Books (South Africa) (Pty) Ltd, 24 Sturdee Avenue,

Rosebank, Johannesburg 2196, South Africa

Penguin Books Ltd, Registered Offices: 80 Strand, London, WC2R 0RL, England

First published by Penguin Group (NZ), 2004
This edition published in 2007
1 3 5 7 9 10 8 6 4 2

Editorial services by Michael Gifkins and Associates
Designed by Mary Egan
Typeset by Egan Reid Ltd
Printed in Australia by McPherson's Printing Group

ISBN 978 0 14 300782 1

A catalogue record for this book is available
from the National Library of New Zealand.

www.penguin.co.nz

To the memory of our dearly loved community member,
Monica Stack rsm
(who made old age look easy)

Introduction

THIS BOOK HAS BEEN IN THE WRITING FOR OVER a year. I began when I was eighty, I've had my eighty-first birthday and now I'm rolling along merrily towards eighty-two. When I started this book on old age, I could only hope I'd survive to see it completed. I've managed to do that, but I've lived old age even as I was writing about it. It's been a struggle and there were times I thought I wouldn't make it, but

I've enjoyed it and I'm grateful for a lot of things. The most important one is that my sight has deteriorated only gradually and I can still read a size forty font on the screen. To help bring this about, I've eaten a carrot a day for the duration. Don't laugh! It's been a serious commitment. I've had a lifelong aversion to carrots, but an eye doctor told me he'd read in a prestigious medical journal that the only thing that could be done for macular degeneration was to strengthen those cells that still remained alive behind the eyes. It was suggested that a carrot a day would help do that. So I've done it. More than that, I firmly believe it's made a difference. All the same, each day when I sat down at the computer I felt I was at risk. My sight could have deserted me at any moment and left both of us, the book and me, up the creek without a paddle. That didn't happen, but the fact that it so easily could have happened gave an edge to the whole exercise.

While I was writing this book, a friend very kindly gave me a delightful piece she had written about her experience of the joys of old age. It seemed that much of the joy of old age for her derived from having grandchildren and it brought home to me that this would be the experience of the majority of old people. Given that I'm a nun it's appropriate that I do not lay claim to grandchildren so I have to acknowledge that this important aspect of the experience of old age is missing from this book. However, there are so many other positive things about being old, that having grandchildren must merely serve to provide an exquisite icing for what is already a very rich cake.

In the course of writing this book I changed computer programmes from Works to Word. It was a good move, but no one warned me that I was about to be bossed about in a way I hadn't experienced since my schooldays. In the end I didn't know who exactly was writing this book, Word or me. Sure, it corrected my spelling and picked up my typing errors and I'm grateful for that, but I could have gladly dispensed with what I considered its misplaced criticism of my grammar, its pedantic correcting of my punctuation, its fussy sniffs of displeasure at what it deemed an overlong sentence and its endless tut-tutting about my spacing. At times it felt close to a take-over. We carried on a love-hate relationship, Word and I, but with countless games of Free Cell to break the tension, together we got there.

I hope this book does not appear in any way to minimise the inconveniences of old age. That has certainly not been my intention. What has been my intention is to testify that there is nothing to fear from this stage of life. The reality from my experience so far, is that old age has so many enjoyable and positive qualities that it's well worth all the effort we've made over the years to maintain good health in order to get there.

1

I TURNED THIRTY LAST WEEK. WHAT AM I SAYING? Something odd happened there. The third finger of my left hand hit the three before the third finger of my right could hit the eight. My touch-typing must be going down-hill as well. Or was it, more likely, my subconscious making one of its more subtle interventions? Either way, I'm eighty. I've always been fairly philosophical about the passing of the years, but it still comes as something of a shock to reach a milestone in your life and see eighty written on it. I go back to the record for verification and sure enough, there it is: 1922 to 2002. I'd better look sharp. They put that kind of thing in Death Notices.

Speaking of Death – here's Someone who quietly asks to join the company at this stage of your life. You find yourself thinking of Death in a way you never did before. In fact, you scarcely thought She knew you existed. But not now. The thought of Death takes up a position at the back of your mind and exerts a new and subtle influence on your consciousness. It's not a cloud, not even a shadow, just another dimension that was not there before. I'll give an example: before I reached this age, I used to read the Death Notices in the paper each day with a kind of detached interest. There just might be someone there that I know, someone whose name I might read with a mixture of regret and sympathy, someone whom Oscar Wilde might have suggested had been careless enough to die. That's not how I read them now. For one thing, they've become a sort of Lotto game. I scan the numbers. I note how many people checked out in their seventies, how many in their eighties and with a momentary flash of optimism, how many in their nineties. If eighty-three seems the most popular exit number (and it's amazing how often it does) that gives me three more years. There's nothing morbid about all this and certainly nothing melancholy, but I suspect it could become an unsettling exercise if I ever begin to believe that I'm actually going to die.

Billy Collins, the poet who more than anyone else these days seems to speak my thoughts – and no doubt, the multi-layered thoughts of all his readers – has this matter of Death summed up

for me in his poem, 'My Number'. Billy Collins, just like the
rest of us, is going to try to talk Death out of it when the time
comes.

> *Or is he stepping from a black car*
> *parked at the dark end of the lane,*
> *shaking open the familiar cloak,*
> *its hood raised like the head of a crow,*
> *and removing the scythe from the trunk?*

> *Did you have any trouble with the directions?*
> *I will ask, as I start talking my way out of this.*

All of this brings me to another aspect of being eighty. It has so
many good features that I'm loath to single one out, but this one's
important: if I hadn't lived to be eighty, if I'd bowed out at
seventy, for instance, I would have missed out on the im-
measurable pleasure of Billy Collins' poetry – and much else as
well.

Old age is not the most romantic subject to write about, that's
for sure. Still, I'm finding the experience sufficiently interesting
to want to do so. It's an intriguing phase of the human journey.
There are so many things about it that are unexpected, so many
parts to the equation that I had no idea were there, so many
unknowns that no one told me about. Was it that I wasn't
listening? Or was it just never considered worth the telling if no
one wanted to hear? Whatever the reason, there are many things
that come as a surprise. For one thing, I had no idea of the sense
of urgency that old age brings, the sense of hidden danger that

comes with living near the edge. After all, it might be tomorrow, or the day after. You feel you can no longer afford the self-indulgent detours you took earlier on the track. You simply haven't got the time. It takes time to indulge boredom, for instance, or apathy, or indifference, or bitterness. When we squandered time so freely on these things in youth and middle age, we did so with the unconscious certainty that we'd come out of them in time. Boredom could be dissipated by some anticipated excitement, apathy could be shaken off if the interest were sufficiently aroused, indifference could be redeemed by a surge of feeling, bitterness could be healed by reconciliation. It had happened before. There was plenty of time.

They were all games we played one way or another, putting human relationships at risk along the way. We gave them space in our lives because we had space to burn – and time unlimited. That's the nub of it. Where time was concerned, we were utterly wasteful – *flahoolach* as the Irish would say. But with old age time is suddenly at a premium. It's not there to be wasted. There simply isn't enough of it. It's a pity we have to wait to become old to put a value on time. Yet in some strange way it can't be properly valued before then. All things being equal, old age makes time a very precious commodity. You can't really complain about a condition that does that for you.

It's claimed that you know you have reached middle-age when you bend down to tie up your shoes and look round to see what else you can do while you're down there. The difference with old age is that either you can't bend down to tie up your shoes at all or, if you can, you need all your concentration to work out how best to straighten up afterwards. At forty, you might be temporarily chastened that the digital timer on your biological clock has rolled over from three to four, but you are not about to give serious thought to your mortality. Not by a long shot. When you are forty you take spring for granted. It does not occur to you that this might be the last time you see those delicate, pink blossoms bursting out of the wood of the apricot tree in the back yard. When you visit another city, you don't find yourself looking back at it as if for the last time.

On election day, the thought never enters your mind that this might be the last time you'll vote. You don't say farewells overladen with anxious cheerfulness to friends leaving for overseas. You don't think of updating your will. You don't know that suppository has very little to do with supposing. When you buy a good suit you don't have the passing thought they might use it for laying you out. You don't start a surreptitious clearing out of the stuff you thought might be useful one day. You don't know the meaning of reflux. You don't do catastrophe checks of your past life. You don't leave an electric blanket on your bed all year round. You don't read obituaries. You don't know that to be incontinent is not always a sign of loose morals. You don't get unaccountably pensive on your birthdays.

2

T TAKES A LOT OF STAMINA TO BE OLD, BELIEVE me. There are just so many things that have to be done if you want to remain operative and each of them takes time. In an earlier age, the old just lived with the dimming of their senses and the frailty of their bodies and got on with it. Shakespeare wrote with philosophical acceptance of the seven ages of man. He avoided women. They have more rites of passage to get through, too delicate it seems, even for the earthy Bard. He kept to the basics for males: the infant, *mewling and puking,* the *whining* schoolboy, the lover *with woeful ballad made to his mistress' eyebrow,* the soldier *seeking the bubble reputation even in the cannon's mouth,* the justice *in fair, round belly . . . full of wise saws and modern instances* until in the sixth stage we find *his big, manly voice turning again towards childish treble* and finally, *last scene of all that ends this strange, eventful history is second childishness and mere oblivion, sans teeth, sans eyes, sans taste, sans everything.*

It's a fair enough account but, given modern medicine, it has to be modified for men and women in the twenty-first century. Thanks to the advances in science, the seven stages are more blurred, less precise. In my case and those of most octogenarians I know, the characteristics of the last stages tend to overlap. There's the fair, round belly all right and the tendency to pontificate, but there are also signs of the alarming attributes of the final stages – the body less agile, the mind less sharp, the senses less fine-tuned. And if we take time to reflect on all this, there's always the poignant reality, the unnerving knowledge that we are in a downward spiral from which there is no escape. It's fortunate for us that those who do such reflections are still in their prime, just as Shakespeare was when he wrote *As You Like It.* By the time we are old ourselves, we are much too busy staying alive to give time to formulating a philosophy of old age.

If in the time of the Tudors, old age brought the gradual loss of all the senses and you ended up *sans everything,* in this age, we have such amazing ways of enhancing our failing senses that the Tudors would be gobsmacked to say the least. They don't come cheap, these marvellous additives, everyone knows that. What is not so widely known is that by far the highest price we pay for them is Time. Take the hearing aid, for example. Here we have one of the most brilliant inventions of the modern age, packaged in the tiniest shell that fits snugly into the ear. The second you put it in, all those half-sounds you hear during the day, all those conversations you strain to catch, every punch-line you miss on TV, suddenly become amplified. You can hear again! A precious sense is restored. How could anyone utter a complaining word? Certainly not I. So, treat this merely as an observation. Night and morning, the dressing ritual has now to be extended to include this tiny object. At night, you take it out carefully, clean it, open it up to save the batteries, store it safely away. In the morning you once again insert it carefully in the ear. Little enough, you might say. But wait.

The hearing aid is a tiny, flesh-coloured, shiny ball, not easy to handle. (Have you tried changing a hearing aid battery lately?) You drop it. At this point it takes on a life of its own. It is endowed with the uncanny ability to merge into the colour of every conceivable floor covering. Your sight is failing. Your joints are creaking. You lower yourself to the floor and begin wide, sweeping movements with the hand. To no avail. Other people join in the hunt. Either one of two things then happens. It is found like the groat in the Gospel amid much joy and relief or, just as you take your first steps away from the scene, you hear a terrible crunching sound. It is found all right, but in several pieces. You lower yourself once more to the floor to retrieve them. When you are eventually upright again, you go to find your magnifying glass to look for the number of your insurance company in the telephone directory and another time-consuming exercise is about to begin.

With the insurance company finally satisfied, you turn to the audiologist. A strange phenomenon now presents itself. Careful fittings notwithstanding, the new case never turns out quite like the original. Either that, or there is some as yet undiscovered circumstance whereby stress can change the shape of the ear. The new one simply does not fit. You keep several appointments until a kind of compromise has been achieved. Yes, you promise, you will come back if you're still not satisfied. There is an unspoken suggestion of neurosis here. You don't go back. If you evaluate this whole process in terms of the time it has taken, you come close to measuring it in days. It gives me pause to think that I have a hearing aid in each ear. That means that this entire procedure is capable of being multiplied by two. Just consider that all this frustrating, time-consuming drama can be applied with equal ease to your glasses (the ones for reading and the ones for seeing where you're going and your old spare pair), your contact lens, your magnifying glass, your false teeth, your support stockings, your orthotics, your enlarging mirror and your tweezers. Some or all of these, like the hearing aid, are a necessary component of old age. All have to be maintained. All are capable of being lost. Most of them can be broken. Along the way, you become very familiar with the waiting rooms of all those professionals dedicated to keeping you alive as long and productively as possible. God bless them! How else could I be sitting here at a computer writing this?

3

VER THE YEARS, I HAVE OBSERVED IN OTHERS AND now, increasingly, in myself, that there is always one particular part of the body that sends out an advance warning of the general breakdown that is to come. The evidence for this is all around us and you can acquire it without really trying. You have only to ask people how they are. You might well be using this question as a polite conversation-opener, a social curtain-raiser to what you really want to talk about. That's not necessarily how others interpret it. There is always a significant number of people who believe that you intended this courtesy to be taken literally. Most often, they respond by taking you on a journey around the crumbling castle. Just when you think you have the entire picture, they inevitably take you into one particular room. This is the place where the harbinger of things to come has taken up its abode. It differs from person to person. For some, it's the hip. For others, it's the knee, the varicose veins, the arthritic hands, the swollen ankles, the bronchial tubes, the heart, the bladder, the bowel, the back. Ask me how I'm keeping these days and the odds are ten to one that within the first thirty seconds you'll be hearing about my sight.

Whenever I gave a thought, which was virtually never, to what my particular affliction might be in old age, the last thing I thought would desert me was my sight. (You did ask how I'm keeping these days, didn't you?) Apart from the need to wear glasses some time after I turned fifty, I had never had a moment's trouble with my eyes. I read anywhere and everywhere, in glaring sunlight, in the half-light at day's end, with a 200-watt bulb, with a 20-watt bulb, small print, large print, dark ink, light ink, type, longhand, any colour, any style. So long as they made words, I read them. I seldom went to the optician. When I finally made an appointment, it was with the vague feeling that my glasses needed strengthening. I was sixty-eight and I was in for the shock of my life.

It took me a while to realise that the optician was taking much longer about testing my eyes than I would have thought necessary. He is a friendly man who, I recalled, had usually made conversation. I became aware of the silence. He hurried from one side to the other, looking intently into each eye. Finally, to break the tension, I asked him if an optician could judge a person's general health by looking into their eyes as he was doing. He very kindly acted as though this were a rational question and indicated that they could not. At last, he told me that he didn't like what he was seeing. Then very gently and with enormous regret he introduced me to two words I had never heard before in my life: macular degeneration. From what he said, I gathered that this condition is generated by a coupling of old age with a rogue gene. I felt appalled, if not betrayed, to hear these two progenitors identified. One made me conscious for the first time that I had embarked on a new phase in my life which other people called old age. The other revealed that this treacherous action came from within the bosom of my own family. Neither circumstance seemed possible.

I cried all the way home in the bus. When I told my community, they were as shocked as I was and we all cried. That night I lay sleepless, with my imagination all but out of control. The next morning, I could see everything as well as usual and I began to realise that I was not going to go blind. Not yet anyway. Not ever, in fact. Not in the manner of those who live in permanent darkness. I assembled the facts as the optician had explained them to me. The cells behind my eyes were dying. Once dead, they could never be revived. This would eventually rob me of my central vision, but my peripheral vision would most likely remain unaffected. I would lose the capacity to make out detail. I would no longer be able to recognise people's faces and to read ordinary print. Here were two things from which I had derived enormous enjoyment all my life. I dreaded such a loss. I need not have worried. My particular brand of macular degeneration has taken years to develop to this stage and my readiness to cope with it has grown with time. I consider myself very fortunate.

There is another kind of macular degeneration that is not so kind. It happens suddenly. The cells behind the eyes haemorrhage and die immediately. The person has no warning. One day their vision is as good as ever and the next, it has gone. They are given no time to prepare either psychologically or physically. Now that, I would find very hard to bear. Yet I've met several people to whom this has happened and I've been amazed and humbled by their philosophical attitude. This must surely mean that human beings are possessed of hidden resources that even they are unaware of until they have need of them. It's a piece of knowledge that I find immensely reassuring.

In the kind of macular degeneration that I have, the cells gradually dry out until they eventually die. It is the kinder form. It takes much longer to develop. It gives you time for preparation and, once you come to terms with your lot, there are many things you can do to prepare. You can join the Institute for the Blind and meet people there who understand the implications of the changes you have to make in your life. They are trained and knowledgeable and compassionate. With their help, you can introduce yourself to talking books, you can learn how to use a computer to suit your needs, you can do things you never thought you'd ever dare to do.

Just to take these last three one by one. If reading the written word has been one of the great pleasures of your life, the transition from reading a book to listening to one is much greater than might be imagined. When you are holding a book in your hands, you develop a relationship with it: its cover, its format, its texture, its colour, even its smell. You can take it anywhere. When you are listening to tapes of the same book, all these attributes are gone. You now have to stay mostly in the same place attached to a machine and you have to accommodate a third party in the process. At first it seems as though the reader is coming between you and the written word. The sense of hearing has replaced the sense of sight. It is a new and challenging experience. It seems unnatural somehow. Yet I used to get a lot of enjoyment from listening to a book read on radio, so what is different? I think it was that the radio provided an optional way of enjoying a book. Now, you have no option. If you want to read a book at all, you have to listen to it. There's a subtle difference.

The greatest obstacle to your adjustment to all this is, of course, your self-pity, all the more difficult to handle because so carefully hidden. It's such a wimpish little weakness, self-pity. Eventually, however, you pull it out, look at it, call it by name and say to it, 'On your bike!' With that out of the way, it's a straight path ahead. In time, you turn your mind to all the people who are involved in making this new experience possible for you and you have the grace to feel ashamed. There's the Institute for the Blind, who provide you with their special machine and the catalogue of their thousands of talking books. There are the public libraries offering a seemingly unlimited choice that you scarcely knew was there. In due course, far from feeling that having a book read to you limits or inhibits your enjoyment, you come to see the ways in which it expands and enhances it. You begin to appreciate the gift of communication that every reader seems to possess, the seamless flow of the story, the technological skill involved in splicing and editing the tapes so that you never know at what point the reader stopped and at what point took it up again. You are at the receiving end of a great number of gifted people, beginning with the creative pen of the writer and finishing with the anonymous faithfulness of the person who posts you the flat, yellow box containing your new book. You might well end with a nod of gratitude to New Zealand Post for allowing it to travel both ways, free of charge. That's not a bad line-up, is it? And all, I remind myself, so that I can read a book.

4

HEN I REACHED THE STAGE WHEN I COULD no longer see what I was typing, I realised that I was barely computer literate. I was instead utterly wedded to my ancient word processor. It was an Olivetti and I knew it inside out like an old friend. It was not given to cranky moods. It suffered, with an uncomplicated equanimity, the less than careful treatment I meted out to it, treatment that more sophisticated machines would not tolerate for an instant. It had an iron constitution and a serene temperament. It wrote five books for me. It was on my side. When I bought it, the young salesman gave me a choice between an Italian and a Japanese model. I said I'd go for the one made in Italy. He was bemused by my naïvety and he pointed out with the knowingness of the young, that most likely, they were both made in Taiwan. Whoever made it, they did a good job. The man who serviced it in its rare moments of need, told me after the first ten years that there were only three machines like mine left in Christchurch. That only increased my affection for it. I had not the slightest intention of parting with it.

Famous last words. In time, my faithful old war-horse, try as it may, could not provide me with big enough print for me to read. I had to let it go and begin the bewildering process of building up a relationship with a second-hand computer. It took more perseverance and patience than I expected and, at times, than I thought I had. It was my friends who had the patience. Sister Teresa sat beside me and would not let me give in. Eventually I had to admit that the computer could do things undreamed of by my cherished word processor. I learnt how to set the size of the font at forty point to do my writing and then, without losing everything I had written, how to bring it back to twelve point to print it off. Every month, it seems to me, I learn a new trick, a new short-cut. I discovered that people who know a lot about computers are possessed of a singular generosity in teaching those who don't. Fickle that I am, I am converted.

I imagine it is common to everyone who acquires a disability in old age, that they come to do things they never thought they'd do, ever. By the time we are old, we have grown used to admiring from a distance the gallantry and skill of those who have to live with disability all their lives. We have seen people who can't walk riding horses; people with no arms painting with their feet or mouth; people who are profoundly deaf communicating fluently in sign language; people with broken spines driving cars. As the years went by, we lost our sense of awe and began to take for granted the courage and the daring that are needed to do all the things that the disabled do. We were able. It seldom if ever occurred to us that one day we might not be. We never speculated on how it would feel to begin learning something new, training for an unfamiliar skill, going back to school in old age, exposing ourselves to failure, daring to try.

My particular act of daring took the form of public speaking without benefit of notes. Even as I write it, I can scarcely believe I have had the audacity to do it. Within the limited parameters of my life, I have done more than my share of public speaking. This has included twenty years of comment on National Radio — but never without a script. Starting from very shaky beginnings some fifty years ago, I grew in confidence and expertise with the passing years. I am a good communicator and I like communicating. For all that, I never took any chances. I always wrote out every word I was going to say. I did this to mentor myself and to be mentored by the members of my community. I also did it to make sure that I kept within prescribed time limits and I did it most of all to prevent the possible nightmare of finding myself stranded in full cry. I could not even imagine giving a talk without a script in front of me.

As my sight failed, I came to the point when I could no longer read from my script and I made the decision to stop speaking in public. That lasted for a year. Then something happened to make me reconsider. That Christmas, my friend, Jenny Rockel, gave me a present like no other I had ever received. She read a book on to a tape for me. The book was called *Ex Libris*, written by Anne Fadiman. It comprised a series of enchanting essays about the Fadiman family, each one of whom was utterly addicted to books. At one point the author told that her father had lost his sight. He could no longer read. Reading had been his life. She told how he used to ring her in New York from California to ask her to read a poem to him that he couldn't recall. Once it was Milton's 'On His Blindness'. I felt their mutual grief as my own. Then, in one of her last essays, she came back to her father to say almost casually, that things were so much better for him. He had discovered talking books. More than that, he had returned to his position at the university and was giving his lectures without notes. Now this was matter for reflection. This was daring that I hadn't even contemplated. It seemed to me that if this man could take a risk like that, then why not I? To date I have undertaken this audacious exercise four times: at a large parish in Wellington, at the UNITEC in Auckland, at a Suffrage Day women's gathering in Christchurch and, most perilous of all, at Sister Monica's funeral. It can only be described as flying with one wing. At any moment you might fall and the ground has never looked so hard. Who knows, perhaps it will happen next time? Whether it does or not, there's a paradox in all this somewhere. I had to get to old age to take a risk as fraught with danger as this one.

5

HILE WE ARE SPEAKING OF RISK, THERE'S one form of risk-taking that some people choose in old age that I admire enormously. They get married. People in their later years make a leap into the unknown. They launch into a new relationship that calls for commitment and intimacy. I think they are wonderful. For them, at the end as at the beginning, life is a living sacrament. Still, it must take courage. Apart from its being a gamble, it takes energy to address all the changes marriage involves and energy is not readily available to the old. They have to balance the loss of their independence with accommodating the wishes of another; they give up their loneliness which is also their known, in the hope of companionship which is as yet unknown; they exchange the familiarity of their daily routine for the upset of new arrangements. They have to consider, amongst other things, what to do about their finances, what to do about their respective houses and trickiest of all, what to do about their families.

Ah, the family. There's the rub more often than not. Their children, well into middle-age in most cases, are the products of the culture in which we live, specifically our pakeha culture which promotes the myth that it is important to stay always young. A multitude of companies dealing in such things as cosmetics, fitness aids and health products depend for their very existence on impregnating the western psyche with the fear of growing old. This fear is so strong in us that we find it hard to accept that in spite of our best efforts, we do eventually become old. Most Western cultures would appear to deny that this is so. That might be why some of them lack a certain humanity in dealing with their old. Unlike Maori and Polynesian cultures which appear comfortable with old age, ours seems to feel some unease with this stage of life and is not entirely sure what to do with it.

The old are very like teenagers in this respect. We find it hard to know where both groups fit into our social context. Both are in-betweens in a way. They are both waiting to enter another phase of life. Neither group has any rite of passage to validate their present state. They can easily become unacknowledged misfits. In those cases where an adolescent shows a close affinity with a grandparent, the mutual attraction might be more than the tie of kinship. Grandparent and grandchild might be aware at a deeper level of consciousness that they have a great deal in common. Their social environment is such that they both feel a certain awkwardness about where they fit. All is well, if both the old and the adolescent keep to their acceptable place in the scheme of things and stay safely within the loop.

Getting married in your seventies or eighties is to act outside the loop. It creates a subtle tension. The children are torn. They want their parent to be happy when they marry, but they can also experience a kind of cultural cringe. They are not sure how other people will take it. Often it shows in how they break the news to their friends that there's going to be a wedding in the family. Sometimes they do this with a kind of wry humour, the kind that parents often use when describing their teenagers' unaccountable behaviour. That's it really. Getting married when you are old is unaccountable behaviour, a form of eccentricity not easy to explain.

Sometimes, of course, the reticence of the children has to do with a very understandable, human dilemma. Who will get the inheritance after the parent dies? Will it go to the partner and subsequently to the partner's family? This is especially relevant when the partner is significantly younger than their parent. It's not an easy issue, this one, but in the end it's for the parent to decide and, in most cases, the children have no need to worry.

Left to myself, I would scarcely have thought of this next possible cause of child-unease over an aged parent's conduct. I picked it up because it was played out with a certain degree of credibility on a recent episode of *Coronation Street*. Deidre's mother went off with her male friend and stayed overnight. Deidre was beside herself and when Ken challenged her about it, she could not say why. She was as upset as any parent might be about the escapade of a teenage daughter and when her mother came home, radiant and excited, Deidre's face said it all. Her worst fears were confirmed. Talk about a reversal of roles. We have to remember, of course, that *Coronation Street* is made in Britain. You don't talk openly about sex in Britain, and certainly not about its indelicacy in old age. 'No sex, please, we're British!' What the British have done as an acceptable alternative is to turn innuendo into an art form. The *double entendre* has become their speciality.

One British poet at least was ready to sing his song about sex in old age. Surprisingly enough it was Thomas Hardy, that most melancholy of writers, who admits to good, lusty yearnings in what are supposed to be his declining years:

> *I look into my glass*
> *And view my wasting skin,*
> *And say, 'Would God it came to pass*
> *My heart had shrunk as thin.'*
> *But time, to make me grieve,*
> *Part steals, lets part abide;*
> *And shakes this fragile frame at eve*
> *With throbbings of noontide.*

The implication is, sadly, that the longings of his throbbing frame went unrequited. But then, given the sense of gloom that permeates his other writings, Thomas Hardy would scarcely have had it otherwise.

6

OR ALL THIS TALK OF THE THROBBING THAT can shake the fragile frame at eve, in the end it is certainly not the loss of sex that causes the most anguish in old age. It is loneliness, pure and simple. It is much more likely that the catalyst that brings a man and a woman together to form a partnership in their later years is not the joy of sex, but the dread of loneliness. Deidre's mother, whose name I have never acquired, bears me out in this. In due course, her relationship with the genial undertaker ended and she was heartbroken. As she sobbed out her distress to her daughter it was not the loss of a valued friend that she was lamenting, but her agony at the thought of the loneliness she was facing in the years ahead. The fear of being lonely in old age is every bit as emotionally debilitating as the loneliness itself. Sometimes, more so. Fear has a destructive quality that corrodes confidence and inhibits all future growth. It is fear of loneliness rather than the loneliness itself that is the greatest contributor to decline.

Before they reach this state in life, very few people have any idea of the kind of loneliness that old age brings with it. It is an uninvited guest that moves in, with little hope that it will ever move out again. But it does send a discreet messenger on ahead to announce its coming. The first intimation of this incipient inner grief comes long before one might be termed old. I have to speak of women here. I know little of men's fears. My perception, right or wrong, is that women in general are much more willing to speak of their fears than are men. Women take the risk of confiding in their friends.

Women in their fifties and sixties will tell you how they feel about the early signs of ageing in their bodies. They describe their first pang of alarm as the evidence grows that they are beginning to lose the person they once were and unconsciously thought they would always be. That person had clear skin, firm breasts, a straight spine, white teeth, well-toned muscles, shining hair, a healthy colour. They have identified with such a person in the most intimate way all their lives. It is this person who has presented them to the outside world. Most importantly it was this person who made them attractive to the opposite sex. Now, it's their familiar body all right, but it begins to show signs of change, and the loss of one's essential persona brings its own special kind of grief, carefully hidden perhaps, but inescapable.

The first thing that women generally notice is that the skin on their hands acquires mysterious mauve-tinted blotches that no amount of expensive skin cream can quite obliterate. Alas, it's only the beginning. In due course, the breasts begin to sag gently and the spine to curve imperceptibly; surplus skin inexplicably gathers on the neck and upper arms, teeth change from the whiteness of enamel to a delicate tone of ivory, a little purple balloon pops out below the knee to announce impending veins, facial hair makes its first appalling appearance and strands of grey appear like fine thread woven into hair that was once a single colour.

Women react to these physical changes in two ways. They either let Nature take its course or they use all the wonderful means now available to stay the hand of change. To me, both courses are equally appropriate because, in my eyes, virtually all women acquire a new kind of beauty in this phase of their lives. I love the lines that come from years of laughter and anxiety and sorrow. I love their interesting, lived-in faces that speak of a healthy loss of naïvety, a tolerance of human foibles, an understanding of the workings of the world, a new wisdom.

But these things are often not much valued by women themselves, not at first anyway. What is most present to the consciousness of a woman at this age is the awareness that she is losing her sexual attraction to men and, in most cases, she is. Men are culturally conditioned to believe that women have to be young and beautiful, with the vital statistics of the magazine model, to be sexually desirable. Very often, their frail self-esteem needs to be bolstered by the attention, if not the company, of younger women. It's when she becomes sharply aware of all this, that the woman in her middle years who is on her own knows intuitively that loneliness will be part of her future life, though for the time being, that awareness is little more than the transient chill of a cool breeze touching her spirit.

One source of loneliness that is seldom revealed even to our closest friends is the loneliness for touch. For the woman who has known the intimacy of a relationship and now for whatever reason is on her own, it can be, as the years go by, a yearning absence in her life. We talk so easily about the loss of the other four senses. We readily remark that with the passage of time we are losing the sharpness of our sight or the edge to our hearing. At different times and seasons we note that our smell is diminished and we perceive that its loss has blunted our taste as well. But we remain reserved about our loss of touch. Perhaps it's because we rely on another to supply our greatest need for this sense, perhaps it's because it's the sense that is most associated with love and tenderness, perhaps it's because it is touch that enkindled our deepest moments of intimacy. Whatever the reason, its loss engenders a quality of loneliness that seems too deep for words.

All this was brought home to me quite unexpectedly on the first programme after Brian Edwards returned to television. Armed with a microphone he was going about the city interviewing people apparently at random. It was obviously a fill-in between the more serious interviews, not the kind of interlude where you'd expect to find your eyes full of tears. He was speaking to a woman who as part of a health service in the central city offered massage to people. She was speaking about the power of touch. To illustrate her point she told of a woman who was over eighty years of age and was visiting New Zealand from England. On the spur of the moment she decided to open herself to this new experience. Some time after the massage began, the masseuse realised that the woman was weeping as though she had never wept before. When the younger woman asked if she could help, the old woman told her that she had been widowed for thirty years and in all that time no one had touched her body until now. It was experiencing the touch of the other woman and the sense of loss it had aroused in her that had released her river of tears. I thought that was one of the most poignant moments I had seen on TV and it spoke to me as little else has done of just how subtle loneliness can be.

By one of those coincidences in life that never cease to surprise us, I was just at this point in my writing when I met a man of some eighty years, whose wife is dead and whose children live away from home. He was looking the worse for wear and, as though he sensed my perception of him, he said, 'I'm drinking too much whisky these days, Sister, but I simply can't bear the loneliness.' Here, in all its stark reality, was the loneliness of real old age. This is no cool breeze. This has the quality of an icy wind penetrating to the heart of the human spirit. It is universal and it differs from one old person to another only in degree.

Loneliness does not induce such desperation in those people who belong to a culture that offers a communal style of life, but even they are not immune from it in their old age. They've told me so, and my own life-style has just enough in common with theirs for me to know that it is so. Those cultures that have based their style of life on family and the community, generally show great respect for their old people. More than that, they rely on their elders to provide them with the wisdom and experience that they lack themselves, they rely on them for their link with the past and for the history of their ancestors and, not least, they rely on them for the safekeeping of their intellectual property. Given that length of days is so honoured in such societies, and given that the old are well aware of their status in the extended family, it would seem unlikely that in such a milieu they would ever be lonely.

In many ways, it is their very way of life itself that contributes to their particular form of loneliness. In old age, they find that Death walks constantly at their side, too constantly. Where the members of the nuclear family experience Death only from time to time, the members of the communal family are seldom free of its visitations. Spouses die. Siblings, with whom they have lived in close proximity for some seven or eight decades, cousins, who were as close as sisters and brothers, all are taken from them one by one. Members of the younger generation, their own children and those whom they reared as their own, are lost to them through accidental deaths and untimely sickness. To be part of the culture of the extended family is to be subject to the pain of constant loss.

Perhaps it's because of this that people like the Maori have developed such deeply human strategies for coping with death. Death is a rite of passage that they have ritualised with profound insight. They have long known that grief has to be released from the depth of the heart and given external expression, and they have created structures that enable this to happen. It is all very human and very healthy. But, for the old, it cannot take from the fact that they have to go on living without people, once so close as to seem like extensions of themselves. Such loss has to bring a degree of loneliness, but it does not bring the frightening sense of isolation that comes from being alone.

From the vantage point of my eighty years, it seems irrefutable that loneliness is an essential attribute of old age, no matter what your life style. I have lived as a member of a religious community for over sixty years. I am not united to the other members of my household by ties of blood. We are, rather, a diverse group of women who chose an idealistic way of life that we were assured would bring us into a close relationship with God. Over the years, two things have become very clear to me. One is that religious life has endured for the best part of two thousand years in one form or another, so it has a rightful place in the spectrum of life choices. The other is that it is just one of many ways of life that can bring us into a closer relationship with God.

What religious life has meant for me is the companionship of like-minded women. Living together as we do, we have to work at our relationships in the manner of any long-term commitment and it is not always easy. We are capable of irritating and inspiring one another in turn. We can understand another Sister and just as readily, misunderstand her. We have to aspire to loving those whom we don't like all that much. We have to come to know that reconciliation cannot be delayed if we are to survive in community life. I remember hearing, as part of convent folklore, the story of an old nun who, when she heard of the death of one of her companions, burst into tears and said, 'She's gone and left me, after all the years we taught and fought together!'

When each of us entered the convent, we spent our first years in a novitiate under the direction of a Mistress of Novices responsible for our training. As part of that formation, we read the writings of the woman who founded the Sisters of Mercy, and became steeped in the tradition, the culture and the spirituality of the Order. We held our old Sisters in the deepest respect as those who had 'borne the burden and the heat of the day' and in whose footsteps we were to follow. We learnt from them our oral history by which we could reach back over long years of time. When I was a young nun in the 1940s, I lived with old nuns who, when they were young, had lived with the pioneer nuns and had heard from them the story of how, in the 1870s, they had come from Ireland to the goldfields of the West Coast. As old women, these pioneers shared what had been their experience with the younger generation in the community. They told of their early years in the convent in Ennis, their call to come to New Zealand to teach the children of the struggling gold towns, their voyage in a sailing ship across the world, the life-threatening drama of crossing the Hokitika bar at journey's end. Back in Ireland they had lived with old nuns who, when they were young in the 1830s, had known Catherine McAuley, the founder of the Order, and had described her to their young listeners. So, in an unbroken line, from 1830 to the present day, I can touch the person of the woman whose vision I espoused a hundred years after her death. That's what oral history is all about.

A shared history creates a strong bond, but even more binding and much more subtle is the connectedness that comes from a shared folklore: the stories and myths that are built up over the years and are told over and over again. Most of these stories are very funny, some are strange, a lot are sad. In the days before TV, storytelling was very important in nuns' lives. It was an art to be cultivated, to be practised, to be savoured. It still holds its place in community life, but not to the same degree as in an earlier time. The telling of a story that is rewarded by a spontaneous shout of collective laughter is one of the most satisfying things on earth. You know you've told the tale well. You also know it when, at the end of a story, no one speaks for a while, until silence gives way to muted murmurs of sadness and regret for sorrows past. From all these things a community builds up a rich store of human experience that provides the raw material from which a culture is created.

But when everything else has been said, I think that the mortar that holds a religious community together more than anything else is its shared prayer. If you sit down every day with the members of your household and pray with them, you are uniting with them at depth. The prayer that religious say together is known as the Prayer of the Church and it has to be one of the most precious gifts that the Church offers its members. Going back long centuries, it has compiled a collection of psalms, poems and prayers for every day of the year suited to each liturgical season, be it Advent, Christmas, Lent, Easter or Pentecost. The daily prayer is so arranged as to allow space for personal intercessions. In those few minutes, we pray in general for the sick, the dying, those who have died, those who are in any need, and in particular for those we name who have asked for our prayer. We pray each day for our broken world that it may know justice and peace. We unite ourselves with all our sisters and brothers everywhere and we pray especially for those who are experiencing pain or sorrow, fear or despair. Not least, we pray for our own special neediness at any given time. Finally, at the close of this vocal prayer, we sit on in silence to meditate together. I had to grow old to recognise that this time of day is invested with a mystical quality that creates a special closeness amongst those who share in it.

As well as prayer, there is the common mission of the community in which every member participates. In our case, it has its focus on the community development of the area in which we live. Bring all these things together then, and you have a group of women who have so much in common that they become bonded in a unique way. Not much likelihood there of loneliness in old age, you might say. But, like the old people of the whanau, loneliness walks with the old in the convent as in any other place.

Much of it is simply part of the human condition common to all old people. Some of it is particular to the religious life itself and some of it can be traced to the personality of the particular person. My own experience is, I would think, common to most people in their eighties.

One of the most disconcerting aspects of this phase of life is to discover with a sudden jolt that you have outlived your generation in the family. At first the very thought of it used to fill me with a kind of dismay. I have survived my three siblings and a bevy of cousins. Many times now I find myself sitting with a letter in my hand, or an article or a picture from the paper that would have been of intense interest to one or all of them. Over the years, I had, without much thought, developed the habit of posting such things on to them and I seldom, if ever, appreciated the pleasure I experienced in doing so. Now, I find myself with no one who would be even remotely interested in whatever it is that is of such interest to me. No one's fault. The members of the next generation simply don't know the people concerned, they don't know the circumstances, they don't know the history, so they can have no idea of the irony or the paradox or the humour that the earlier generation would have enjoyed in it. On these occasions, I find myself, with enormous regret, consigning the cutting to the waste-paper basket. It is just a passing sadness, but it is part of my dying.

7

THE CONVENT HAS MUCH IN COMMON WITH the extended family when it comes to deaths. They have a lot of them! They generally come in batches and you might have three in as many months. They each bring their own degree of loss depending on how well you had known the Sister over the years. But they only begin to bite deeply when members from your own vintage start coming up to the barrier:

those who were your friends from the day you entered the convent, those who passed each milestone with you as your birthdays came up in the same year, those who would have made it to eighty this year, your peers. The day we entered the convent, we were allotted a number to sew on our clothes, instead of having to print our full name on them. They were given in order and I was 102. In the past year, 99, 101 and 104 have died, good friends with whom I shared memories of sixty years. The convent is the only place I know where your number comes up quite literally. 102 is waiting its turn.

All of which brings us back to the man who was drinking too much whisky. This is the loneliness of old age that is the lot of the majority of people and all other loneliness pales in comparison. Here is the person who has known the kind of love that comes from commitment in marriage or any life-long partnership. It means that, over and above a general kind of loving, there has been a particular loving of the most intimate nature. We all have a deep, human hunger to be loved in this exclusive way. Out of the intimacy of this love, children are born and the aura widens like a warm, amber light to embrace the family circle.

It would, of course, be unreal, not to say sentimental, to suggest that there is no room for suffering in the domestic community of the family. There are the hurtful pinpricks that can occur every day to roughen and irritate relationships, and there is the heartbreak of tragedy that can occur from time to time and threaten to tear the fabric of relationships to shreds. Few families are exempt from either. Still, no matter how rugged the journey, the ties of blood which are the mortar that binds a family, remain the closest bond in the human condition. The loneliness of old age stems from the gradual breaking of these ties through conflict or through death.

If a couple has stayed together into old age, they can generally claim a companionship in the end that is comfortable and comforting. They have learned to come to terms with the things that might have divided them in the past. They have children and grandchildren in common who bring them untold joy and they share the unique satisfaction of continuing a line. They have acquired a tolerance born of life experience that makes them readier to accept the foibles of human beings in general and of their partner in particular. If one of them precedes the other in physical or mental decline, they almost unconsciously begin to live out the vow they made in marriage and which is implicit in every committed partnership: for better or worse, for richer for poorer, in sickness and in health. Strangely enough, they were seldom called on to honour those vows to such an extent in their earlier years. In many ways, they have moved from the being in love with each other of their youth, to the loving each other of their old age. It sometimes happens that those on the outside, even their children, who might have thought their parents' relationship to be dried out of emotion, are amazed and moved to see the selfless devotion with which the one can care for the other.

Such was the case with the man I met that day. He had cared for his wife for years when she scarcely knew who he was. Now, with her gone and his children scattered, he was in a state of utter desolation. That's what the loneliness of old age can be like. I was at a loss to know what to say to him. I tentatively put forward the idea of a rest home. We both knew this would mean breaking up his own home and we both knew that whatever he left behind, it would not be his loneliness. It's possible that he will choose that solution and it's possible that the company of others, the activities that such places provide, the security of being cared for, will take the sharp edge off the bleakness of his spirit. I certainly hope so and I hope that the nips of whisky he imbibes will be for the pleasure and spark that honours a great drink and not for the compensation and befuddlement that dishonours it. Both the man and the drink deserve that.

8

$\mathscr{F}$OR ALL THAT LONELINESS IS AN INTEGRAL part of old age (and I have touched on only a few of its aspects here), it is balanced by all the positive things that are an integral part of old age as well. Wisdom is one of these. Of course old people are wise. They can scarcely be otherwise. Mind you, not all old people know just how wise they are, or knowing it, they are reticent about claiming such a lofty human attribute, but they can't live for eighty years and not accumulate some wisdom. For that reason I count myself wise.

That said, I hasten to add that I'm not speaking of the wisdom born of a lifetime study of philosophy. The wisdom of the aged is not to be confused with the wisdom of the ancients. Between ourselves, however, I don't think it's really all that different. It's just acquired in a different way, the one from a lifetime of learning, the other from a lifetime of experience. Old people of the twenty-first century AD may not be as articulate as the sages of the sixth century BC, but the advice they give is, most likely, just as sound. They are not bent on leaving memorable one-liners to posterity, as their illustrious forebears seem to have been, but their grandchildren may well remember for the rest of their lives what they quietly advised them one day and then pass it on, in their turn, to their children. It's a humbler outreach maybe, but not without honour.

I would not find it a difficult exercise to imagine the grandmother or grandfather of today offering advice in contemporary vernacular that equates with the lyrical gems in Greek, that have come down to us across the centuries, be it Cleobulius of Lindos saying, *Avoid extremes;* or Pittacus of Mitylene giving the hurry-up, *Seize Time by the forelock;* or the financial guidance of Thales of Miletus, *Who hateth suretyship is sure;* or Solon of Athens (and later Shakespeare), *Know thyself!* My father wrote those two words in the autograph book I got for my ninth birthday. At the time I was sorely disappointed in him. It made no sense to me and it didn't even rhyme. All I wanted to hear was, *Roses are red, violets are blue, sugar is sweet and so are you,* or any of the variations on that theme that were popular in 1931. The autograph book disappeared long years ago, but it seems worth noting that his is the only autograph in it that I can now recall, written diagonally across the page in his bold hand and signed with his formal signature as though I were sixty-two like himself.

One aspect of the wisdom of old age is that you become more and more aware with each passing year, that relatively speaking, you know nothing. You might put it a little differently, but most old people would echo the modest response of Socrates when the Oracle of Delphi declared him the wisest man in Greece: *'Tis because I alone of all the Greeks, know that I know nothing.*

In modern times, the people who seem to have won most respect for their wisdom are the old people of indigenous cultures. Not only are they wise, but they are blessed with poetic language in which to couch their deepest thoughts. It is part of the wisdom of the Maori people that they would not dream of making an important decision in their lives without first talking it over with their kaumatua or their kuia and tapping into their precious store of wisdom. Not long after the attack on the World Trade Centre in New York on 11 September 2001, I read this story. A native-American grandfather was talking with his grandson about the tragic event that had just taken place. He said, *I feel I have two wolves fighting in my heart. One wolf is vengeful, angry, violent. The other wolf is loving, forgiving, compassionate.* The grandson asked him, *Which wolf will win the fight in your heart?* The grandfather answered, *The one I feed.*

We may not be able to match that depth of thought and it's unlikely we have the same poetic quality of speech at our disposal, but I don't think it's all that hard for the old to be wise. Common sense is important, intuition plays a part, a sense of humour is useful and, of course, you have to have a good memory. It's like history in that regard. It's said that if the people of a nation don't know their history, they are doomed to repeat the mistakes of their past. History is nothing more than the memory of a people. In the same way, your memory gives you your personal history and can save you from repeating your mistakes over and over. That alone makes for wisdom.

All this is possible because, in a world that is changing with almost terrifying rapidity, there is one great constant and that is human nature. If, over long years, you live with people at home, engage with people at work, mix with people on social occasions, co-operate or compete with people in sport, you come to know a vast amount about human nature as perceived in yourself and in other human beings. You learn what to say and what not to say, what to do and what not to do. You learn when to speak and when to be silent, when to lead and when to follow, when to stand alone and when to merge, when to press a point and when to keep your mouth shut. You never learn it perfectly, of course, but you do learn enough, and for this priceless education the pub is as good an academy as the university. Better, most likely. Wisdom is accessible to everyone and it's the one area of life where the poor have a distinct advantage over the rich. The poor have not had the buffers to life's knocks and bruises that money can provide. They have had a less sheltered journey.

When I think of the advantages of old age, I often think of Queen Elizabeth II. We could just as easily go back to her illustrious namesake, Elizabeth I. It would be hard to match the consummate shrewdness (one of the lower branches of the wisdom family) of the first Elizabeth as she outwitted all those men who plotted to unseat her. Her courtiers came and went, she played one off against the other, she found it necessary to behead a few of them, but she herself survived. A woman could not have stayed on the throne for forty-five years in that dangerous age if she were not growing in wisdom with each passing year.

But we'll stay with Elizabeth II. Every so often a cry goes up that she should resign. Why? Not because she is physically unable to carry out her duties. Not because she is mentally incapable. Not because she has started acting strangely or saying inappropriate things in public. Not because she is a secret alcoholic. Not because she is having an affair with a married man. None of these things. The only reason is because she is perceived to be old. She is in her mid-seventies. In my opinion, she is just at her best as a monarch and she knows it.

It's unlikely that anyone on earth understands the workings of a constitutional monarchy as well as Elizabeth II does. No one else could practise the role of monarch within such a sophisticated system with her ease and flair. With the experience of over fifty years on the throne, she has acquired wisdom. I remember when I was doing a paper on constitutional history at the end of the 1940s, I read of an incident that had happened a few years before. The young Princess Elizabeth had committed a serious constitutional blunder. It appeared that when she heard the outcome of the 1945 election, she gasped audibly! Her beloved Winston Churchill had been defeated and Clement Attlee had become Prime Minister. Labour! What blue-blooded princess would not gasp audibly? Yet, here was her gasp recorded in a serious tome on constitutional history and, according to the historian, she was very severely reprimanded. The royal family, and certainly the heir to the throne, is never to give the slightest indication of which political party they prefer. The line is as fine as that and she has walked it successfully for over fifty years.

We might be inclined to think, on evidence such as this, that the Queen has played no part in British political history for five decades. If we did think it, we could not be more wrong. During her reign, by my counting, she has put no fewer than eleven Prime Ministers through her hands. Each Prime Minister has met with her once a week to give her a full report on the domestic and foreign policy he or she is planning or implementing. This has to be an experience without parallel. Elizabeth must have unique insights into what is the best course to take, what has worked in the past and what hasn't, even what has won and what lost past elections. After each change of government, as she faces her meetings with a brand new Prime Minister, quite possibly a constitutional greenhorn, I can hear her pained sigh of resignation, silent of course, as she prepares to train him.

The press has no access to these private meetings between monarch and premier, but it is not all that difficult to imagine what might ensue. Her role is not a silent one and although she has no power over government policy, she is allowed to have an opinion.

'I recall that Mr Eden discussed that course of action with me in 1956. He told me later that he regretted it.'

'It might interest you to know, Mr Blair, that Mr Callaghan suffered a backlash from a similar policy in the 1970s.'

'Mr Heath worked hard to win the people to that point of view.'

'Yes, of course, Mrs Thatcher!' (We are talking wisdom here.)

The simple fact is that this woman is as wise as she is, because she is as old as she is. Why would they ever want to get rid of her? Britain should not be asking her to resign because she is old, it should be asking her to stay because she is old.

I would be more than a little dismayed if anyone perceived all this as a defence of monarchy. It is quite simply a defence of old age. I could just as easily have chosen the example of Golda Meir, who was leading the state of Israel when she was in her seventies, or Pope John XXIII who, in his seventies, initiated long-overdue reform in the Catholic church that set it on its ear, or Catherine Graham who took over the *Washington Post* when she was in her sixties and remained a powerful influence in its publication until she died in her eighties. There are any number more I could have cited, but I'm not aware of their being called on to resign because they were considered too old for the job. Old age, rather than being a handicap in one's work, can be a priceless advantage and that goes for the engineering bench as much as for the Presidency of the *Washington Post*.

I felt pleasantly affirmed in this view when I read in the *Listener* an interview with the Australian genius, pianist Roger Woodward. He is a Commander of the Order of Australia and one of their 'living treasures'. He is director of the School of Music and Dance at San Francisco State University and a director at Santana Arts Foundation in Tokyo. I mention all these things to ensure that he is taken seriously, because this is what he has to say: *Pianists only come good in their late forties, getting really good in their fifties and sixties, and in their seventies and eighties they are at the top. They are at their most famous when they reach their nineties and still smoke cigars like Rubenstein. It's like the ripening of fine wine. You are absorbing more and richer experiences as you age and this comes out in your music.*

So much for wisdom acquired by human means, through learning or living, but there is a Wisdom that surpasses all other wisdom. It can neither be earned nor learned. This Wisdom is not the prerogative of any class or any age or any person. It is accessible to everyone, to the very young as to the very old. It is pure gift. It is the very breath of God, freely given, freely received. I think we are talking of holiness here.

If your Bible is one that includes 'The Book of Wisdom', you have only to turn to Chapter 7 of that Book, beginning at Verse 22, to read the praises of this Wisdom sung in ecstatic language. The author is unknown although, following the tradition of the Hebrews, 'The Book of Wisdom' is published under the patronage of a sage, in this case the wisest of them all, Solomon himself. Scholars can discern that it was probably written in the first century BC and that the author was a Jew, well versed in Greek.

> *Wisdom,* he writes, *is a spirit, intelligent, holy,*
> *Unique, manifold, subtle,*
> *Holy, active, incisive, unsullied,*
> *Lucid, invulnerable, benevolent, sharp,*
> *Irresistible, beneficent, loving humanity . . .*
> *She is a breath of the power of God*
> *Pure emanation of the glory of the Almighty*
> *She is a reflection of the eternal light . . .*
> *Image of God's goodness . . .*

This Wisdom lives with the Spirit of God and is ready to make her home in every human heart. She is not bound. She breathes where she wills, or as James K. Baxter wrote of the Spirit, she

> *blows like the wind in a thousand paddocks*
> *Inside and outside the fences.*

I like those last three words best of all – *outside* the fences. Everyone.

9

HEN YOU FIRST NOTICE IT, YOU THINK IT must be your imagination. When it happens again and then again, you go through a phase of fearing paranoia. Perhaps, you think to yourself, you are becoming paranoid because you are old, that it's one of the side effects as it were. It can become very worrying. In the same way, some old people think, when they are tending to be forgetful, that one of the side effects of old age for them is going to be Alzheimer's disease. You have a lot of anxiety about things like these in your seventies and eighties. It's uncharted territory. Eventually, however, you decide you are not paranoid, you dismiss the idea that this thing is your problem and become quite certain of its reality. You are not imagining it. People actually are using a different tone of voice when they are speaking to you.

I find this doesn't happen with my family or friends. It happens mainly with people I don't know and who don't know me. To explain it to myself, I sometimes try to form a mental picture of what the other person sees when they look at me. They see an elderly woman, white hair thinning at the crown, sight obviously going, hard of hearing, not standing quite upright, short (and getting shorter all the time), a bit rickety. That's not how I perceive myself, strangely enough, but it's what other people see. It's understandable, then, that they feel a certain concern for me and reveal it in their voices.

Many things compound this situation. To be old often means to be out of touch with contemporary language and idiom. For instance, members of the older generation are likely to go into a café with nothing more on their minds than a cup of coffee or a cup of tea. Suddenly they find themselves facing crisp, quick-fire questions indicating that they have a wide range of choice in the matter. The mysteries of flat white or long black may still be hidden from them and if, to cover their embarrassment, they make a quick decision and choose one or the other, they can become even more bewildered. They find that the coffee they are served is neither flat nor long as the case may be. If they did French in Form Three seventy years before, they have a fair idea that a latte is most likely connected with milk and they are pretty sure that an English Breakfast is not a boiled egg. But, what used to be a simple situation for them has been turned inexplicably into a complex one. Situations like this one can undermine one's confidence at a time in life when it's already slipping away.

Old people, because they are no longer in a hurry, give much more time to making up their minds. They no longer have to make snap decisions as they did in the past when they were pushed for time. When they were younger, it always seemed there was something else waiting to be done, or they were running late for an appointment, or they had a bus to catch, or they should have been at work. Now, none of these things apply and the old actually have time on their hands. It's a mixed blessing, part luxury, part loss. Whichever way they see it, the effect is much the same: they are more inclined to take their time. Unfortunately, this apparent indecisiveness can give an impression of mental slowness. People behind the counter in shops and professional people behind their desks do not have time to spare. They are trying to survive in a market economy where time is money. There's another customer in line who might go elsewhere, or a client arriving who might not appreciate being kept waiting. In these matters, the palm has to go to doctors because most doctors realise that the words *patience* and *patients* can become synonymous where the old are concerned. Older people have more things wrong with them and it takes longer to describe the symptoms. For all we know, any one of our ills might be life-threatening. Anxiety can make us less coherent than normal. Apprehension can make us want to put off hearing the diagnosis. This, after all, might be the beginning of the end. We are always aware that it has to come sometime and it will be sooner rather than later. We need more time, not less. I would that every old person had a doctor like mine. She could easily be my grandchild, but I always come away from her with a sense of being healed in more ways than one.

If there's one thing that can temporarily rob us of our mental faculties, it's the feeling, real or imaginary, that the other person is impatient with us. The feeling that you are the cause of suppressed annoyance in another is disturbing at any time, but it is maximised with age. To know that the other is itching to hurry you up is to be thrown into a crisis of confidence that inhibits normal thinking processes. If you were not confused before, you fast become so in that context. It's in moments like these that I feel most like a child and therefore, most belittled. It has to be said that old age has a lot in common with childhood. When I analyse that tone of voice that so diminishes me, I realise that it's the tone that adults use when speaking to children.

I'm loath to say it, but it has to be said: many people do patronise you when you are old. Looking back, I think I first noticed this phenomenon when I was about seventy-five. I have not the slightest doubt that the motive is kindness itself and it seems less than gracious to take exception to it. But it's too much a part of being old to pass over for reasons of delicacy. The assumption behind this voice or this body language is that because you are old, you must be a little short on marbles. I'm not all that sure that we don't lose a few along the way, but most old people who are getting on buses and taking taxis or enquiring about their pension or buying their own groceries are still far from senility. Yet in all these situations, they are at risk of being treated as though they have never done any of these things before; yes, like children.

Are you all right there, dear?

Here we are, love!

Getting to town on a children's ticket are we?

What's Grandma been doing with herself today?

This is a straightforward form, but it may be a little complicated for you.

On one occasion, I took a taxi after taking part in a protest march against military intervention in Iraq. Some of the marchers were still on the street and as we passed them, the taxi driver said, 'Bloody stirrers!' and turned to me expecting agreement. I felt constrained to say that I had just been one of them, a remark that activated his latent sense of humour. *Are you scared they're going to send old ladies to the front line these days?* Generally, I think of my best lines some time after the event, but on this occasion I thought I did quite well. I said, *No, I'm too old to go to war, and so are you, but we need to do what we can to stop our young people ever going to war again.* I was particularly pleased with the *and so are you* bit, even if it did me no credit. He took my fare without another word. But you can see what I mean, can't you?

There's another type of condescension that is harder to take than the more direct line of the taxi driver. It's not just what's said, it's the voice in which it's said. I think it's called 'talking down' to someone. It has a dimension of patience to it, a nuance of care considered appropriate when speaking to the disabled, a subtle suggestion of pity. It's as though the person has moved into a different gear which calls for the practice of virtue. It's hard to counter this approach, it's too well-meaning to be taken amiss.

One reason why I try not to take any of this amiss is that I have no guarantee that I didn't act in the same way towards old people when I was young. In fact, I have a distinct feeling that I did. When I think of all those old nuns I lived with in my youth, I have to wonder. They had all the characteristics of old age. Their bodies were infirm and their minds less sharp than those of the young women in the community. They were, in short, rather like what I am now. I remember one old Sister who was cheerfully abstracted and forgetful. She had a sister who lived in Paraparaumu. Once a month without fail, after she had written a letter to her, she would come into the community room and ask if anyone knew how to spell Paraparam, as we used to say in those careless days. I would dearly love, at this moment, to hear my tone of voice when I was the one who painstakingly spelt it for her yet again. What I hear across the years is that tone of gentle forbearance that is just another form of talking down to another. I wonder if she noted it. I have no doubt she did, as she graciously thanked for the favour for another month and went off to address her envelope.

10

IRONICALLY ENOUGH, KEEPING YOURSELF ALIVE becomes progressively more costly the older you get. No one ever tells you in advance just how expensive it can be in your seventies and eighties, to keep the show on the road. There seems to be no limit to the things that can go wrong. Either your blood pressure gets too high or your blood count gets too low. Your bowel becomes tighter and your bladder becomes looser. You need medication to make the one work and medication to make the other stop working. Then the stomach decides to join the action. It goes into revolt and starts to return its contents in what the medical profession rather graphically describes as reflux. You have to take medication to put down the rising, as it were. The medication in its turn can get stroppy and react badly to certain foods that you like. I've always been particularly fond of eggs. At first you attempt to defy the recalcitrant organ and eat what you like anyway. It won't have it. You only need enough acid in your throat at night to know who's going to win this argument. Like a child who has answered back to its cost, you toe the line smartly and take your medicine. And as if all this were not mortifying enough, you now have to go looking for two big telephone directories to put under the head of your bed so that you can sleep on a downward incline. It's not all that conducive to sleep, but it's an attempt to outsmart the stomach by requiring it to push its wares uphill. All this is only a small part of the drama. Your back, your hips, your knees, your lungs, your heart, your kidneys, a huge cast altogether, is assembled in the wings waiting to come on stage. At any given time, at least some of these have a speaking part and the director, in the person of your GP, can have a difficult job controlling them.

And they cost money. Mind you, most of the medication prescribed is subsidised by the government, for which we should be very grateful. This is made easier for us because the chemists have devised an ingenious way to keep us in a permanent state of abject indebtedness. They print the real cost of what you are getting beside the actual amount you are paying. I never fail to be profoundly chastened by that information. Without those subsidies, I'd be gone long since. Only the rich would survive. Even so, given the range of pills and potions we are taking at any given time, there's always a good chance that at least one will not have an approved subsidy and we get a taste of paying the full amount. I sometimes wonder if I'm worth the cost. But I don't ponder it for long. When it's a matter of staying alive, such ethical considerations are strictly for the birds, or maybe for philosophers under sixty.

I've only recently discovered that people who have to go to the doctor at least every three months can get a disability allowance. My guess is that virtually everyone of my age is eligible. It somehow implies that old age is a disability, but let's not quibble. Every little helps. The allowance is given to help meet your medical and prescription costs and other expenses such as hearing aid batteries. In my case, it helps with some of the expense incurred by my loss of sight. For instance, there came a time when cutting my own toenails became a less than prudent exercise, given that I could no longer see my toes. There was nothing for it but to go to a podiatrist. To begin with, this experience is positively surreal. You are sitting there paying some one else to cut your toenails. Unbelievable! But in no time at all, you find you're quite at home having your nails filed and buffed as though you've lived the life of Riley since birth. Once I'd caught on to this idea of a disability allowance I became quite enthusiastic about it and began making suggestions to my GP. For instance, I think it's a real disability not to be able to see what is sprouting on your chin. The fear that you might be growing a mini beard could bring on panic attacks which could seriously undermine your mental health. Could we not claim for chin waxing? My GP appeared to give this some consideration, but finally she thought not. A pity. Still, waxing aside, old age does have its compensations to be sure.

I have to say, though, that the compensations barely cancel out the losses. Each loss that comes with old age gradually whittles away your independence. It's the first stage in the process of dying. You are stripped little by little of your self-sufficiency and you have no idea how much value you have placed on this self-autonomy until you begin to lose it. Even having no option about a small thing like cutting your toenails is a loss of autonomy. However, things like that pale into insignificance beside the loss of independence you suffer the day you can no longer drive a car. The truth is that most of us have become so dependent on the car that we can feel its loss like a death. It's all out of proportion, of course, but it's the reality of things. I have the good fortune to live with three women who are generosity itself in responding to my requests to be driven somewhere, but it's never easy to ask. The spirit of independence dies hard. It has saved us over a lifetime from having to express a need and ask for help. It has distanced us from the experience of the poor. It brings us back in many ways to the state of childhood. Suddenly we have to dig deep into our spiritual lives to find the simplicity and humility that we need in old age, that came so naturally to us as a child. We find to our cost that the more independence we have practised in life, the further we are from these profound qualities.

It's a disconcerting fact that just when you think you have most things in life sussed out, you find how little you have understood anything. Nowhere is this revealed more clearly than in the reading of the Scriptures. It's part of the pattern of my life that I read Scripture every day and what a trap that can be. Because you hear the Word so often, you can be deceived into thinking you understand what is being said. There is great wisdom in the claim that we don't read the Bible, the Bible reads us. Did I really have to get to eighty years of age to come to any understanding of what Jesus had in mind when he said, *Unless you become as little children, you shall not enter the kingdom of heaven*? Of course I always knew he didn't mean that we give away our wisdom, our maturity, our whole precious store of adult experience. That would be nothing more than the senility of second childhood. So what did he mean? I had a vague feeling he was asking us to trust others the way children do and to trust in God's love for us, in the transparent way that children trust in the love of their parents. But I didn't make it a lifelong goal to practise it. What I think I can discern happening now is that I'm being given an opportunity late in the day to practise this childlike trust in others and to trust completely in God's love for me. When I view things this way, I see the loss of my independence, not as a door that has been closed on me, but as a window of opportunity opened for my spiritual growth.

As I was writing this, I tried to recall any times in my adult life when I could have been said to have acted with child-like simplicity. Out of a rather mixed bag, I decided on two. Towards the end of my teaching life, I did a two-year stint as principal of the convent secondary school in Timaru. On one occasion in the winter term, I went with the seventh-form girls for a day out at Lake Tekapo. We spent most of the day at a little outdoor skating rink near the lake. We had it to ourselves. The girls were all expert skaters and they found it hard to believe there were people walking this earth who had never been on skates, not even roller ones. They felt it their mission in life that day to teach me. The other adult present prudently decided to observe the lesson before committing herself. I gave myself into those girls' hands and the circus began. They tied me firmly into skating boots and gave me my first instruction. It was easy, they said. I stepped on to the ice and simultaneously, my feet shot from under me and my legs spread in a wide V. The girls caught me just in time and held me upright. We proceeded in a series of such Vs around the rink. The only way they could get me steady in order to issue further instructions was for four of them to hold me in a standing position, one on each side, one in front, one at the back. To add to the indignity of the scene the sound system was playing a Strauss waltz. I loved those girls. They were so serious about it and they really believed that they would succeed. After several ignominious circuits, I begged them to give up, but not they. I was doing very well, they assured me. All I knew was that I was in the middle of a skating rink with no possible means of escape. In the end I think I did manage a step or two and they heaped me with praise. As for the other adult, she sat in the viewing stand and became so hysterical that she had a little accident which must have made her a tad uncomfortable for the rest of the day. At the time, I sincerely hoped so.

On another occasion, some years later, I was on holiday at the Hahei home of my nephew Paul and his wife, Mary Varnham. Mary was determined that I was going to enjoy every wonderful experience that Hahei had to offer and indeed I did, with just one small reservation. It had to do with a walk to Cathedral

Cove. It was, she said, a place of breathtaking beauty and she would never forgive herself if I didn't see it. It was, she said, not far to walk. Child-like, I gave myself into her hands. It was a hot day, but what else do we ask of summer? We walked and talked and the miles flew by. Did I say miles? The first little warning bell began to ring. That prompted me to realise that the track led downhill all the way. That could mean only one thing when it came to returning home. Finally, purple in the face and knees buckling, I followed Mary through a majestic archway of rock to a dream place of gold and blue. I lay on the sand and dozed. I dreamt that a helicopter had landed on the beach to pick us up, that a boat had come into shore, that a flight of angels was carrying me home. The journey back is best forgotten except that it provided a classic example of an adult motivating a child, and I was the child. Mary would walk on ahead and say things like, 'Pauline, you're doing brilliantly! It's just a little way now!' and I would stagger the next few yards to join her. Or she would say, 'You're amazing, Pauline, the way you're doing this walk!' and I would rise to the bait and continue to amaze her. For me, the most memorable part of this event came later in a postscript that took my breath away. After I'd returned to Christchurch, someone sent me a cutting from the *Evening Post* where Mary was a columnist. She was writing about all the attractions of the Coromandel, one of which was the beauty of Cathedral Cove. It was, she wrote, a relatively easy track. Her aunt, who was over seventy, had done it quite easily in the summer, and had enjoyed it. Words fail me!

11

THE OTHER DAY I RECEIVED A CARD FROM MY niece, Mary O'Regan. It has a picture of four old people, three men and a woman, sitting on a bench. The inscription inside reads, *The nice thing about getting old and losing your memory is that you meet so many new people!* It's cheeky, of course, but it gave me a good laugh. Sure, as many of us get older we tend to forget people, but we perfect some pretty smooth strategies to cover ourselves. 'I know your face so well, but just at this moment your name escapes me!' 'It feels like only yesterday since we last met!' With that one, I secretly dread the day that someone replies, 'It was yesterday!' Still, forgetfulness apart, we old people actually do meet a lot of new people precisely because we are old. Lovely people, whose paths we would never otherwise have crossed.

Take my podiatrist, for instance. He's a young man, both serious and light-hearted, a nice mix. He is very serious about the state of the world. He has travelled widely and he reads well. I never cease to be impressed with the breadth of his knowledge. As he clips and files and buffs his way across my nails and massages my feet, he enhances his craft with good conversation. Could any pair of low-vision feet ask for more?

In recent times, I've developed an ingrown nail on my big toe. He tells me that nails tend to curl inward in old age. Well, they would, wouldn't they? After several fruitless attempts to curb the curl, he persuaded me to let him do an operation that would outwit the offending nail. It meant cutting off a thin strip, the length of the nail where it joins the quick. Even writing it makes my skin crawl. The fact that I agreed to it at all says a lot about him. On the appointed day, I found I was more than a little nervous. He came to the waiting-room door, rubbing his hands in anticipation and said with obvious relish, 'D Day!' He was enjoying himself. Before he gave me the local anaesthetic, he enquired what I'd like to do for the duration: listen to the radio? Talk? Sing? I told him that what I'd really like to do was to say a Rosary. 'Ah,' he said, unfazed, 'at that rate I'd better get my Rosary beads!' While he was in the house I remembered that he had an aunt who was a nun. What nephew of what self-respecting nun has not got a pair of Rosary beads stored away somewhere? He came back, ostentatiously blowing the dust off them and the operation was conducted in silence. A good job he made of it, too. My big toe has been duly chastened. And I've met another new person whom I like. You do meet a lot of them in your declining years. What a wonderful paradox life is!

Let's go back to that card that Mary sent me. It put old age and loss of memory together, as though one were the inevitable consequence of the other. I don't quite accept the logic of that. Memory is too mysterious an element of the human mind to be open to such generalisation. For one thing, everyone is different. I have met many old people who have sharper memories than their children. Teresa, a member of our community, is fond of telling us about a relative of hers who was 104 years of age. Once, when his son was visiting him, the older man was speaking of a family event that his son of seventy-five could not recall. The father said, 'What's the matter with you, boy? Are you losing your memory already?' In my own case, a lot depends on whether you're talking about the day I climbed the windmill at three years of age, or my very first book which I learned off by heart and can still recite, or my First Communion day, or the 1929 earthquake. They are just a fraction of the videos I can play in my mind at a moment's notice. If, on the other hand, you're talking about where I've put the key of our letterbox, which is lost at the moment, or even if I were the one who collected the mail yesterday, then that's another matter altogether.

I have developed a theory that everyone is getting more forgetful these days and it hasn't all got to do with age. You have only to mention in company that your memory is not as good as it used to be, to hear cries of, 'Join the club!' from people in their forties and fifties. I think it's possible that people of the modern era suffer from mental overload. Life is moving so fast and there is such a mass of information being fed into the computer of the brain, that human evolution has not yet caught up with it. Your mind simply cannot cope. How else could it happen that a name or a place that completely eludes memory when needed, will suddenly pop back into the mind unbidden when it is no longer relevant? It's not all that different from the way a computer will sometimes take a little time to process information it has received.

Recently, I was listening to a tape on which Billy Collins was reading his poems to a live audience. One of the poems was called 'Forgetfulness'. There was no indication that his hearers were old. On the contrary, they sounded young and lively, yet their response to that particular poem was remarkable. Their shouts of laughter revealed that mixture of ruefulness and delight that spring from an authentic and spontaneous recognition of one's self. That poem was about them no less than about me.

> *The name of the author is the first to go*
> *followed obediently by the title, the plot,*
> *the heartbreaking conclusion, the entire novel*
> *which suddenly becomes one you have never read*
> *never even heard of . . .*

Despite what evidence I can muster to the contrary, there can be little doubt that the memory loses its sharpness as you get older. It's the everyday things: the key of the letterbox, the magnifying glass, the spectacle case, the sunglasses, all in hiding somewhere in the house. Add to that the gloves, the umbrellas, the cardigans, the cake plates, that are distributed around the houses of other people. As the years chip away at the memory, you have to work harder to keep ahead. I have no fewer than four little whiteboards set at strategic places in our house. I rush to the nearest one to record every new appointment as it comes up. By this means, I manage to keep my head above water, but the fact that I have to resort to such secretarial ploys makes it quite clear that I'm drowning, not waving.

There are some brighter moments though to this growing forgetfulness. There's the thrill of triumph when you are the one to remember the name or the place that other people are trying in vain to recall. I have sometimes held back for a moment before supplying the information. The idea is to convey a certain nonchalance that is intended to indicate that such things are not a problem to me. I've stopped doing that. It happened too often that someone else beat me to it by that split second. I can't afford to have that happen, it's too frustrating altogether. As it is, I have to suffer the frustration of very often being able to supply the first letter of the name or the place that everyone is trying to remember. Generally, it takes only that initial prompt on my part for everyone else to immediately announce the wanted word in unison. It's not a lot of fun being a catalyst to the action. Into the bargain, I always have to remind the company afterwards that they remembered that Nicosia was the capital of Cyprus, only after I'd said it started with an N, or they remembered the girl's name was Juanita only because I'd said I thought it started with a

W. I find that providing the first letter of the missing word seldom gets the credit it deserves.

When advice on their health is being handed out to senior citizens, the catch-cry is very often, 'Use it or lose it.' This applies to the arthritic hand, the rheumatic joint, the stiff shoulder, the gout that has nothing to do with high living. 'Use it or lose it' also applies to the brain. Most people who do word games took them up in the first instance purely for pleasure. It's highly unlikely that they did it with their future mental health in mind. Whatever their motive, it was a good move. Those games of Scrabble or chequers or chess are first-class brain sharpeners, as important to the mind as exercise is to the body. You have only to play a game of bridge or 500 or euchre with crafty old-timers to know how fast the brain has to work to prevent a complete rout of your self-esteem.

For me, the main source of mental exercise is the cryptic crossword. I began to do these about twenty years ago when we had two bright young people from Massey University doing a placement with us for three months. We were supposed to give them a hands-on experience of community work to complement their degree in social work. I have no idea what they learnt from us, if anything, but I do know what we learnt from them. Before they had left our house, we were hooked for life on the cryptic crossword. It's a daily ritual faithfully observed that Helen and I do the one from the *Press* together every day. There is something singularly enjoyable about reading a clue and immediately sending the brain off to find the solution that is not where your normal thinking pattern would expect it to be. Cryptic crosswords demand that you think laterally. I do this exercise each day, first and foremost for the pleasure of it, but with the secondary motive of keeping my brain in good working order. There's enormous pleasure in getting such enjoyment from something that the geriatric nurse claims is good for you. It's a bit like taking a good toddy for a cold.

The concept of lateral thinking has always interested me. I remember, in my teaching days, hearing a lecture by a visiting educationist. He was talking about the importance of recognising the lateral thinker in any group of students, someone who well might not appear one of the clever ones in the class, but whose mind did not follow the conventional pattern of collective thinking. He told us the following story. The Crown Prince of some small European state was visiting one of the towns in the realm and the people had gathered on the streets to cheer him. As his car drove slowly by, he saw a country fellow standing on the corner and realised he was looking at someone who was the image of himself. Intrigued by the closeness of the likeness, he thought he'd like to meet the fellow and dispatched an aide to bring him to his hotel. When the embarrassed peasant came into his presence, the prince did his best to put him at his ease. Finally he said to him, 'Tell me, my good fellow, did your mother ever work in the royal kitchens?' The man shuffled round for a bit and then said, 'No, Sire, but my father did!'

It was a marvellous illustration of what he was talking about. A large audience had followed the story and had obviously made a collective assumption before it was finished. Given that history is replete with kings who have sired royal bastards, it was to be expected that we would not readily have suspected the queen, but the point was made. I had to wonder how many lateral thinkers were in the audience that night. I was not one of them.

I don't know just what is the interrelationship between memory and the brain. It's a mystery to me, but I work from the premise that if the brain is kept alert and sharp that the memory will follow. They are in partnership. My sister-in-law, Cassie, confirmed me in this view. She lived to be eighty-eight, with a mind and memory that never diminished with age. She had a fine brain and she honed it constantly. She didn't do that in a conscious way, she was the least self-indulgent woman I have ever known. It was rather that because of a good early education or a gene that thirsted for knowledge, or a lifetime of practice, or all of these things, she was never satisfied with not knowing. The moment she came on a new word, she was out of her chair and over to the bookshelf for a dictionary; when it was an obscure place, out came the atlas. Her book of quotations was falling to pieces on the shelf. It was only in the light of her instantaneous action that I saw how mentally lazy I was myself – physically lazy too, in fact. I wanted to know all right, but I was mostly too tired to go and look at that moment, which meant that, too often, I didn't go at all. To the day she died, Cassie's mind and memory were intact. I believe that she herself played a big part in that blessed consequence.

One thing I did have in common with Cassie was that we both knew screeds of poetry by heart. She had an edge on me in that she also had a store of children's poems, having read them to her children over the years, but the others we most often chanted in unison. Because we just loved saying those poems, we often told each other how glad we were that we belonged to the era of educational thought that encouraged – no, actually required – children to learn poetry by heart. I know there are excellent reasons why this practice was abandoned. Children are now encouraged to write their own poems. It is believed that their own creative writing is inhibited if they learn off other people's poetry. I'm not all that sure of the merits of this argument, but what I do know is that to be in possession of lovely poems is to have a store of treasure for life.

There's nothing to quite equal the pleasure of finding someone who knows one of your favourite poems by heart. This pleasure is greatly enhanced for me when the other person is a man. I think that's because so many men are still in the closet when it comes to poetry. I remember with enormous pleasure, the day that one such friend suddenly said, apropos of something we were talking about:

> *We few, we happy few,*
> *We band of brothers . . .*

and we both went back to the beginning and declaimed Henry V's speech together. Incidentally, I always think that if the modern marketing guru wants the secret of how to motivate those under him, he could do no better than take a lesson from that famous address before the battle of Agincourt. It successfully fired a hopeless, ragtag, weary bunch of soldiers to win a great victory in the face of a superior force.

I get even greater pleasure when the man in question is a young one. I remember my delighted response when someone unexpectedly began to recite that delightful Belloc poem:

> *Do you remember an inn, Miranda?*
> *Do you remember an inn?*
> *And the tedding and the spreading of the straw for a bedding*
> *And the fleas that tease in the high Pyrenees*
> *And the wine that tasted of the tar?*

Much of my pleasure on that occasion came from the fact that this man was in his thirties and had memorised the poem. I had rather assumed that it was only the older generation who committed things to memory for future enjoyment.

I grew up knowing old men who had only a few years' schooling, my father one of them. Their childhood and youth belonged to the last decades of the nineteenth century. They all equated education with literature and jealously safeguarded the poems they had learnt during their brief schooling. Often they didn't recite the entire poem but would, quite naturally, insert appropriate extracts from them into their everyday conversation. They had been treated mainly to the ballad and, in the absence of any significant body of New Zealand poetry in their early years, they made the Australian ones their own, with poets such as Henry Lawson, John O'Brien and Banjo Patterson their favourites. I can remember one day, after a visit from a neighbour whose main grasp on the art of conversation was to state the obvious, hearing my father say to my mother, without any explanation:

> *It's dry all right, said young O'Neill,*
> *With which astute remark,*
> *He settled down upon his heel*
> *And chewed a piece of bark.*

The men in that particular John O'Brien poem had been discussing the ruinous drought they were experiencing.

I have tried to recall if any of those old people whom I knew ended up with dementia of any kind. I cannot think of one, even though many of them lived to a good old age. I wonder if one contributing factor could be, in an era of few books and no TV or radio, that their memory was very important to them and they used it far more than we do. In those days, before the computer and the media supplied us with mechanised information, they committed many things to memory. In the small country community where I grew up, there were people who could tell you every All Black score for the previous twenty years or more. There were others who knew every winner of the Melbourne Cup for the same period and others again who could give every statistic of the world boxing championships of the 1920s, when the famous Jack Dempsey and Gene Tunney dominated the boxing ring. In casual conversation, any of our neighbours would toss out a statistic to have it debated or accepted: the weight of a champion steer, the average butterfat return or the price of wool in a given year, how many ounces of gold came out of the Lucky Strike mine. They had all these things stored in their memory and prided themselves on the accuracy of their recall. I believe it was things like these that kept their minds alive and well into old age.

For all this, I have to acknowledge that you can have a good memory and still be forgetful. I don't have to go past myself for evidence of this. Take the key of our letterbox as a case in point. It turned up on the ledge behind the curtain in my bedroom. Its proper place is on the ledge behind the curtain in the lounge. I should be worried about that. More to the point, I should be worried that I'm not worried. I'm not worried because I remind myself that I've always been capable of acting in an abstracted way when my mind is fully occupied with other things. I remember once, when I was a relatively young principal of a school, being worried that the school year was about to begin and we were short of a biology teacher. I was so preoccupied with the problem that I drove a carload of nuns almost to the gate of an old friend whom I visited regularly, before I realised that I was supposed to be taking them to the railway station on the other side of town. I would have taken them even further, had not one of them remarked on the rather unusual route we were taking to the station. It was a group of Sisters returning to the Coast after the holidays. Fortunately they had insisted that we leave home in good time. As it was, they ended up clamouring on to the train with only seconds to spare while we threw their bags on after them. One of them, a meticulous woman, was taking a pot plant home with her. It was too fragile to be thrown aboard and I was left holding it after the guard had closed the doors. He grabbed it from me and set it on an outside ledge next to the driver, then swung himself onto the moving train. We watched it until it disappeared round a bend, with the precious fern blowing wildly in the wind as the train picked up speed. To complete this undignified spectacle, the other Sister who was present and I collapsed on a station seat and became hysterical. You can see why, with a track record like that, I refuse to attribute every forgetful thing I do to old age.

12

’M PREPARED TO ACCEPT THAT WHAT I'M ABOUT to describe is personal to me rather than an outcome of old age, but just in case other old people have the same experience, I want them to know they're not alone. The reason I believe it could be my particular problem is because I'm what I've heard described as a height-challenged person. In short, I'm short.

I think my lack of height is compounded by my slightly tentative manner in shops. I don't like shopping at any time and I don't prepare myself well enough beforehand. There has to be some explanation for the recurring experience of having people feel so sure that they know what is best for me. I was put in mind to write on this matter because of an incident that happened yesterday.

I had a very early appointment and didn't have my breakfast. At eleven o'clock I went into a local café, very hungry, with a clear picture in my mind of what I wanted. I wanted some toast with a piece of bacon on top and a pot of tea for one. My mental picture was of sweet, crispy bacon and my stomach had caught on to the idea and was all but aching in anticipation. The place was not busy and a man and a woman both took an interest in my order. I told them, quite unnecessarily, that I hadn't had any breakfast. The woman said, 'Wouldn't you like a sausage with it?' I thanked her, but said, no. The man said hopefully, 'Hash browns?' No, thank you, no hash browns. The woman pointed to the little blackboard, which I couldn't read anyway, and said, 'We can serve eggs with the bacon?' I felt a wild desire to tell them about my reflux, but restrained myself in time. By this time I was beginning to feel I'd asked for caviar by mistake, but I said, 'No, just the bacon and toast if that's not too much trouble.' At this point, the woman said to the man, 'She'd be best with a toasted bacon sandwich.' And the man said to me, 'And it's cheaper.' He didn't know that, at that moment, I would have paid fifty dollars if I had it, for a piece of crispy bacon. I gave in. I don't like toasted sandwiches, the bacon was salty and flat, not a crackle anywhere, and I was left to ponder glumly, what is it about me?

On another occasion, I was going to make cheese scones for Sunday night tea. We were out of cheese. I went to a store nearby and, amongst the cheeses, I spotted a packet of cheese that was already grated. I suddenly felt overcome with tiredness and needed to take things easy. I took the packet to the counter. The woman serving me looked at it with utter distaste and said, 'Do you really want that?' All the evidence seemed to indicate that I did, but in the face of her obvious disfavour, I found myself conceding that I had thought I did. She said, 'It's terrible stuff. We have to eat it for Weight Watchers. It has no taste whatever.' Hadn't I noticed that a large block of tasty was on special? And she went herself to get it for me and I went home and got out the grater.

On another occasion, I was home by myself and my nephew was coming for a meal. I had been attracted by ads on TV at that time for tinned fruit set in jelly. Things like guavas in lime jelly or nectarines in raspberry jelly. Right now, as I write this, it all sounds rather revolting, but at the time it felt like a good opportunity to try out this new product. I went to our friendly grocer across the road and asked if he had them. Yes, he had them all right, but he said, 'You don't really want those, do you, Sister? They're ridiculously expensive for what's in them and you could make a jelly that is every bit as good yourself. I've got tinned apricots on special and a packet of jelly would only cost you 65 cents.' I slunk home and made a jelly.

I could go on almost indefinitely, but the point is made. The question I sometimes ponder is this: is it my height? Is it the lack of certainty in my voice? Or is it kindly people being good to old ladies? Most likely it's a combination of all three, but I'm quite sure that when I was younger it didn't happen as often as it does now that I am old.

I have tried very hard in describing these events not to use the word 'assertiveness', but it's perfectly clear, even to me, that it's assertiveness that was called for in each of these situations. I consider assertiveness to be one of the most important of human skills. Too often, people of my generation confuse it with aggressiveness. It could not be more different. Aggressiveness has to do with confrontation. It stems from anger. Assertiveness has to do with quietly standing your ground. It stems from self-confidence. I have considerable admiration for assertiveness in other people and considerable regret when I perceive its lack in myself. It is a social skill that can be acquired. Many people in the generations after me seem to have it quite naturally or they make it their own through consciously practising it. The skills involved in acquiring this virtue are now accessible to virtually everyone. Even the smallest town offers courses and programmes in confidence-building and how to become assertive. They are as available as any other form of adult education and vastly more rewarding than most, because once you begin to regularly practise these skills, you have them for life. It's like learning a musical instrument. Practice is everything. The good thing is that, once acquired, self-confidence can have a transforming effect on your daily life.

Some old people participate in these courses, but they are often at a disadvantage. They are coming from further back on the track, with more hurdles to surmount. I think that many people in their seventies and eighties and even those in their sixties had the kind of influence as children that looked on any form of assertiveness in young people as highly undesirable. Any sign of self-confidence in the young was anxiously perceived as over-confidence. Old nineteenth-century adages such as *children should be seen and not heard* were still considered to have merit. The mouse was often the model. The more little girls and boys resembled a mouse, the better brought up they were perceived to be. They were the 'nice children' that most parents aspired to rear. The school system of that period tended to reinforce these mores. Pupils sat quietly in desks and were 'taught'. This meant, on the whole, that the teacher imparted knowledge to a passive audience. Of course nothing was ever as black and white as this. There were many exceptions, but this was, in general, the norm. The marvel is that so many bright-minded achievers came out of this particular era. They were people who succeeded in their fields, and success is by far the quickest and most effective generator of self-confidence. It goes without saying that the confident person becomes by natural progression an assertive person.

There's a certain irony in my inability to be assertive in given situations, because I conducted my first assertiveness course in 1982 and our community has been running similar courses for local women ever since. It is an integral part of our work in community development. We realised early in the day that before women could become leaders in their community, they had to attain a certain level of self-confidence themselves. We took a book by Marjorie Manthei, recently published at that time, entitled *Positively Me*, and ran with it, devising our own programmes as we went.

Because we were living in a new suburb, we were surrounded

by young mothers living at home with small children and we looked to their needs first. They were often women who had held responsible jobs. Some of them had been professional women, but once they became lost in the suburbs, it made no difference. At home all day with small children, deprived of adult company, they seemed to lose every vestige of self-confidence they had ever had and often became depressed. They became victims of what became known at the time as suburban neurosis and they urgently needed the skills to combat it. We gave all our attention and energy to them. It was some time before we realised that old people could profit greatly from acquiring the same protective skills.

When we did begin to cater for old people in our courses, we found that the particular skill that most old people were interested in acquiring, especially if they were retired and living at home, was the ability to say the little word *no*. We used to call it how not to say *yes* when you want to say *no*, and how not to feel guilty about it. This is not easy to do at any time and it is particularly difficult when it involves your own family.

There's a strange phenomenon that has developed in modern times, greatly exacerbated by the economic necessity for both parents to go out to work. It is that people need child-minders. One of the worst aspects of the market economy is its disregard for children. Children have been given virtually no place in the market equation. The social and economic structures that would take their interests into account have never been seriously developed. The demands that are often made on employees simply ignore the fact that they might have responsibilities to their families that, in any civilised society, should take precedence over their ability to increase profits.

There's a simple logic in what follows from this. Younger people see their parents, now retired, as relatively young and in good health, with what appears to be very little to do. There can be no doubt about the fact that these grandparents adore their grandchildren and the little ones are happy and secure with them. If the older couple live in the same town, they are easily accessible. It's the most natural thing in the world for them to become the people who get called on to do most of the child-minding.

The assumption behind the request is absolutely correct. The older couple do love having their grandchildren, they idolise them, but there is a *but*. They had also hoped to have time for themselves after their retirement. They had plans, perhaps savoured in anticipation for many years. It might well have been the stuff of their fantasy life that they would do so many things when they stopped work, and all on weekdays. The luxury of it! They would play bridge, they would play bowls, they would play golf, tennis, croquet; they would join a tramping club, a reading club, a craft club, a music club; they would learn French, they would learn woodwork, pottery, computer skills; they would study genealogy, organic gardening, creative writing. The pos-sibilities were unlimited. To take up even one of these activities means that, on certain days and at certain times they are simply not available. When the request comes, they want to know how they can possibly say no without running the risk of hurt.

Many old people have told us of this dilemma and it's a psychological minefield. It calls for a sophisticated balance of their own interests against those of their children. But it can be done in a way that does no harm to relationships. The chances are that their own daughter, coming out of a more up-front generation, already has the skill required and uses it herself. Part of the problem for us old people is that we come from a generation that was never up-front. We were brought up to be nice, which means we were expected to say yes to everything and everyone. It was the Christian thing to do. Never mind that you could be driven mad in the process, or worse still, become the kind of person you never wanted to be. It could make you devious. When we didn't want to say yes to a request, politeness required of us that we make up some kind of excuse. If someone asked if they could come to stay and we didn't want them for very good reasons, we might elaborate our regrets with a fictitious story. We had someone else coming. We were going away ourselves that week. We were doing up the house. We had no skill with which to say we were sorry, but it would not be convenient, though we'd love to have them for a meal while they were in town. In other words, we'd say no. It follows from this, that when we do say yes, which is most often, it is completely authentic and open-hearted and leaves no residue of resentment.

This need to be truthful and, at the same time, sensitive to the other's feelings, becomes imperative for the well-being of people who live in close proximity to one another. I am thinking especially of housing complexes for the old. It most often happens that women (and a few men) move to live in these houses after the death of a spouse. They are most often living alone and it can make them very vulnerable. If things go well, the housing complex can be a delightful place, where the need for some community life is balanced nicely against the need for some personal space. If things go badly and the complex provides either too much 'community', which is socially suffocating, or too much personal space, which is socially isolating, it is not a health-giving environment for old people.

It makes all the difference in the world if the residents of such a complex have some skill by which to keep control of their own lives without having to cut themselves off from everyone else in order to do so. What people of my generation often don't realise is that there is a way to counter virtually every problem. It can be learnt. And it takes care of our relationships with other people. We can, for instance, learn what to do to counter the person who, to assuage her own loneliness, comes to visit too frequently and stays much too long. There is a way of discouraging the neighbour who borrows too often and then has a prolonged bout of amnesia. There's a conversational ploy with which to divert conversations that are veering towards gossip. There are ways of dealing with the good-hearted woman you are visiting, who presses food on you when you've already said you've had enough.

When we are devoid of these basic skills, we often feel the need to run away, sometimes quite literally. I knew more than one woman who kept her coat near the door so that when she saw a particular neighbour coming to visit yet again, she'd be putting it on as she answered the door, saying she was just going out herself. Another woman used to grieve that the only time she got back the things she had lent was when she got angry enough to demand them. An elderly woman who was overweight and wanted to do something about it, had to do many role-plays before she was practised enough to cope with her sister-in-law who baked a wide variety of cakes for their weekly visit and got upset if they weren't all eaten. When women find they can successfully deal with these situations without damaging important relationships, there are few things that can match their excitement and delight.

I've often thought what a creative thing it would be if those responsible for housing the old could provide a trained facilitator to help make these complexes more health-giving and human. It would be a sound economic move as well as a social boon. When we are in a healthy environment, we have no need of a social worker. When we are happy, we are not likely to have mental health problems. When we have the opportunity to meet one another in a safe setting, we won't feel the need to keep bending the ear of our GP. True, not every problem would be solved by possessing these human skills, but even with a few basic ones, old people would feel better able to call the tune when it comes to their own lives and feel themselves empowered in the process. They would not be so fearful of making new friends and much less inclined to keep to themselves and suffer loneliness and isolation in the few years that are left to them.

I suppose every generation bears the mark of the type of child-rearing that was being promoted when they were children and, in this regard, most of us in our seventies and eighties still can't resist the need to be 'nice'. One of the side effects of this social conditioning is that we often find it hard to express our own needs. We prefer to project the responsibility on to someone else. I might say something like, 'The Sisters think I should have a holiday.' Others of my age might say, 'My daughter persuaded me to buy this new suit.' 'My family insisted I get a new car.'

We would find it hard to say, 'I want to go for a holiday.' 'I liked this suit so I bought it.' 'I decided to get a new car.' Niceness seems to make us pathologically incapable of owning our own actions. The self-effacement that won us so much approval as children has become, a lifetime later, something very near to self-dislike. We are saying in effect, that we're really not worth the money that these things cost, that we feel guilty about spending money on ourselves (in my case, the community money). At the same time, it has to be faced that, if we hadn't really wanted our holiday, our new suit or our new car, we wouldn't have acquired them. We just needed to have our actions legitimised by others. To put these things into some perspective, try to imagine a twelve-year-old today saying, 'Dad persuaded me to get a new bike!'

Many people of my age are loath to spend money on themselves because they feel they should be leaving it to their children. The implication is that their children are more worthy of it than they are. They forget that, in most cases, they have already given their children a better education than they were able to have and they are earning more money than their parents ever did. A friend was discussing this with me on one occasion and she took me over to the sideboard where she had a framed card from her daughter, a leading New Zealand academic. It read in bold letters: *Always travel first class!* and underneath, *Your heirs will!* The message was clear. Spend it on yourselves. That's my idea of a daughter.

13

WE OLD PEOPLE, WITH OUR LIVES BEHIND us, harbour the fond hope that the generations coming after us will benefit from our experience and profit from our wisdom. In our more honest moments, we hope that they'll learn from our mistakes. Few things cause us more regret than to see younger people, especially those we love, reinventing the wheel when we have already done it. We sigh in resignation. We can't help feeling we could have saved them the trouble. In the midst of all this, we tend to overlook one important truth. It is that, if we had a mind to do it, we have much to learn from the younger generation.

Take, for instance, the matter of direct and honest communication with others. They have sussed out how important this is in relationships. They don't come at things as obliquely as we tend to do. They are more ready to own their actions. They are more assertive. They are more up-front. Dare I say it, they are more honest. We older people could do worse than to take a leaf out of their book.

There's another leaf we could take while we're about it: we could learn to take better care of our mental health. Most people of my generation have no difficulty about caring for their physical health. We don't find it difficult to go to the doctor. But when it comes to our mental health, we are much more reticent about approaching a professional. In this matter, we carry a lot of baggage from our early years. The chilling expression 'lunatic asylum' was still in common use when we were children. Even though it was most often referred to as the asylum, we knew there was another word in that phrase. When the asylum became a psychiatric hospital, things were only marginally better. The shame attached to any suggestion of mental illness remained with us. This is a piece of baggage that mercifully the younger generation seems to be shedding along the way. They are more matter-of-fact about their mental health. They travel lighter, which is nothing short of a blessing for them, as it could be for us, if we followed their example.

The young are more inclined to place their mental health on a par with their physical health. Both are likely to need professional help at one time or another. If they perceive that their mental health is in poor shape and is affecting their daily life for the worse, they are more likely to make an appointment with a psychotherapist or any other appropriate person such as a counsellor. This may not be true of everyone, of course, but it's the modern trend and it's a good one. I have known many people whose lives have been completely transformed by psychotherapy. With their mental balance restored, their general health improves, they are happier people and all those close to them feel the benefit.

I myself have taken the plunge only once. I use the word, plunge, advisedly. I went in the deep end with a six-week course in psychodrama, the only person over sixty in a group of thirty-somethings. At the time, I wanted to clear a shadow on my spirit that tended to come between me and the sun and at the end of those six weeks, the shadow was on its way. I've been an advocate for therapy ever since.

I work right next door to a psychotherapist. There are two outside rooms in our back yard: I write in one and Marie, a member of our community, does whatever psychotherapists do in the other. It happens from time to time that, as I come across to my room, I meet people coming or going from hers. I can't help noticing that they are virtually all middle-aged or young. Yet, I wonder, in a society that is becoming more secular by the day, where the peace acquired in the confessional is the preserve of the very few, if the therapist and the counsellor have a part to play for people in old age. Each day, one way or another, we face the reality that death can't be all that far away. It prompts us to ponder the mystery of life and death in a way we have not done before. Yet we seldom reveal our hopes and fears to one another. We could find much peace from a listening ear and from wise counsel in a setting as safe as any confessional. Ah well, perhaps that has to wait for future generations grown old.

In the meantime, it's sometimes assumed that there are no challenges left for old people to face. Some would say it's challenge enough to live as full a life as we can within the confines of a creaking body. But there are many more challenges than that, and one of them could well be this matter of observing the younger generation with openness and interest to see what we can learn from them.

14

HERE'S NOTHING MORE DISCONCERTING, NOT to say irritating, when you grow old than to open the paper in the morning and read the exploits of someone older than you, a lot older. It can spoil your day. You've just reached the stage when you secretly want to start milking your advanced years for a few geriatric Brownie points, when there they are, smiling at you from the front page, smarter, brighter, healthier, more adventurous than you are, and in their nineties. You're lucky if they're not a hundred. They are telling the reporter that they're still driving the car, they haven't been to an optician in their lives, they can hear the grass grow and, what is hardest of all to bear, they still have their own teeth.

Take yesterday's *Press*. He's 101, he lives alone on top of a hill, he grows his own vegetables and does his own cooking, he's vegetarian, he divides his time between gardening and reading the Bible and some years ago, he threw away the glasses he used to wear. And you can tell from the half-page picture that he has his own teeth. Before that it was a sprightly little woman who didn't look a day over seventy-five, being interviewed after her first flight in a hot-air balloon. It was a present from the family for her ninety-fifth birthday. She loved it and she hopes to take it up as a hobby. The camera did not indicate if she had her own teeth, but I'm sure she did. You wouldn't want to risk dentures in a hot-air balloon, would you?

It makes a difference, of course, when you know the person, someone like Letty Herbert who died recently at the age of 106. She lived in our suburb and we met her from time to time at the home of a mutual friend. She was a Scot, with one of those wonderful accents that come out of Scotland, crisp, clear, concise, with laughter always annotating the margin ready to be part of any story she was telling. She had family in Canada and she made her last flight there to celebrate her 100th birthday with them. When she returned from that trip she had a chest infection and the doctor gave her a course of antibiotics. They worked like magic because she had never had an antibiotic before in her life!

Today, as if on cue, someone sent me a cutting from the *Timaru*

Herald. It was an article on the well-known Timaru personality, Rita Minehan. Mrs Minehan had just retired as the bell-ringer at the Sacred Heart Basilica. She was ninety-seven years of age! A campanologist from the age of nineteen, Rita Minehan climbed the sixty-six steps to the belfry every Sunday, year in and year out, to play the bells. In the interview, she made the point that she was not retiring because of the stairs. They were no trouble to her, but she feared she might fall at that great height. I have a memory of a woman of erect carriage with flair and style that she has carried into old age. There was a nice postscript to the profile. Rita Minehan had never seen the bells she rang so brilliantly. The photographer from the *Herald* climbed the five-metre ladder, opened the trap-door and with the aid of his flashlight illuminated one of the giant bells for her to see.

Who could feel anything but warm admiration for such women, even if they do make my eighty years feel a bit like adolescence?

And then there's Alistair Cook. With Alistair Cook, it's something else again. He's the star of my geriatric heaven. He makes old age look like a piece of cake. In my book, he's still the best broadcaster on air and a political commentator without peer: wry, wise, well-informed, with a perspective that comes from nearly sixty years of broadcasting *Letter from America* for the BBC. He is ninety-five years of age and I want him to be still on air when he's a hundred. He's our flag bearer.

In a recent broadcast Alistair Cook did what was for him a rare thing: he spoke about himself and the effect of old age on his life. He quoted someone as having said, 'A man should repair his friendships.' Woman that I am, I recognised the wisdom of this immediately. He is saying that, as one by one the friends of our own age are lost to us through death, we would do well to make friends with those younger than us. Alistair Cook certainly thinks so. He told us that he has made very good friends with 'a couple of kids in their sixties'.

I paused here to go back in my mind to people I've known in my life who, in their old age, appeared to have 'repaired their friendships' in this way. Two women stood out, one of whom I knew personally and the other by repute. The first was the late Elsie Locke: writer, feminist, environmentalist, peace activist. She died at eighty-eight. Most of her peer group had gone before her, but when she was old she had friends of every age. I think it was her life-long commitment to building a better world for future generations that won her so many friends amongst the young. She was as passionate about the environment as she was about writing; as committed, from the 1930s, to the cause of women as she was to the cause of peace. Age didn't seem to matter to her, neither her own nor yours. You were simply her friend.

The other woman was someone I never met, but always hoped that I would one day. Too late now; she was Davina Whitehouse. She was a woman who had a life-long, single-minded passion for the theatre. If there's one walk of life where age appears less important than in any other, it is the theatre. It might be difficult for older actors to get good parts, but nothing seems to diminish the sense of belonging that actors, old and young, appear to experience. It's as though they have a secret we don't know. It is no coincidence that all I know about Davina Whitehouse came through a mutual friend who was thirty years younger than she, and the gap in their years was of no consequence. The young were received into the circle of her friends as generously as the old. Both those women would have known what Alistair Cook was talking about when he advised the old to 'repair their friendships'.

Two other people who would not see themselves as an Elsie Locke or a Davina Whitehouse come to mind. Sister Monica was an ardent member of her parish. All her life she had a gift for friendship and she liked men. She made no bones about that. For her eightieth birthday, ten men from her parish, most of whom would be forty years younger than she was, came together to sing her favourite hymn, 'Lead Kindly Light'. They made a tape of it and gave it to her to mark the occasion. It was good too, good enough to be played on *Hymns for Sunday Morning* on National Radio. When she died three years later, they sang it at her Requiem Mass and a young priest left the sanctuary to join the singers as a mark of his friendship and he was followed by one of the funeral directors. Alistair Cook would have liked that.

The other person who did the same thing as brilliantly was my sister-in-law, Cassie. She lived to be nearly eighty-nine and she had seen almost all her peers die before her. But she always had friends. I used to tell her she had the art of making friends without really trying. Her secret was to be simply herself for everyone. Things like status, money, power or personality cut no ice with Cassie. She was happy simply to have you as a human being. In the last seven years of her life when she was very frail she employed a woman in her thirties to clean for her. In due course Joy's husband Lou joined the team on a voluntary basis as handyman *extraordinaire* and laughter-maker. Joy and Lou were to become such friends of hers that it seemed only right they take their place beside her children as pall-bearers for her final journey. They were amongst the closest friends of Cassie's life, but it couldn't have happened if she had not at eighty-two been open to making new friends who were forty years younger than she was.

I count it as the richest of blessings that I have friends who are 'kids in their fifties'. The parameters of my life would be much, much narrower without them. They keep me in touch with a life that could so easily be lost to me because I tell myself I am old. I have only to think of the past month: one friend rang to invite me to go with her to the theatre to see *A Room of Her Own*. I would never have gone out on a cold, autumn night otherwise. It would not be good for me. As it was, I had a magic evening with Virginia Woolfe. There are those who claimed that the woman on stage that night was an actor, but not for me.

It was another friend who first introduced me to Glen Colquhoun. She rang me a few nights ago to read me a poem from his latest book, a salty, audacious, profound poem about dying. He's a GP who is healing the people of Northland through his medicine and the rest of New Zealand through his poetry. I would dearly love all people over eighty to have the experience of a younger friend reading them a poem over the telephone.

One of the perks of losing one's ability to read is that people read things to you. Our community went for a picnic last Monday which was a holiday for the Queen's Birthday. As we sat on deck-chairs in balmy sunshine on the second day of winter, Helen came and knelt beside me to read me a paragraph from her book. It was about Glen Colquhoun in a way, about poets and artists everywhere and their empathy with all humankind. In this piece, the great Chilean poet Pablo Neruda described what he termed a momentous moment in his life. A miner came out of the tunnel into the sunlight, his face blackened with coal dust, his eyes bloodshot. He saw Neruda and came to him reaching out his calloused hands and said, 'I have known you for a long time, my brother.' For Neruda it meant that this man, working all day in the depths of the earth for scarcely a living wage, had felt he was not alone. There was a poet who understood his suffering. To cover the fact that I was crying, I said to Helen, 'You have never seen men coming home from working in a mine and I have.' I think I was crying not just for the childhood memory of blackened faces and sunlight denied, but for gratitude that I knew someone younger than myself who could read something like that for me in my old age.

In spite of all this, I have to concede that, members of my community apart, there's one inhibiting aspect to making friends with younger people when you are old and I would be less than honest not to acknowledge it. It comes in the form of self-doubt. You look at these younger friends and see them living attractive and interesting lives, you know that life has so much more to offer them than it has to you, so much vitality, so much energy, so many opportunities that are no longer yours in old age, and you can't help wondering. You ask yourself, what can there possibly be for them in this friendship? Are they, after all, just being kind? It's something that doesn't seem to trouble the Alistair Cooks of this world. Perhaps it's a gender difference that women are more introspective in these matters than men? Whatever the reason, it could well hold people back in old age from taking his advice to 'repair their friendships' by making friends with those younger than they are.

I put all this to Jenny, a very close friend. She would have none of it. Age, she said, has nothing to do with it. I believe her. The members of her generation are too honest to indulge a close friendship for any motive other than genuine affection. So I write this to encourage all old people like myself to put aside any anxieties in this matter and to embrace every opportunity for friendship that is offered them regardless of apparent differences and especially a difference in age. Old age is too bleak a prospect to be countenanced without the company of friends.

15

ONE OF THE THINGS THAT ALISTAIR COOK FINDS difficult in his old age is that quite often, when he mentions a well-known name of his earlier life, his younger friends don't know who he's talking about. The one that seemed to hurt him most was when he made a casual reference to 'The Babe' and one of them asked him who was this Babe he was talking about. I have to admit to being a bit staggered myself over that one. Even I have heard of Babe Ruth, arguably the greatest baseball player of all time, and I'd know as much about baseball as those friends of his would know about rugby.

I would say that virtually every person of my age would identify with Alistair in this matter. (I feel first names could be in order now, we have so much in common.) My Babe Ruth is a film star. Take the film *A Star is Born*. If you're in your forties you think the stars of this film were Barbara Streisand and Kris Kristofferson. Fair enough. They did their best in the seventies version. If you're in your sixties you're likely to recall Judy Garland and James Mason in the starring roles. No one would dare to ask, 'Who's Judy Garland?' surely. But I think I can already hear, a faint, 'James Mason?' But for us in our eighties only one star was ever born, the incomparable Janet Gaynor. 'Janet Gaynor? Who's Janet Gaynor?' The dream girl of all my teenage years, that's who. And the ageing actor whose star was on the wane in that 1937 version? Frederick March, who else I ask you? All right! All right! You've never heard of him. And that's fine, as long as you don't expect anyone to know who Russell Crowe is in sixty years' time.

I've just re-read the transcript of the *Letter from America* of 31 March 2003 and I think I'll have to revise my assumption that first names might be in order. Apparently Mr Cook deeply regrets the passing of formality in social intercourse. In this matter, I don't identify with him, but I know where he's coming from because I come from the same era. I grew up hearing my mother address her friends in the local community as Mrs Walker, Mrs Buckland, Mrs Cohen. Friendship was one thing, familiarity was quite another. I've often thought, looking back, that perhaps this formality was prompted by an intuitive fear of invasiveness in the relationships of a closed, rural community where mobility was restricted and outside influences few. Needless to say, children never addressed an adult by a Christian name. Even within the extended family, a certain formality was required. When I was a child, we had an older cousin who was married and because he and his wife were adults and we were children, we called them Cousin Helen and Cousin Pat. By the time we were adults ourselves, the habit was so ingrained that they kept that title to the end of their days.

I have no regrets about the loss of all this formality although I value a sense of the appropriate above most other things. I think I had rather too much formality in my earlier life. From the time we entered the convent we were always addressed by the religious title of Sister and the religious habit tended to distance us even from our friends. Intimacy was not encouraged. It came as a breath of fresh air, then, to be called by our Christian names when we moved out of the classroom to the suburbs and began to mix with people in daily life. I can recapture across thirty years when we first moved to Hampshire Street, the surge of delight I experienced when little children on the street would call out as they all did, 'Hi Pauline!'

I think there's little doubt that my taste for informality is rather more a reaction to an overformal past than a sign that I have fully accommodated myself to modern culture. There are plenty of indications to the contrary. One of these has to be my passion for correct grammar. I love grammar, every jot and tittle of it. I loved learning it and I loved teaching it. I love the good order it imposes on the English language, its structure, its logic, its common sense. Here was a taste for the formal that I never lost.

My primary school years were from 1928 to 1935. For the first four years at school we did all our work on slates about the size of an A4 page. We were supposed to have a small, damp cloth on our desk to rub off one set of work to make way for the next, but we were not past using a blob of surreptitious spit for the purpose. Everything we did was obliterated shortly after we did it. There was never any work to take home to show our parents. We were learning one important lesson unawares, the practice of detachment.

I recall a story I printed laboriously on my slate when I was about seven. The topic was 'I am a Pet Lamb'. I told how the lady chased me with a broom when I nibbled the leaves on her roses. I finished the account of the chase by writing *oo oo oo* on a line by itself at the end. Mr Stanley took my slate pencil and put an exclamation mark after each *oo*. I could never forget the excitement I felt over acquiring that punctuation mark. For me that day, grammar was born!

If you say a particular word to people over eighty years of age you might well see them change colour. The word is Proficiency. The Proficiency exam was the one you had to pass at the end of your primary school career. It was the dark cloud that hung over the head of every New Zealand child. You had to have your Pro even to get out of primary school. If you were fortunate enough to be going on to secondary school you had to have your Pro to get in. It was the requirement for virtually every job that young people wanted. You sat it in two subjects only, English and Arithmetic, and a significant part of the English paper was taken up with grammar. We had to know that two singular subjects joined by *and* take a plural verb, that the verb *to be* takes the same case after as before, that the apostrophe comes after the last letter in the name of the owner, that when you use *its* in the possessive it does not take an apostrophe, that the collective noun for geese is *gaggle,* to mention just a few of the things that equipped us for the question on the Proficiency paper that read: *Correct the following sentences with reasons.* I have to admit that crosswords apart, I've had little occasion in my life to speak of a gaggle of geese or a pride of lions for that matter, but that's not the point. Just what the point is, I'm at a loss to say. But I have been known to use a stealthy hankie to rub out the apostrophe on the word *cabbage's* outside a shop; I still get a small pleasure writing such phrases as *men's shoes* or *sheep's clothing* and I cry out the word *fewer*, as if in pain, when the reporter on TV says there were *less* people at the festival this year. All this might well sound excessive to some people, but I feel confident that those over eighty who sat the Proficiency exam will understand.

Incidentally, I have the honour of being in the last batch of New Zealand children to sit a public examination at the end of primary school. Proficiency was done away with after 1935, but it was not all over. After two years at secondary school, at the end of fourth form, there used to be another public examination. Once again I was in the last batch to sit it. It was called Intermediate and was abolished after 1937. I'm no Harry Potter, but I used to feel I was possessed of some hidden magic for the benefit of all those coming after me. It seemed I had the power to destroy examinations simply by sitting them. Still, at the time, it was a deflating experience to have expended blood, tears and sweat on passing exams that were immediately declared redundant. For all that, I have long since recognised and readily concede that this over-examining of the young gave a far too narrow focus to learning and is not conducive to good education.

16

A LONG LIFE IS RATHER LIKE AN EXTENSIVE TRIP overseas. There is enormous pleasure to be had in looking back on it. In both cases, the people, places and events can be enhanced by the memory and be even more satisfying than the experience actually was at the time. In the act of recall, we can cancel out the drawbacks: the aching feet in Paris, the spasms of panic in the traffic in Rome, the language difficulties almost everywhere. Rather, we recall our delight at seeing the Eiffel Tower, our awe at the beauty of the Sistine Chapel, our excitement at encountering people and cultures so different from our own. These are the things we recorded on film and they are the things we can picture at any time in our minds. It's very much the same when we look back on the journey of life. We can unconsciously black out the financial difficulties of a given time, the strain in our relationships at another time, the fear of illness at another and remember instead the thrill of graduation, the excitement of a wedding, the wonder at the birth of a baby. As with the overseas trip, these are the things we have recorded for posterity and they are the memories we can recapture in an instant without benefit of technology.

Looking back is one of the pleasures of old age and having scorned it in my earlier years, I've been surprised and chastened to find just how pleasurable it can be. I don't know at what point in life we stop looking forward. In our fifties perhaps? Too early? Our sixties maybe? Certainly, by the time we get to eighty it's a practice that, for obvious reasons, has lost much of its appeal. By the time you get to that age, it's one day at a time where the future's concerned. But the past is a different matter. It is always there, stretched out like a large canvas in full colour to be pondered on, discerned, enjoyed. It's the work of our own brush. There are parts of the picture we wish now we'd taken more care over and parts we could have done much better and there are other parts again where we're secretly delighted that we did so well. The past is very different from the future. The future, of its nature, is 'the stuff that dreams are made of', and dreams are insubstantial things that may or may not come true. But the past is substantial. It happened. It is real. It is unique. It is mine.

The events of our past are at their most vivid and alive when we are sharing them with people of our own age who had the same experience. The event might be the same, but we each see it from a different perspective. It makes each story the same and yet different. Just mention some outstanding happening from the past and you have the perfect conversation opener even amongst strangers. A middle-aged dinner party can ignite like a match if someone asks, 'What were you doing on 21 November 1963 when you heard that President Kennedy had been assassinated?' Whatever we have heard to the detriment of John F. Kennedy since that time, it can't obliterate the shock of that moment and our deep sense of loss. I was making my bed about 8 o'clock in the morning in a dormitory I supervised in the Villa Maria boarding school. Suddenly, a girl came racing in, breathless and crying and announced, 'President Kennedy has been killed!' I stood with a blanket suspended in my hands, completely stunned. When we had begun that day we expected nothing more of it than the usual routine. There was no way we could have known that a moment of that day would be carved into our memory so that, forty years later, we can remember exactly what we were doing in it as though it were yesterday.

As you get older, the people with whom you can share a memory of a distant past become fewer. By this very fact, the memory becomes increasingly more precious. Very soon, you realise, there will be no one left who experienced this particular event and, in the meantime, these are the only people who can validate your own account of it. Such is the case for those who can still remember the great earthquakes of 1929 and 1931, the one in Murchison, the other in Napier. The first was felt all over the South Island and the second all over the North Island. Ask any group of people in their eighties if they remember that day and you are sure of a response. I will tell of a girl, a week away from her seventh birthday, writing on her slate in a country schoolhouse, eighteen miles as the crow flies from Murchison. At precisely 10.19 a.m. on 17 June 1929, there was an eerie, preternatural booming sound and the building began to sway drunkenly on its foundations to the point where it must collapse. I will tell how we ran outside and had to lie on the ground because it was moving in undulating waves across the playground. I will tell how we were sent home that day to find every chimney down, everything in our house smashed to pieces and our mother weeping in the woodshed.

If people are too young to remember those two unforgettable events, let's say they're in their seventies, the question that will bring them alive is, 'What were you doing on 3 September 1939 at the precise moment you heard that war had broken out?' It often happens that at the moment when we hear some earth-shaking news, we are engaged in the most mundane activity. I was ironing at the end of the kitchen table that day, when our neighbour, Jack Coghlan, opened the door off the side veranda and put his head in. Even before he spoke, I knew from his face that something terrible had happened. He said four heart-stopping words: 'We are at war!' I felt my whole body begin to tremble.

In 1939 there was never any doubt that this war was going to be our war, that young men of my age would go to it, that some of them would be killed and that those who came home would be scarred for life one way or another. We knew all this because we had grown up seeing what had happened to the men a generation before us who had also gone to war. Even in our small country community we had our quota of men who had been shell-shocked, men who had breathed in poisonous gas and could never draw an easy breath again, men who never knew a proper night's sleep because they had seen things that became their nightmares for life.

Our family was already preoccupied with death that day in September. Our Uncle Jim was dying. He was a favourite uncle, my father's younger brother and my godfather. It was a day of dark foreboding in our house as we pondered the implications of a world at war and waited to hear the news of our uncle's death. My father sat beside his bed that day, more aware of a present sorrow than of a future cataclysm. He told us that about an hour before he died, Uncle Jim opened his eyes, looked at Dad and said in a weak voice, 'They'll have to do something soon, Jack, about that Hitler fellow!' Neither knew at the time that 'they' had done it that same day.

In past years, it always seemed to me that wars were written into the New Zealand psyche. People quite naturally used to define important events in life according to wars. I grew up hearing that such a one was born just after the Boer War, another was married just before the Great War, and yet another died the day that war was declared. They could just as easily have given the years: 1902, 1914 and 1939, but they didn't. It's a significant footnote to our nation's story that people in New Zealand, for the best part of a hundred years, were able to measure their lives by one war or another.

My father was the first to introduce me to this idea of using war as a point of reference. He used to say with a certain amount of misplaced satisfaction that he was born in the same year as the Franco-Prussian War. As a young child I used to think that the two events were related in some inexplicable way. Had my father somehow ignited a war by being born? Or conversely, was a war responsible for his birth? Either way, the Franco-Prussian War broke out in 1870 and simultaneously it seemed to me, my father was born. I was arguably the only five-year-old in the country to have that historic date lodged firmly in her mind. In later years, as a history teacher, I taught the events that led up to the Franco-Prussian War and explored with sixth forms the profound effect it had on the future history of the world. I could seldom resist telling them of its intimate association with my own life even though they promptly added at least twenty years to my chronological age. After all, if her father was born in 1870 she must be . . .? As for my father, I've often wondered if, in later years, he ever perceived the connection between Bismarck's war that ushered in his birth and the war of 'that fellow, Hitler' that was declared the day his brother died, sixty-nine years later.

Now that I'm in my eighties, I look back and find myself quite appalled at the number of wars our country has participated in during my lifetime. It has to be a measure of our national insecurity that we were always so ready to help our Big Brothers win the fights they mostly started themselves. It's the playground syndrome, of course. We are a small and vulnerable country, and as every undersized kid in the playground knows, if you side with the bully he's less likely to bully you and he might even come to your aid if some other big kid attacks you.

To give us our due, we had little choice about the first two wars of the twentieth century, both of which were part of my childhood consciousness. New Zealand was a member of the British Empire when the Boer War began in 1899 and again when World War I was declared in 1914, so we were bound by our constitution to follow the 'Mother Country' into war. I was not alive for either of those wars, but I lived with them just the same because my generation grew up with their aftermath. As children, we all knew some middle-aged men who had gone in their youth with the New Zealand army to join the British war against the Boers in South Africa. In that more jingoistic age, people would sometimes give the names of famous battles to their children, generally as a second Christian name. As a result there were people born at that time who had to write that particular war into their signature for the rest of their lives. I knew of more than one person who was given the name Mafeking as a second name. Some of them carried it for the best part of a century, long after the relief of Mafeking in 1899 had been lost to memory and the Boer War itself mercifully forgotten. Over the years I have noted in death notices the passage of Mafeking as a given name. It is only in the last ten years that it has disappeared, as men dying in their nineties took the last remnant of the Boer War out of our living history.

We, who are now in our eighties, knew a great number of men who had returned after 1918 from what was still being called the Great War. When we were growing up in the 1920s we knew little of the terrible details of that war, but we sensed its horror in the haunted, inarticulate men who had fought in it. Their silence spoke more loudly than any words the terrible things they had endured. Most of them would never have permitted their children to carry any vestige of the memory in their names. That particular form of jingoism came to an end in the horrors of trench warfare in World War I.

I was seventeen years of age when World War II broke out. In those years before 1939, Germany seemed a long way from New Zealand and despite our history, I was still naïve enough to think that events in a country so distant and so foreign could never impinge on our lives down here in the South Pacific. So, in those days before the advent of TV with its daily news programmes, we teenagers went to the pictures and without any real sense of impending doom watched the newsreel that was shown before every film. As we got deeper into the 1930s, the news increasingly focused on the rise of Hitler. Most often the newsreel would show huge rallies in his honour, with rows of people, thousands on thousands of them as far as the eye could see. Their response when the Führer made his appearance was always one of near-delirium. We were not too young to recognise mass hysteria when we saw it. He himself was a small, insignificant man with a toothbrush moustache who compensated for his lack of natural presence by wearing military uniforms adorned with ribbons and medals. He ranted and raged, it seemed to us, incoherently. Had we understood German, we might have got at least a glimmer of how dangerous he was. As it was, we found it hard to take him seriously. We used to wait for the moment when he would pause dramatically in his frenzied oration and on cue those thousands of people would rise as one to give the Nazi salute. A titter of amusement would go through the theatre in Reefton. But our complacency was to be shattered all too soon.

On a day in early spring 1939, we turned on the radio to hear the flat, strangely uninflected voice of our Prime Minister, Michael Joseph Savage, say the fateful words: *Where Britain goes, we go!* Reality could be deferred no longer.

When I look back across sixty-five years to that time, World War II always seems to be epitomised for me by Bill Andrews. Not that I knew Bill Andrews all that well. He was someone we knew quite a lot about without actually 'knowing' him. He was the son of a Scottish couple who came to New Zealand and took up land in an isolated part of the Inangahua valley, 'across the river at Rotokohu'. A place more remote from Berlin, or London for that matter, could scarcely be imagined. Through that mysterious bush telegraph by which information was dis- seminated in rural communities of the time, we all knew that Bill Andrews was a mass of brains; a chance remark by a country schoolteacher perhaps, the chatter of his classmates at mealtime, it didn't matter how. The fact was that Bill Andrews was very clever, and knowing the Scots' passion for education, it was a foregone conclusion that he would go to secondary school. When that time came, we saw him biking past our house to Reefton District High School every day for five years, in all weathers, fourteen miles each way on unsealed roads. In due course he went away to university, not a common practice in the Inangahua of that time and we then began to hear news of his academic success. We were proud of him.

One day in the early months of the war, the astounding news went through the valley that Bill Andrews had enlisted. Enlisted! We were dumbfounded. The general consensus in a predom- inantly Irish community was that no one in his right mind chose voluntarily to go to war. You waited to be conscripted. More than that, those less acquainted with the ease with which politicians can change their colours when it suits them, firmly believed that the Labour Government would never have the face to introduce conscription. Hadn't many of the current cabinet ministers resisted conscription in World War I and, in some well-known West Coast instances, gone bush? So why, in all that was sane, would Bill Andrews want to enlist? But enlist he did. He came back home on leave before going overseas and we had a send-off for him in the Rotokohu school. It was about five miles away from where we lived, cars were few and petrol rationed, but there was railway line for miles, undisturbed by trains after mid-afternoon. Accordingly, two jiggers were duly commandeered from the railway shed and one summer's evening, with young people hanging precariously from every available foothold, we made our illicit way by rail to Bill Andrews' send-off.

It was to be the first of many such farewell gatherings in the next few years. When a community assembles to send off its young to war, a new dynamic is released. Everyone moves into a gear hitherto unknown even to themselves, to make this a night never to be forgotten. The result is a strange, rather desperate mixture of forced merriment, barely suppressed anxiety and a kind of collective protectiveness so powerful as to be almost tangible. It's as though the community wants to put its arms around this young man and refuse to let him go. But eventually, the words have to be said: goodbye, God speed, safe return. But it's the unsaid words that hang in the air and speak most potently: don't go!

Bill Andrews was killed in action as soon as the fighting began. It was my first experience of the reality of war. We know now that terrible things happened in World War II, but Bill Andrews was for me its first tragedy and by that very fact, its most lasting one.

In the three succeeding decades after World War II, our country found other wars to go to. We had a new enemy and we'd changed partners: Communism became the enemy and the United States the new partner. But it made no difference. Men still got killed. Only the venues changed. There was Korea at first and then Malaya and then Vietnam. The need to go to war seemed to me like a hoodoo that had been placed on our country. Then, in a new century and a new millennium, something changed. The unbelievable happened. New Zealand refused to go to a war. We, who had responded for a century to the call to arms first from Britain and then the United States, suddenly said, 'Enough!' In 2003, when it was not one or the other of our former allies, but a coalition of both of them that looked to us to fight with them, we finally said, 'No!' We did not go to war against Iraq and I have lived to see the hoodoo lifted.

17

I'VE ALWAYS THOUGHT THAT PEOPLE OVER eighty should stop going to funerals. There's a limit to how many curtain-raisers you can watch. But, strangely enough, I haven't stopped. When it comes to the crunch you feel you can't desert your friends at the finishing line. It's disloyal somehow and discourteous, it's unworthy and uncivilised. Most of all, it's an act of unadulterated cowardice.

The day you stop going to funerals, you look in the mirror and see a wimp. So I go. I went to three last week.

There can be little doubt that the funeral you go to when you're in your eighties is a vastly different experience from the one you attended in your forties. The middle-aged at a funeral suffer no foreboding that they will be playing a central role in a similar drama to be staged uncomfortably soon. At forty you are a detached spectator. At eighty you're a potential participant. But even as you attend successive obsequies that bring you into closer proximity to your own, you have to concede that a funeral is a social event like no other. That's because no other social occasion brings us face to face with death, our own included.

Death is the one dramatic moment in life for which there is no rehearsal. It is the ultimate rite of passage. It's the most profound mystery in life. All of which should make funerals very serious, if not sombre occasions. Yet, as an inveterate funeral-goer over a lifetime, I have discovered that many of them can prove to be strangely enjoyable. It's that mix of laughter and tears that is the story of every life, and laughter and tears mingle in a unique way in that moment of formal closure which is the funeral. If we dare to admit we can enjoy a funeral, we are testifying to the fact that life itself is one huge paradox. I could scarcely bring myself to write all this were I not secure in the knowledge that in virtually every case where I've had this experience, the deceased would not have wished it otherwise. I know I would be very disappointed myself, if my friends don't come away from mine saying, 'Pauline had a good send-off!' which, being interpreted, means that all sadness notwith-standing, they enjoyed it.

Needless to say, when I speak of enjoying funerals, I am not speaking of the ones where I have been engulfed in grief or where tragedy has devastated my friends. I am speaking rather of those where I am sad at the loss of a family member or a friend, but not distraught. These are the funerals where, in the midst of tears, we are able to enjoy meeting the people who are there. They might be friends we haven't seen in years, cousins we barely recognise, old school mates from decades ago, student friends from a half-forgotten era, former teachers grown ancient, colleagues from an earlier job or neighbours from our first street. Only a funeral is capable of drawing such a network of people into the one place at the one time. Each one represents a living chapter in the life of the dead person. And because most of them are mutual friends of ours as well, they are reminders to us of the many and varied paths that we ourselves have walked so far. Such an awareness of the tapestry of life, seen in the context of a death, invariably catches us unawares and is charged with emotion.

Funerals are invariably full of surprises. There are all the things we didn't know about the deceased when we thought we knew everything. The eulogy always holds at least one revelation. *I had no idea that Fred played the violin as a young man! She was married before? I never knew that! Did you know Joe had been a prisoner of war? How sad that she lost a child at birth! I had no idea he was adopted.* Then there are all the people whose presence there we can't explain and who provide us with a distraction we could well do without during the service. (How do they come to be here, for heaven's sake?) *I didn't know you were related? Not really, she was my brother-in-law's sister. He was my first boss. She was my mother's best*

[133]

friend. We were in the same class at school. Mostly though, we come away with our curiosity unsatisfied, which is just as it should be, and with the chastened awareness that there are many strands, even to the life of a friend, that reach far beyond our knowing.

One of the advantages of going to funerals in your eighties is that you can always spend some time during the service making remote preparations for your own obsequies. You like that particular choice of music or there's a hymn that you would never have thought of or you think you'll copy that reading. You come home determined to make an immediate note of these things for the benefit of those who'll be preparing your own funeral, but by the time you've had a good cup of tea, debriefed to the people at home and rested your feet, you seldom think of it again. It's just one of many indications that, even in old age, you find it hard to take your own funeral seriously. A priest told me once of an old man who came to discuss his funeral plans. He had everything well thought out. He didn't want a funeral procession. He was prepared to leave all that to the undertaker. He said, 'After the service, the hearse can drive off and we'll all come back inside and have afternoon tea.'

At the same time, human nature being what it is, you come home from a funeral much more convinced of what you don't want at your own than what you do. You are certain, for instance, that in spite of an ego that not even old age can diminish, you do not want them to go on talking about you for too long. By now, you have sat through too many drawn-out, repetitious eulogies to ever want to inflict one on your friends. At least in my case, my friends will be spared a procession of grandchildren thanking me belatedly for always having cookies in the tin. When that happens, I have a wild desire to stand up and shout, 'There was more to your grandmother, baby, than a full cookie tin!' It's a scary thought. It could be that I have to lose only one more marble for this to happen. When I ponder that possibility I find it a potent argument for not going to funerals in your eighties.

Still, in all fairness to eulogists, it must be said that it's never easy to choose the right words at the time of a death. It's a tightrope. You always run the risk, on the one hand, of not doing justice to the deceased or, on the other, of seriously overstating their virtues. When we fall short of a true assessment, people can go away with feelings ranging from vague dissatisfaction to actual hurt that their dear one was so poorly served. But that has to be preferable to the irony that is engendered in one's hearers by attributing to the dead, virtues that in their life were most notable for their absence. It always seems to me that poetry can come into its own at the time of a death. The poets of the centuries have given beautiful expression to every human emotion and poets are at their best when plumbing the depths of loss and sorrow. Nothing demonstrated this more clearly to me than the film, *Four Weddings and a Funeral*. Lightweight and unremarkable as it was, those who saw it are unlikely to forget the moment when the eulogist read a W. H. Auden poem at the funeral of his friend and lover:

> *He was my North, my South, my East, my West,*
> *My working week and my Sunday rest . . .*

Most of us I'm sure, have a memory of a particular poem which, quoted at the time of a death, said what needed to be said as nothing else could have done. In this regard I remember the letter written by his great friend, Graham Speight, when my brother Barry died. They were two men wedded to the law, lovers of language, dripping with priceless anecdotes, different enough to spar but possessed of such humour as to be quite incapable of taking themselves or each other too seriously. They could talk together for hours without any accounting for time. The letter of sympathy opened with the first verse of a poem written by William Johnson Corey:

> They told me, Heraclitus, they told me you were dead,
> They brought me bitter news to hear and bitter tears to shed.
> I wept as I remember'd how often you and I
> Had tired the sun with talking and sent him down the sky.

Strangely enough, the poem that I find full of consolation in a time of sorrow has no title and is without the name of a writer. It is, I'm told, a yachties' poem. The first verse describes a white yacht leaving harbour and heading out to sea until, for the watchers on the shore, it is nothing more than a speck that disappears over the horizon:

> Then someone at my side says, 'There, she is gone!'
> Gone where? Gone from sight, that is all.
> Just at that moment there are other eyes watching her coming
> And other souls taking up the glad shout: 'There, she is coming!'
> And that is dying.

If at any point of my past life a clairvoyant had told me that in the twenty-first century there would be a TV series about death and corpses and undertakers and the hidden intricacies of their craft, I would have seriously doubted her claim to second sight. If she had added that it would be immensely popular so that people wouldn't miss it for anything, I would have laughed. But she would have been right. *Six Feet Under* became an enormously successful TV series and I'll have to leave it to the psychologists to tell us why. There is no doubt, however, that it brought a taboo subject out into the light of day and made death and its immediate aftermath a normal part of life. In a culture that has been in denial for a long time about these things, that was no ordinary feat. That particular TV series also required of us that we see the undertaker and his more euphemistic persona, the funeral director, as a compassionate person doing a pastoral work of singular service to society. Perhaps less often recognised is that *Six Feet Under* has also made it possible to tell funeral anecdotes without appearing ghoulish.

During my eighty years, I've had some strange things happen to me at funerals. On one occasion I was kneeling in a church after a vigil service. The members of the deceased person's family were gathered around the coffin before it was closed. I became aware of some agitation and then of the undertaker walking towards me. He was very pale. He asked if I would help him wheel the coffin into a side room. Once in the sacristy he said in an urgent whisper that the family didn't think this man was their father. He asked me to look and tell him what I thought. As it happened, I had come to honour this good man for kindness done a long time before and I had not seen him for some years. I closed my eyes, conjured up the face I remembered and then looked at the face in the coffin. He was not unlike the man he was supposed to be and he certainly looked every inch a Catholic in his brown shroud with his rosary beads entwined in his fingers. But was it he? The more I looked the more convinced I became that it was not. I said as much to the shaken young man on the other side of the coffin.

He didn't want to hear it. He asked me to hold up the man's legs while he examined a name-tag around his ankle. The name was the right one. So, he declared, I had to be wrong. I knew I was not.

At this point he lost his nerve altogether. He asked me if I would go out and tell the family. I became aware then of how young he was and how shocked. I mustered up a tone of authority long out of use. I said that something like this might never happen to him again and he'd want to look back and know he'd handled it well. To that end, he needed to pull himself together, get out there to the waiting family, tell them the simple truth and then get going, fast. By this time I was feeling more than a little shaken myself, but it was not quite over. As I prepared to follow the family out of the church I heard a voice call in unmistakable panic, 'Sister!' It was the undertaker. He grabbed my arm, 'I've just promised them that I'll find their father and bring him back here. What will happen if he has already been cremated?' He took one look at my face and fled.

He worked for a highly respectable firm of undertakers and I sensed they would need a head to roll. I badly wanted it not to be his so when I got home, I sat down and wrote a letter to his boss commending his handling of the crisis. I then had a good strong drink for medicinal purposes. After that, I sat with the two Sisters in my community and talked for a long time as we explored various scenarios. One of them was that the man in the coffin might conceivably be a Grand Master of the Orange Lodge, the Saint Francis' shroud and the rosary beads notwithstanding.

There was one postscript. Sister Teresa went to the Requiem Mass the next morning. She arrived just as the first hymn was being sung. It was 'Amazing Grace'. Teresa is not one given to levity, but she told us later that she knew all was well when she got to the door and they were singing the line, 'I once was lost, but now I'm found.'

I've heard it said that every person in the funeral business has at least one nightmare in his career to match that of the young man that night. Another undertaker told me once of an episode that cost him hours of sleep. Early in his career he was entrusted with driving the hearse and even though he had memorised the route to the cemetery, he made a wrong turning. To his horror he discovered he had driven into a cul-de-sac. There was nothing for it but to keep going. As he drove the hearse out from this unaccountable detour, he found himself facing the long line of cars in the funeral procession that was still following him in. He said that for a long time, whenever he found himself behind the driving wheel of a hearse, the questioning faces of the mourners that day would return to haunt him.

There can be little doubt that some undertakers are more unconventional than others. I remember seeing such a one in action. It was a small funeral. When we arrived, the undertaker was playing the organ and the familiar strains of 'Over the Rainbow' filled the church. The service began. He left the organ and became the altar boy, swinging the thurible with such enthusiasm that we were completely enveloped in the sweet-smelling, blue smoke of burning incense. I couldn't help wondering what he would do at the end of the service. He had no dilemma. He directed the pallbearers on their way and walked across to the organ again. As we filed out, he was playing something that as a choice for the occasion, left much to be desired. The person was going to be cremated. He was playing 'Smoke Gets in Your Eyes'.

The next day I met someone who had been there. He said, 'That was an unusual funeral yesterday. The undertaker was the organist and the altar boy and the priest drove the hearse.' It was only much later that I realised that the hearse was a left-hand drive.

When it comes to the unusual though, nothing I have experienced so far compares with a funeral that a friend of mine attended recently. It took place in a funeral chapel and she did not notice at first that there was a large screen at the front. The woman who lay in her coffin under a mass of flowers, silenced one would have thought for life, was about to conduct her own funeral! Which she proceeded to do. She had made the video well in advance and entrusted it to the undertaker of her choice. She announced the hymns and actually accompanied them herself on the piano, she did the readings and she gave her own eulogy. She addressed the members of her family with what for some of them must have been disconcerting frankness and she included subject matter that a conventional eulogist could well have considered too delicate to touch on. She told her mourners when to stand and when to sit. She thanked them for coming to her obsequies. She said a final prayer of dismissal. It was, my friend told me, the only funeral she'd ever been to where people were sitting on the edge of their seats. She sensed that some of them were sweating although it was not a warm day, and the almost audible sigh of relief that came when it was over was too real to be imagined. There are those who might claim that what this woman did gave new meaning to the term 'control freak' and there are others who might see it as a novel piece of lateral thinking about the possible uses of modern technology. The jury, of which I'm a member, is still out on this one.

That's enough about this topic although there's a lot more I could say. I actually did go to those three funerals in case you had your doubts. It's just that I belong to the generation whose numbers are coming up with alarming rapidity. If you insist on going to funerals in your eighties, you have to expect to go to more of them than at any other time of your life. It does tend to hammer home the reality of old age rather too effectively though. Writing about the topic has had much the same effect on me. I'm beginning to take the imminence of my own demise a little too seriously and I can't afford to have that happen.

18

GIVEN THAT DEATH OFFERS INCONTROVERTIBLE evidence that one's body is in very bad shape, I suppose it's understandable that old people spend a great deal of time worrying about the state of their health. They also talk about it a lot. In fact, I'd venture to say it's their most popular topic of conversation. If it's true that a trouble shared is a trouble halved, then that's not such a bad thing. What I don't like about it is that all this talk about our health can develop into an obsession. We can spend our time in endless exchanges on what to eat and what not to eat, what potions to take and what not to take, what's good for us and what's not good for us, what this doctor said and what that doctor said, what the woman in the health shop advised and what the man in the pharmacy advised, what we heard on National Radio and what we heard on radio talk-back, especially what we heard on radio talk-back.

It never ceases to amaze me the extraordinary credence that people give to what they hear on radio talk-back programmes. I often wonder if it has something to do with the fact that these opinions are being offered on air, that they are somehow associated with the media. The media, after all, is where we hear what the experts have to say: the professor of medicine, the doctor, the head of the Medical Association. They all speak on air at one time or another. It so happens that the talk-back host also speaks on air as do all those who ring in to talk to him. They are all using the media to put forward their views and, through association, they are all somehow treated with equal respect, the talk-back host and the caller as much as the professor of medicine. There's a problem here, though. While each of them speaks on medical matters with very much the same tone of informed authority, they have not all spent long years studying the subject. Since the invention of the talk-back, it could be argued that radio offers the greatest opportunity there has ever been for people to freely share their ignorance with one another.

I came to realise on one occasion how influenced a person can become by constant listening to these radio discussions on health matters. I had a close friend who, in her old age when she lived alone and was less active, became quite addicted to radio talk-back. She was an intelligent woman with a bright and lively mind, an expert at cryptic crosswords, someone who would not be easily influenced, or so you'd think. She was the last person I thought would ever believe anything that was patently silly. But she did.

She told me quite seriously that she'd heard a discussion on a talk-back session on the subject of soap. 'You really should be using liquid soap when you wash your hands after using the toilet,' she said. 'I heard on talk-back that it's not wise to use cakes of soap because there could be other people's germs left on them!'

'You're joking!' I said.

No, she assured me, she was not joking. I couldn't believe it. I reminded her that we'd both been brought up on farms in the 1920s. We'd drunk milk straight from cows milked in what would now be considered unhygienic cow yards, we'd pulled carrots out of the garden and wiped them on the grass to eat them, we'd sucked sour grass, we'd eaten meat from beasts our fathers had killed in less than sterile conditions, we'd drunk water from the creek with no thought that it might have been contaminated upstream. As for this matter of liquid soap, as she'd recall, there was no such thing in existence seventy years ago and anyway, it's quite likely we didn't use soap at all to wash our hands, if we washed them at all.

I reminded her of the old saying that we all eat a peck of dirt before we die and if that were the case, we country children had surely eaten our quota before we were five years of age. And, as she must have noted, we'd survived. And why was that?

Because before our childhood was over, people like the two of us had built up an immunity system that no self-respecting germ would look at. At the end of this unsolicited tirade, she laughed and I knew the danger was over for the time being. But for the first time I came to realise the power of talk-back radio.

Still, none of this can take from the fact that radio plays an important role in the lives of old people, especially those who live on their own. For one thing, it can fill in the long hours of night when sleep simply will not come and it's during those lonely vigils that talk-back radio in particular comes into its own. The talk-back offers to the insomniac the priceless knowledge that there are other people who can't sleep either. There's a vast company of people out there in the same situation as herself. It tells her she is not alone and this awareness can bring such a sense of solidarity as to assuage the worst pangs of loneliness and alienation that the night can bring. The caller who picks up the phone and rings in at three o'clock in the morning could not possibly know the comfort he is offering to another person by that very act. And the radio host who treats the caller at 3 a.m. in the same way as he does the one at 3 p.m. is offering as much consolation to others as any social worker might have done, or any counsellor or pastor sleeping soundly in their beds at that moment.

19

I'S A PITY THE WORD 'PHENOMENAL' IS SO OVER-used and misapplied these days because I can't find any other word which will cover what I want to talk about. I want to talk about change. In particular I want to talk about the changes that have taken place in the lifetimes of people of my age. Eighty-year-olds of past centuries saw nothing to compare with it, and as for what the eighty-year-olds of this century will see, the mind simply jibs at any attempt to imagine it. To get the full impact of the changes that I have known I have only to dip back into each decade of my life, to the 1980s, the sixties, the forties, the twenties, and recall the way things were. It's one of the most fascinating aspects of being old. The changes that have taken place in my one short lifetime have to be described quite precisely and irrefutably as phenomenal.

You tell me about the Porsche or the Mercedes of today and I'll tell you about the Model T Ford of my childhood. My first decade of life was the 1920s and in the district where I lived, that was the transition time from the horse and trap to the car. I remember well, seeing people trotting smartly by our house in their trap, fast enough to raise a small film of dust from the unsealed road. It was a matter of pride to have the bodywork of the trap shining, the brass accessories polished and, not least, to have the horse sleek and well groomed. I always regret that Stanley Austin, the Reefton undertaker of my childhood, was such a progressive man. Otherwise I would be able to recall a horse-drawn hearse. I'd like to be able to do that, but Mr Austin was too smart for me. He got a motorised hearse in the early 1920s when I was very young and it was still something of a novelty by the time I first recall it. I regret not having a memory of those horses with black accessories drawing a hearse at a mourner's pace.

We must have had our Model T Ford in 1922 because it features in all the stories I've been told about my birth. Skinny Wright was the driver of the car that night and years later, when he was an old man, I had the opportunity to visit him and thank him. He told me that it was a fierce frost and he was called from his warm bed in the early hours of the morning to drive my mother the seven miles to Nurse Crowley's Nursing Home in Reefton. He was looking back over sixty years as he spoke, but I could still detect in his voice a slight note of reproach that I'd been careless enough to be born in the heart of winter. He remembered that my dear eccentric Aunty Katy, who had come to mind the other three children, was showing signs of hysteria, that my mother was laughing at the drama Katy was creating, that my father was hounding him to hurry up, that he couldn't find the crank handle in the dark, that the car was cold and wouldn't start, that once on the road, the windscreen kept frosting up every few minutes so that he couldn't see where he was going, that he had to keep stopping the car to get out and rub it with the half-potato that was always carried for that purpose, and that he was in a state of panic at the thought of what might happen before he got there. When I congratulated him on the fineness of his memory, he remarked wryly that it was not a night he could easily forget.

In the early days of the motor car, not everyone presumed to drive it. My father, who could break in horses and ride any one of them, never drove a car. He always had a young man to help on the farm and one of the big attractions of the job was that the farmhand also became the official driver. I doubt if any of them ever held a licence to drive a car. So long as they could make it go forward, could reverse, knew the vagaries of using a crank handle, could be trusted not to smoke while pouring in the kerosene, didn't skid on the loose gravel that heaped up on either side of the road and never put the car in the ditch, that was considered enough, they could drive. Having to have a licence was not part of the deal. Even when a licence was made compulsory, the test was anything but stringent where it was applied at all. Sister Teresa tells that sometime after 1925, when it became compulsory to have a licence to drive, her father went in to Timaru to get one. Before he left home, his wife asked him to pick one up for her too and that's exactly what he did. He came home with the two licences and Mrs O'Connor drove a car for the next fifty years.

The Great Depression changed things somewhat for us. During those years we did not have a car at all and farmhand-drivers became a thing of the past. But by 1938 when I was sixteen, things were looking up again; we now had an Austin and my father was looking for a driver. He did not have to look far. I was a more than willing candidate. By this time, cars were more common on the road and the licence to drive was being taken more seriously. By this time too, freshly coined words belonging to the brave new world of the motor car began to enter our vocabulary, words like petrol, bowser and traffic cop. Reefton by now had its own traffic cop, but the new title had no threatening overtones for us because it belonged to a man whom everyone liked called Curly Palmer. It was known that even if you were not too good behind the wheel, Curly would send you off with the licence tucked safely in your pocket and a store of tips about what you still had to learn.

I regret to say that when I came to get my licence, my state of unreadiness was too much even for the kindly tolerance of a Curly Palmer. The preparation, such as it was, consisted mainly of reversing the car out of the garage and then driving it in wide circles round and round the paddock. I presented myself, overconfident and unprepared, at the county office and we set off on the test drive. By the time I had effectively demonstrated that I was not fit to be on the road, even the redoubtable Mr Palmer had had enough. He had asked me to stop on a rather steep hill. Then, to my alarm, he asked me to go forward again. This was a far cry from the home paddock. We began to run backwards in the general direction of the ditch and my examiner just had time to grab the hand brake to save us both.

Undaunted, he instructed me to drive into a narrow gateway with the ubiquitous ditches on either side. I was to pull out to my left. At this point I lost all touch with what was my left and what was my right and we returned to base with a much mortified me in the passenger seat.

There were no reproaches. Curly said simply that he had too much respect for my father to deliver him into my hands. I was to go home and learn how to drive and come back in a fortnight's time. A much more chastened candidate presented herself the second time and the reward was a brand new driver's licence and a head crammed with helpful advice.

When the Concorde landed at Christchurch airport I went out to see it. It seemed important to do that somehow, given that I could remember the aeroplanes of the 1920s. They were such a novelty then that people would travel a long way to see one. It was always a great attraction at any country fair to advertise aeroplane rides. We could not afford the five shillings it cost, but I doubt if I would have had the courage anyway. Those early planes always looked to be made of papier-mâché. I remember on one such occasion in a paddock at Ikamatua, following the antics of a rowdy group of young men who had dared one of their friends to 'go up'. They in their turn would put up the five shillings. The pilot had obviously been given his instructions. The young fellow in his innocence took up the bet, fortified himself in the time-honoured way of young men and climbed aboard to the loud cheering of his companions. Then began the most breathtaking performance one could ever wish, or not wish, to see.

The pilot looped the loop, turned the nose of the plane upwards into a steep climb and then nose-dived down to the screaming crowd. He turned on his side, straightened up and waggled the wings. He flew upside down. He swooped low and skimmed the tops of trees and fences. For fifteen minutes of madness, he flirted with death. Finally, he came into land and his shattered passenger stepped ashen-faced on to the ground and stood for one triumphant moment facing the expectant on-lookers. Then, as if in slow motion, his knees buckled under him and he collapsed in a heap beside the plane.

Some sixty years later, when I began to hear about deregu-lation with its implied suggestion that there had been much undue regulation, I realised that on the day of that country fair I had seen what could happen in a world where there was no regulation at all.

The Concorde was almost passé by the time I saw it. I no longer needed it as my measure of change. I had seen pictures of a man walking on the moon by then, and one early morning in the northern spring I had arrived in London from Singapore in a jet plane carrying the population of a small New Zealand township. When we touched down at Heathrow airport it was as if a butterfly had landed on a flower. From a paddock in Ikamatua to a tarmac at Heathrow. That is change.

You tell me about the wonders of the Internet and I'll tell you about the wonders of radio in the 1920s. We had a crystal set, whatever that meant. It had a shelf of its own in the corner of the living room with a little curtain hanging from the shelf to hide the two big batteries underneath, on which it was run. The batteries had to be put in the car from time to time to be recharged. The radio had three dials and each one had to be in exactly the right place to tune in to the different stations. It took a lot of concentration and much delicacy of touch to go from one dial to the other until the balance was right. Barry was the eldest in our family and at twelve years of age, he had perfected this art of tuning in.

It then became his exclusive domain. No one else was allowed to lay a finger on those dials. This may not appear now to be such a privileged assignment, but believe me, if you have all the men of the district gathered around your radio to hear a Dempsey and Tunney world title boxing match and they have their money on the outcome, it could become a huge responsibility. Barry thrived on it. He was treated with much the same respect and awe that is now afforded the child in the house who knows more than anyone else about how to activate the manifold possibilities of the Internet or the mobile phone.

The constant bane of those early radios was static. Static, we were told, was caused by the weather conditions and it could all but ruin the reception. The quality of each reception was measured by the one thing. 'The static is bad tonight' could be countered another night by, 'Oh, good, there's very little static!' We got our best reception from Australian stations. For listeners on the West Coast, the Tasman Sea generated less static, it seemed, than the Southern Alps. There was much rejoicing on my mother's part when Barry discovered how to tune in to 2SM, the 'Catholic station' in Sydney. We children were less enthusiastic. We would get on to our knees in our living room to receive a blessing that was being given in distant Sydney and hear the tinkling of the bell from the altar of St Mary's Cathedral. Sometimes we were called in to join in a Rosary which was being lead by the Archbishop of Sydney no less, and my mother braved the static once a week to listen to a programme called *Dr Rumble's Question Box* where the passionately convinced Dr Rumble answered all sorts of esoteric questions about the doctrines of the Catholic church. It's a relief to me to know as I write this, that such a programme is as much a thing of the distant past as is the radio set that transmitted it.

One of these religious events on radio stands out clearly in my memory. For one thing we were called to listen to it at three o'clock in the morning and for a household that loved its bed, that had to mean it was a very special occasion. And it was. The year was 1933. In the thirty-third year of every century, to mark the anniversary of the death of Jesus, the Church celebrates what it calls a Holy Year. At the opening of such a year, a particular door in St Peter's in Rome is opened by the Pope and at the close of the year he seals it again, not to be opened until the next Holy Year. So it was that in 1933, bleary-eyed and half-awake and feeling less than religiously inclined, we were called from our beds because through this marvellous new invention, the radio, we were going to Rome to participate in the opening ceremony of the Holy Year.

Because it was so late at night the reception, courtesy of
Sydney, was almost perfect. Everything was in Latin, but the
English commentary kept those who were awake in touch with
the unfolding drama. My mother saw to it that we were all awake
to hear the knocking on the Holy Year door as the Pope called
for it to be opened. She wanted us to hear the Pope's voice and I
can only regret my lack of enthusiasm then because, seventy
years later, I'm more than a little pleased to be able to say that I
heard the voice of Pope Pius XI. He was the first of the six Popes
who have occupied the Chair of Peter in my lifetime. In 1933
though, when we looked towards Italy, it was Marconi whom
we saluted, the inventor of the radio.

It is obvious to me now that our sense of wonder at the
invention of radio went deep with us. I remember our surprise
one night when we were talking about it and our brother Pat
quietly began to recite a poem by G. K. Chesterton:

> If radio's slim fingers
> Can pluck a melody from night
> And fling it o'er a continent or sea
> If the petalled notes of a violin
> Can float across a mountain or a city's din
> If songs like crimson roses are culled from thin blue air
> Why should mortals wonder if God hears prayer?

I'm sure someone has written a poem in praise of the Internet.
It's just that I haven't come upon it yet. It deserves it so. As I
look back over all the improvements I have seen in my eight
decades I feel nothing but the most profound gratitude for

change and specifically for all the changes I have seen. By far the great majority of them have been for the betterment of humankind. That surely is reason enough to embrace any future change I might have the good fortune to see in what is left of my life.

20

OF ALL THE LITTLE DEATHS THAT WE DIE IN OLD age, and there are plenty of them, it seems to me that the one that causes the most grief is the breaking up of the family home. Most people in their seventies and eighties live in fear of such a moment. Their home is so much more than a house. It is the repository of their best memories. It is a living mosaic of their lives. They know the day they moved in, they know what it took to pay it off, they know the day it became fully theirs, they know every stick and stone of it. Its contours, its colours, its character are as familiar to them as their own, sometimes more so. It is an extension of themselves. To give it up and take their body out of this safe, familiar shell is the most potent metaphor there is of Death itself. No wonder people try to put off such a moment.

All this is especially traumatic for people who have stayed in the one house for most of their adult lives. They have brought up their children there and known joy and pain under this same roof. It has been the centre of countless family celebrations. Both Birth and Death have visited them there. When they come in the door of this house, it's like opening the pages of a book that they themselves have written. It holds the story of their life. Now, suddenly, everyone is telling them it's time to move on, the place is too big for them, they need something smaller. 'You can't stay in this house on your own, Mother, it's not safe: what if you were the victim of a home invasion? What if you had a fall? What if you had a heart attack? (Pause) What if you died? Can't you see how worried we all are?'

But we old people refuse to be motivated by fear and an impasse generally follows, an uneasy truce during which we carry out a rearguard action worthy of any military strategist. We find ourselves calling on a cunning unconsciously acquired over a lifetime of survival that we didn't even know we had — until now. Our children waver between frustration and admiration as they find themselves outwitted on every front. But it's only a matter of time and one day we have to give in and the For Sale notice goes up on the fence.

They have a new word now to describe what happens next. It appears we have no option but to downsize. Downsize! What a word! Whoever coined that one had neither imagination nor feeling. It's a word that belongs to the tough environment of the marketplace. It has no place in things so deeply human as breaking up a home. It cannot hope to encompass the depth of discernment and detachment and strength we now have to summon up from deep within ourselves. It means, of course, that we can't take everything with us. We are off to a rest home or a council house or a retirement village or a granny flat. 'It's just too small for all your things!' becomes the mantra we now hear. Stating the obvious is easy, but someone needs to tell us where we're going to find the resources we need for the decisions we now have to make. How do we decide what to leave behind when everything suddenly seems too precious, too saturated with memories, too much part of ourselves to be discarded?

But we do it! And in the process, we learn a lot of things we'd never even remotely suspected. We learn, for instance, that things we thought were valuable are now worth very little and things we thought were not worth all that much, 'would bring a mint'. That old table in the kitchen which is scored and stained with living, apparently 'needs only a sandpaper and a polish to bring a thousand'. It's all a bit too much for us, but our steepest learning curve is the discovery that our children are not all that captivated by our taste in pictures or our style of furniture, they really don't want the chiming clock, the silver service, the china tea-sets, the collection of teaspoons, the tea wagon, the damask tablecloths, the starched linen serviettes, the embroidered pillow cases. They are not all that attracted to the wedding presents that were in vogue in the 1940s and 50s and, regretfully, they haven't got the space for the upright piano. It takes a little time to digest all this, but the message is clear and you find to your surprise, that in a strange, freeing kind of way it gives you a new perspective on everything.

I have observed this process over and over again in the lives of people I know. It's a time when most people are desperately in need of a confidant and for once, a family member is not a suitable choice. They are too much part of the problem to be confided in. So who better than an elderly nun who has no children of her own to love her enough to tell her what she can't see for herself? 'They're telling me it's time to move out of here!' is the typical opening statement to what has become an easily recognisable first step of a familiar process. I know now that to walk with an old person on this particular journey is to accompany them into some very dark valleys. But I also know that if I stay alongside long enough I will, in virtually every case, eventually see a ray of light appearing over their skyline. It's a comforting conviction born of experience.

I count it as a special grace that I've come to see how Nature with exquisite delicacy reveals to us a wonderful spiritual reality about life. The truth is that at many different points of our lives we have the experience of dying in one way or another. We suffer a period of sorrow and grief and paradoxically it most often has its source in our love of another person. Later we come to realise that out of that particular death, we are born again to some aspect of a new life and with it, to some new dimensions of our own self. Often we find we've become more understanding, more compassionate, more tolerant, of others' weaknesses, more accepting of our own, more at peace. It's a pity that the phrase 'born again' has been turned into a kind of religious cliché that irritates us far more often than it inspires us. But that in no way takes from the experience itself.

I am writing this on the first day of spring. We have just come through a hard winter of cold and sunless days. All around us Nature died. But today, the first pink blossoms are beginning to show through the wood in the apricot tree in our back yard and the first spring flowers are in the garden. The rebirth has begun. It will be the same next year and in all the years after that. And that's how it is with life. Even in old age the pattern continues. I look at the apricot tree, dead yesterday and alive today. I look at myself, depressed with the cold and darkness yesterday and alive with the hope of spring today, and I see these recurring deaths and rebirths as one rehearsal after another for playing out the final drama of Death itself and the rebirth that follows to a new life.

It's precisely for this reason that I do not feel hopeless for my friends as they go through the pain and loss of breaking up their home to move to a new place. Given a little time, it most often happens that they find enormous relief in the security they are now experiencing, that there is unexpected pleasure in having others do things for them after a lifetime of doing things for others, that they can give themselves permission to stay in bed in the morning, that they can waste time and call it leisure, that they can read or watch TV at ten o'clock in the morning if they so wish and sleep in the afternoon without explanation or apology. They find that no one has expectations of them that they feel they must meet, that they can learn new things like painting or petanque, that even at this late stage of their lives, they are capable of making new friends; especially that. They make new friends. In this new role, in this new place, they are discovering things about themselves that they didn't know. Whether they acknowledge it or not, they are experiencing new life. It's true. I've seen it happen too often for it not to be true.

Lotte is not quite my best example, but she's too interesting to pass over for the sake of making a point. She was a close friend of ours and we knew what very few others knew about her life. We knew how, one day in the 1950s, to escape the Communist regime, she and her husband and two little children walked out of their home in East Berlin leaving everything behind and risked their lives in a daring escape. We knew of the privations they experienced after coming to New Zealand, how her husband had worked in menial jobs before being able to follow his professional career, how she had cooked and sewed and mended for other people and struggled to learn English. Later, when we first came to know her, we used to feel that to go into her home was to be in Europe. It is an English adage rather than a German one, but Lotte's home was every inch her castle.

Already, once before in her life she had been forced to leave behind everything that was precious to her and she was not going to do the same again without a struggle. When at last she had no option but to break up her home, she took every lovely thing she possibly could and somehow fitted it into one small room in a rest home. Each time we visited her we had to marvel all over again at the flair with which she had done it. Every centimetre of wall space was covered with photos and her favourite pictures and every other space held one precious object or another. Although anyone else would have considered it a logistic impossibility, she somehow created the space for her visitors to be entertained as if in her own home. It was a triumph. Lotte would not easily have admitted to being content in her new life although there was plenty of evidence that she was. I have an uneasy feeling she might have scorned my claim that she discovered fresh interests there, but more than anyone else I have known, she successfully transferred the unique atmosphere of her home into a single room.

It's scarcely a coincidence that I'm reflecting on the phenom- enon of breaking up a home at this particular time. As I write, our community is in the process of selling our house. I've just this minute vacated my chair in this little outdoor room where I write to make room for two prospective buyers to come in. I'm amazed how protective I feel about the place. Fortunately it's the estate agent's job to do the talking or I'd be pointing out all the things I love about it. It's strange the way each one of us is reacting to this business of selling the house. One Sister feels a moral need to confide even the smallest defects to those who are coming to look at the place. I suggested to her this morning that she take up her post at the gate to warn them off before they come in. As for me, I couldn't help seeing the looks of surprise and dismay on the faces of the other three when I announced with emphatic conviction that I didn't like the signature of our first prospective buyer. Moral scruples in one, irrational prejudice in another, it takes everyone differently. It's just another way of saying that we love the place, we've been happy here and we don't really want to leave it. But even without benefit of children to counsel us, we've been forced to the conclusion that it's too big for us now and we need a smaller place.

We'll be gone by Christmas. By that time this book should be well finished. If you recall my earlier assertions that old age generates its own kind of wisdom, you'll be justified in thinking that those claims look rather hollow in the light of what's happening. How could anyone with so much as an ounce of wisdom find herself meeting a deadline for a book and be part of selling a home at one and the same time? It makes me nervous to think of it, and so it should. There's that matter of aversion to the buyer's signature to be reflected on, for one thing. And this is only the beginning. We still have to make all those tricky decisions about what to take with us and what not and what to do with the what not. This is going to come close to our final clean-out. This is when we'll find out once and for all if consensus really works. This is what so many of our friends have already done. This is the experience of breaking up a home. This is the reality of old age.

21

*I*T HAS TO BE ONE OF THE MOST SATISFYING
pastimes of old age to tell yarns garnered from the
past. Old people enjoy it most when they tell them to
one another because often it's only another old person who has
the leisure to listen and the time it takes to spin their own yarn
in return. When old people get together, no one is ever satisfied
with the one yarn. You tell me your anecdote and then I match

yours with one of my own. To do that, you need time. Generally this is available in sufficient quantity only within the peer group of the old. Younger people simply don't have the time it takes to spin out the thread of more than one yarn. They have to get back to the office or they're due at the gym or it's their turn to pick up the kids.

Telling yarns belongs to the old for another reason as well. When you tell a story from the past you can dip back into any one of seven or eight decades. Only someone of the same age knows the context in which your story is set. If it's from the thirties they can remember what it was like to live through a Depression, if it's from the forties they know how it felt to be at war, if it's from the fifties they can recapture in an instant the feel of a society that saw everything as black or white. You don't have to spend time explaining to them how things were and they don't sidetrack you with questions just as you're warming up to the punch-line. Yes, spinning yarns is definitely for the old.

Things generally go something like this: you tell me about an embarrassing thing that happened to you in your early days and I'll tell you about the time in the 1940s when we were coming home in the tram and a drunk got aboard at the next stop. For us, in the days when the religious habit proclaimed to the world that we were nuns, there was only one thing worse than travelling with an inebriated man and that was travelling with a Catholic one. There was often someone the worse for drink on the trams in those days and it seemed to us that the number was unfairly weighted in favour of Rome. We knew the signs. On this occasion when the man caught sight of us he immediately began to intone, *Kyrie Eleison, Christe Eleison*, and we knew it was only a matter of time before he would announce to all and sundry that he'd been an altar boy. This he did, but he had more laurels than that to his crown. He proceeded to tell us all that he'd been taught by Sister Augustine and he'd gone to school with Jimmy Liston, he being the Bishop of Auckland at the time. He was launching into an account of the time he went to Confession to Father O'Brien when my companion hit on a bright, if somewhat desperate ploy. She took out a little black book from her bag and asked him if he'd be quiet now because she wanted to say her prayers. He was silent for a few moments, digesting this important piece of information. Then he slowly stood up. He steadied himself for a moment and then turned to face the tram full of people. He put his finger to his lips and let out a prolonged *sh . . . sh . . . sh . . .* Everyone stopped talking and looked expectantly at him. Then in a loud and commanding voice with only the slightest trace of a slur, he said solemnly, 'I want you all to keep completely silent now for the rest of this trip because Sister here is saying her prayers.' The tram fell into silence and we got off at the next stop and walked the rest of the way home.

You were once a teacher and you tell me about an incident that happened in one of your classes that makes you laugh to this day. When you are done, I'll dip back into the fifties and tell you about the time I was reading *The Tempest* with a fifth form. If you had taught in a state school I'll have to remind you that at that time there were no government subsidies at all going into private schools, no money towards building classrooms, no money for teachers' salaries, no money to help buy textbooks. To use the expression of the time, 'No state aid!' On the first day of each school year we would welcome the pupils, give them a list and send them off post-haste to town to scour the second-hand bookshops for their textbooks. That's how it came about that the girls had any copy of Shakespeare's plays they could lay their hands on. Many of them carted the family tome of the *Complete Works of Shakespeare* to school. It was no time to quibble about using the sanitised version courtesy of Mr Thomas Bowdler who in the nineteenth century had removed all the Bard's earthy innuendoes and bawdy quips for what he called family use.

In the 1950s our pupils were exposed to them all. Most of them passed completely over their heads and more than likely the majority of them went over my head as well. There would be frequent interruptions as voices complained that 'that bit isn't in my copy' and on other occasions, outraged cries of deprivation such as when some lucky reader with the unbowdlerised version got to order the servants to 'Lug out the guts!' as Hamlet dismissed the corpse of Polonius. It all helped to brighten up the English class.

Eventually the government came to the party and provided us with free textbooks all appropriately abridged. Shakespeare was never the same again. But this yarn is about *The Tempest*. One of the girls was reading the part of Trinculo where he claimed to be offended by the smell in the cave of the monster Caliban. The reader took great offence on Trinculo's behalf, complaining loudly that he could smell hot pies! Not an eyebrow twitched and the reader went on her dramatic way. Somehow her sub-conscious had prompted her that it was not permissible to be talking about horse piss in a convent school in the 1950s and her eyes automatically provided something more acceptable. A little anachronistic maybe, but a brilliant substitution all the same.

Across fifty years I can still salute her unconscious acumen and laugh at the memory.

Most old people have a great store of stories about their grandchildren. Those of my generation can claim to have great- and even great-great-grandchildren as well, and given that little children are getting wiser by the year, it gives them an unfair advantage over people who have no grandchildren, like me. One of the yarns I bring out of my store comes from a time when the Villa Maria boarding school took in very small children. On this occasion there were five of them all five years of age, two sets of twins and a little girl whose father had recently died. She was the one who opened the batting. She announced solemnly, 'My father didn't go to the war because he was dead!' This being 1951, her father had died six years after the end of the war, a small point that was lost on her hearers. There was a respectful silence for a while after this and then one of the twins said, 'Our father didn't go to the war because he was sick!' That left only one father to have his name cleared. An even longer silence ensued. Then a little voice said, 'Our father didn't go to the war because he didn't know where it was!' That settled it. Every father's honour had been vindicated and everyone was happy.

What that loyal little girl will never know, she being a grandmother herself by now most likely, is that her brilliant saver passed into the folklore of our community. We have over the years, not attended this meeting, not gone to that social event, not turned up for this practice session, not been part of that reunion, not gone to this church gathering and our justification to one another is always the same: 'Yes, I would've gone, but I didn't know where it was!'

You tell me you had an interesting experience on your first visit to London? Strangely enough, so did I! Lorraine, my travelling companion and I were invited to lunch with an old family friend whose husband was at the New Zealand High Commission. They lived in Kensington. Mary rang me the day before and gave me the number of their house. It was No. 12. We walked into a lovely, leafy street with tall white houses and found the one with a shining brass twelve on the gate. We were a little taken aback to find a spanking new Rolls Royce parked on the street outside. We wondered aloud what the New Zealand taxpayer might have to say about that.

As we turned in the gate a man materialised from nowhere, fell into step beside us and escorted us up the drive. He was a muscular, handsome young man and I could see a distinct likeness to the family of the house, most likely a son. I said to him, 'Well, it's easy to see that you're a Fogarty!' He gave me a bemused look and said nothing. We rang the bell. A man answered. This must be Mary's husband whom I had never met. The young man remained standing beside us and if they looked at each other in any meaningful way, it was lost on me. I was too busy announcing our arrival.

I reached out my hand and pumped that of the man at the door, aware that my enthusiasm was not altogether reciprocated. I put that down to the reserve appropriate to diplomats. It took some time for me to realise that we were still standing on the doormat. It took a few moments more to take in that they were saying that no one of that name lived at this address. Was this No. 12? It was! I pulled out of my pocket the crumpled note on which I'd written the number the day before. Sure enough, there it was,

No. 12. They expressed regret but no such people lived in this house. My dismay must have been palpable. If this were not the house we had not the slightest idea which one was.

I asked if they'd mind ringing the New Zealand High Commission to make enquiries for us. The two men at this stage had a whispered consultation and came to a decision. They asked us to come inside and they'd ring for us. It was at this point that our dismay gave way to amazement. We were taken into a large drawing room and the two men withdrew. Our first impression was that it was a florist's shop. It was a veritable bower of flowers. Glorious arrangements in huge bowls and tall vases were everywhere. Where on earth were we? We began to talk in whispers.

Lorraine pointed out that everything in the room was brand new. And so it was! The Persian carpet on the floor still had its fold marks showing. We had no idea what period the furniture belonged to, but even to our untrained eye it was exquisitely beautiful. The pictures on the walls were all originals and all unknown to me except for the large, luminous one over the fireplace. It was unmistakably a Rembrandt. Lorraine tiptoed across the pristine carpet for a closer look and came back to report that it was encased at the back with burglar alarms. We froze. We felt that one movement could set the place alive.

The two men returned. They had spoken to Mary's husband. The address we were looking for was No. 21. I was mortified beyond words. All I wanted was to be on our way to what was by now a very late lunch appointment. But our two new friends were loath to let us go. They pressed us to have a cup of tea. They asked one question after another about New Zealand. They might be visiting there some time in the future, they said. The Maori, were they as interesting as they sounded? Our ski fields, were they as good as everyone said? Our scenery, was it as breathtaking as the tourist hype would have us believe?

We answered yes, yes, yes, to every question, our patriotic spirit struggling with our desire to be gone. Finally, we sang a last hymn of praise of our homeland, thanked them over and over and made our way to No. 21. We arrived breathless and apologetic to a worried hostess. What had happened to us? There was nothing for it but to confess my embarrassing reversal of numbers and to tell about our visit to No. 12.

At this point, Mary stood stock still with serving spoons suspended in her hand. 'Did I hear you say you've been inside No. 12?' she asked, and then appearing to address someone in the ceiling, 'I don't believe this!'

Our bewilderment grew when she collapsed into a chair with a delighted shout of laughter. 'Aren't New Zealanders wonderful?' she asked of no one in particular. 'You,' she said, 'have just been into the house that everyone in this street would give their eye teeth to see!'

It appeared we had just paid a visit to the brand new London home of one Rod Stewart. He himself was not in residence but it made no difference. We were instant celebrities. The teenagers in the family had been entertaining their friends upstairs. As the news spread they all came racing down to gather around and ply us with questions. I left it to Lorraine. I didn't want to run the risk of revealing that I didn't know who Rod Stewart was. Nuns have never been much good at keeping up with pop stars and this was twenty-five years ago. Rachel Hunter mightn't have known who he was in 1979. She would have been about nine years of age at the time.

22

IT SEEMS THAT AT LEAST ONCE IN EVERYONE'S lifetime there's a traumatic moment when we lose something and the ensuing drama becomes a story told for the rest of our lives. There's the bag that was snatched in Rome. ('He actually cut the shoulder strap!') There's the expensive camera stolen from the rental car in Paris, the wallet lost in Auckland, the passport in Warsaw, the purse in Cairo. I'm at home in this company. I know all about that trauma and all about the ensuing drama. I lost my purse once, not in Rome or Cairo, but at the Warehouse. Well, strictly speaking, I didn't lose it. It was stolen from right under my nose.

It was early December two years ago. It happened to be my month in charge of the community finances. In December, we always add some extra money to the monthly budget we each get in order to cover Christmas presents and other extras. I sensed that the others thought I'd be slow off the mark in handing out their budget so, to prove them wrong, I went to the bank on the first Monday of the month and collected it, that and the housekeeping money for the coming week. It was all in my purse, some $350 of it. Considering that generally I have only the remnants of my budget in my purse, this was a large sum to be carrying round.

While I was out and about that day, I went to the Warehouse and it all happened at the check-out counter. I presented my purchases, my purse was safely tucked under my arm and I knew the familiar routine. But on this occasion the routine was momentarily suspended. The assistant asked me if I'd like to buy a raffle ticket. It was, of course, for a worthy charity of which Mr Tindall is, no doubt, the patron. I needed both hands for the exercise, one to hold the book, one to write my name, both to tear out the slip. I put my purse on the counter beside me.

It was not a busy time, but I became vaguely aware that someone had come in beside me waiting to be served. I was anxious not to hold them up. Then I heard one of them say in an urgent whisper something that sounded like, 'Go!' and the two women moved off at speed. It occurred to me that I had indeed held them up. Perhaps they had a bus to catch or were late for an appointment. I looked up from the raffle book to see their rapidly receding backs and called out that I was sorry. It simply never occurred to me that my purse was rapidly receding with them.

We all rather fondly think we have a good idea how we'll react in such a crisis. At that time, I'd already had nearly eighty years to acquire this self-knowledge. It turned out that I knew nothing about myself at all. If you'd asked me, I'd have said that my inclination would be not to make a scene. I thought I had too much human respect to draw attention to myself in public, that I cared too much what people thought about me. I would have thought I'd ask quietly to speak to the manager or the security guard or the shop walker and tell them in cool, accurate detail of my problem.

So, what did I do when the time came? I created a scene to end all scenes, that's what I did. The assistant who was serving me had just begun to invoke the blessing, 'Have a nice day!' when I began to shout. I yelled to the startled girl that my purse had just been stolen. And I kept on yelling. I went from counter to counter looking accusingly at each customer, demanding to know who had taken my purse. I finally got to the information counter and expected action. Action was what I didn't get. They all looked back at me as though rooted to the spot. By this time, everyone in that vicinity knew that someone had stolen my purse. I could see nothing was going to be done and the enormity of the situation grew on me with each passing second.

Still in full cry, I announced to all and sundry that all the Sisters' Christmas money was in that purse, that our food for the coming week was in it, that I couldn't afford to lose it, that someone had to do something about it. I shouted all this and any other unsolicited and irrelevant information that came into my head to an increasingly large audience. Finally, someone brought the shop security man.

Somewhere along the line, Sister Teresa had joined me from another part of the shop. She'd been talking to a friend when she became aware of the commotion, recognised the voice that was reverberating down the aisles and feared the worst. I ignored her efforts to soothe me. We went with the security guard to his tiny 'office' and there we stood for the next hour amid piled-up packing boxes while he played the security camera for me to recognise the culprits. It was twenty-eight degrees in Canterbury that day.

We stood beside the guard seated at his screen and watched the procession of people coming and going to and from the Warehouse that afternoon. We saw people walking forwards and then watched them walking backwards. We saw them racing in and out of the shop and then saw the same people barely moving in slow motion. He pleaded with me to say I could recognise the offenders. Was it this one? That one? The next one surely? I couldn't do it. I'd noticed only one thing from the brief glimpse I'd caught when I'd looked up to apologise to them. One was short like me and not young. The other was a young woman. Finally, almost dropping with heat and exhaustion, we begged the man to give up. They were well away by now anyway. He would not stop.

Suddenly I saw her! She was walking out of the shop with what was unmistakably my purse, carrying it just as I always did with the shoulder straps hanging down in front of her. The man was elated. His machine indicated that the two women had stayed in the store for at least half an hour after the heist. They were experts, he declared triumphantly. I could scarcely match his excitement. As far as I was concerned they were well away and my purse with them.

At this point I learnt a salutary lesson. I had not had a lot of faith in the security guard. He didn't fit the stereotype. He was too young and too slight, not a muscle in sight. As it turned out, he was also very astute. He said, 'I saw that woman earlier on the screen. She came into the shop about two hours ago and she had nothing in her hands!' He put the machine onto fast replay for several minutes. Suddenly he hit the stop button. Sure enough. There she was coming into the shop with her young companion and her hands were empty. He raced the video forward to inspect her leaving the shop. She was our woman all right. After that, it was all slow motion. He took us on a conducted tour of their movements. See, there are the two of them standing by that huge box full of packets of Christmas cards. There's the younger woman walking out. Watch closely. See her nodding imperceptibly to her companion that the way is clear. There are the two of them going out to the car park. And thought I, there's my purse going with them!

Our friend made two further observations: 'We walked past those two women on our way to this office!' and 'Your purse would have been in that big box at the time!' He would blow up a picture of these two, he announced with excited relish and he'd send it round all their other shops. They'll be caught! He was a happy man. I was an unhappy woman.

So much for the trauma. Now for the drama. A little later,

Teresa and I were at the bank across the street from the Warehouse, she trying to be philosophical, me trying to remember what had been in my purse. I had often suffered jokes at its expense. It was widely believed to carry everything with the possible exception of the kitchen sink and the parachute. I could replace the Sellotape and the Band-Aids and the pens and the tape measure and even the money, but there were things I could never replace and my address book was one of them. Now to add to the gloom, the teller was showing signs of a long, hard day. She seemed unable to take in that everything she required of me was in the purse and repeat, the purse had recently been stolen. Yes, I was carrying the chequebook in it at the time. Yes, I did have a Bankcard that needed to be cancelled. No, I had no idea of the numbers of either. Yes, I was who I said I was. No, I had no ID. It was all in the purse, remember?

We seemed to have reached some kind of impasse when there was a commotion outside and the door behind us flew open. A man's voice was shouting, 'Stop! Stop! Don't carry on with that!' Everyone in the bank froze in their tracks. This must surely be some kind of a hold-up. It was the security guard from the Warehouse. 'She's brought it back!' he shouted at us, scarcely believing his own words. We stood there dumbfounded. It couldn't be true. But it was true. A short, elderly lady had handed it over a counter and disappeared before anyone could speak to her. The assistant thought she'd mumbled something about making a mistake. Not a thing in that purse had been touched. Every dollar could be accounted for, every Band-Aid, every pen, every rubber-band. The address book and the little diary, every last thing was there.

Now, why did she do that? Everyone we told had a theory. Some thought that obviously, she was a Catholic and the sight of *Sister Pauline* written on everything in the purse unnerved her. Others thought we might have done a good turn to someone belonging to her sometime. One singularly sly suggestion was that she had been one of my pupils at Villa Maria years before. The more religiously inclined believed she had undergone a conversion experience. In the end, the security guard could well be the one who got it right. He made his first delicate reference to my embarrassing part in the affair. He thought the two women would not have expected 'all that noise'. It would have unsettled them, made them fearful there might be a witness and they could be apprehended. They would not have been prepared, he thought, for all that talk about the Sisters' Christmas budget, not to mention the money for the week's food. Had I really said all those things? It seems I had.

I was too relieved, too overcome with gratitude, to even care. I wrote a letter to the Warehouse top brass telling them what a superb security man they had at Linwood. Much later, when I brought myself to visit the Warehouse again, he came running after me to say my letter was sent round all the other Warehouses as an example of how it's done. More power to him! As for us, we prayed for that woman for some time afterwards. We christened her *Kitty* because she'd had the opportunity to keep the community kitty that day and she decided against it.

I have a back-up story to this one if anyone has time to listen. Strangely enough it happened only a couple of weeks later. I had often felt I didn't do enough in service to my parish, so I put my name on the list to count the weekly collection on a Sunday morning. It had two advantages as service goes: your turn came round only a few times in the year and it's a sitting-down job.

On this particular Sunday morning, two other women and I were ensconced in a back room of the presbytery counting the money, not an onerous job and we enjoyed one another's company. We had the notes tied up in bundles of $100 each and had just dealt with the silver. We were nearing the end of the exercise and were talking quietly together as we did the paper work.

What happened next took place with such speed that we couldn't take in what was actually happening. The door behind us opened quietly, and in one practised sweep of a hand the bundles of notes were scooped up off the table before our eyes. It was as swift, as defeating of the eye, as a sleight of hand. We each had an impression of seeing a young man with a baseball cap pulled well down over his face, but then again it could have been a mirage. But it was no mirage that said, *Merry Christmas!* as it flew out the door. I realise now that cheek must of necessity be part of a thief's stock in trade, but at the time we simply couldn't believe our ears. We couldn't believe our eyes either as we gazed in shocked silence at the empty card table where the $100 bundles had been. Out the window I caught a glimpse of a slight figure racing down the street and out of sight. He didn't even have a get-away car!

I leave you to do the detective work needed here.

No, the suspect wasn't a Catholic! But he had been known to visit the presbytery for no good reason. No, the front door was not locked. Yes, he had correctly discerned that church collections had to be counted. Yes, he may well have observed unsuspecting cashiers carrying the loot into the presbytery. Yes, once inside, he most likely identified the room by the murmur of voices and the companionable gusts of laughter. Yes, any thief worth the name would consider it a safe risk. No, he was never caught!

Those are the two 'how I lost' stories that I generally tell when such stories are going round. In the first case, my goods and chattels were returned and the money as well, and in the second case the money wasn't mine anyway. It's generally agreed that I came out of these catastrophes better than I deserve.

23

I ALWAYS FEEL AT A DISADVANTAGE WHEN A STORY-
telling revolves around what exercise people have
done during their lives: tramping, swimming, weight
lifting, rowing – there's no end to what most people have done
either for their enjoyment or to maintain their fitness, or both. I
encourage them to tell another yarn, lest they expect one from
me. I can hardly tell them about the time I decided to take up

walking, strictly for fitness' sake. I can never conceive of walking for pleasure. I looked up the paper to find a walking group. There it was, centred at Queen Elizabeth II Park right near where I was living at the time. What appealed to me most, however, was their name. They were called the City Strollers. I envisaged leisurely walks around the Botanical Gardens and other Christchurch scenic spots. I had no way of knowing that I was about to encounter the misnomer of all time, the kind that gives new meaning to a word.

I arrived to find the group already gathered, all of them reassuringly as old as I was, some of them significantly older. I was in my sixties at the time. They greeted me enthusiastically. There was nothing they liked more it seemed, than a new member. I tried to maintain a little reserve of manner. I had no desire to become too friendly too early in case I didn't want to come back.

It was announced that we were going that day to French Farm. French Farm? That was about thirty miles away on Banks Peninsula. There had to be some mistake. They were the City Strollers, weren't they? What happened to the Botanical Gardens? I tried to hide my dismay.

By the time we were all packed into cars and heading out to the country, my worst fears were taking shape. I looked closely at my companions to see which one looked as decrepit as I. I chose an elderly woman in a longish skirt and an unlikely pair of shoes. Hypocritically, I made advances of friendship to her. To my secret joy, she told me she was seventy-four years of age. She was my woman. When we arrived at Little River I heard we were going to climb the hill. I was horrified. It was at this point that my new friend dropped her skirt to reveal a pair of workmanlike shorts and sat with unbecoming agility on the ground to change into her walking boots.

Worse was to come. They were a competitive lot and amid much laughing and bantering they were making bets about who would get to the top first. I felt the cold hand of despair. In due course, those who were still interested in the new member realised they had a problem on their hands. Two leaders told everyone else to go ahead and they stayed back with me. They were kindness itself and as if this one fact explained everything, they told me I was not suitably dressed for such a climb. They advised me what to wear next week as though there were some likelihood of a next week. I did my best for someone who had not willingly climbed a hill for years. Pouring sweat and purple in the face, I tried to keep up with my virtuous mentors whose day I was successfully ruining. Eventually I declared that I was going to turn back and after some earnest expressions of regret they turned and virtually raced up the steep incline in pursuit of their party.

I strolled slowly back to the cars feeling that at least I was giving some meaning to their unfortunate and misleading title. I was scarcely back, sitting on the grass leaning against a back tyre, when I was alarmed to hear a clamour of voices on the still air and then the first of the pack appeared. For one shocked instant they thought I'd beaten them to the top and was back ahead of them. 'Did you go right to the top?' one of them asked accusingly. I had just enough energy left to laugh.

I didn't return to the group and I gave up all idea of exercise. But it was not quite over. The leader and founder of the group rang me up each week for the next month. They were missing me. Had anyone offended me? Could I not try again? She so obviously felt she had failed me in some way that I had the grace to feel ashamed. I last saw her in the local bookshop where I was hiding furtively behind a stand of books.

It's even worse when the yarn has to do with prowess in sport, the medals won, the records broken, the shield their team took home. Someone tells me of their triumph at swimming and I don't feel inclined to pull out of the bag the story of the one competitive event that stands out in my memory. It took place when I was five years of age and had just started school. The venue was the Inangahua River where swimming was in progress and certificates were being handed out to the older pupils who had swum fifty or one hundred yards. No one actually swam the distance given on their certificate. To get a certificate for a fifty-yard swim, you either swam twenty-five yards upstream or one hundred yards downstream, but never just the fifty yards. It was a matter of choice and I noted that each member of my family chose to swim upstream.

At the end of the day, the teacher asked if any of the new entrants could swim. My family announced that I could; I had just found I could swim underwater in a creek near our house. I was called out and with my knees shaking I was directed to a shallow, fast-running channel of the river. To maintain the family tradition I told the teacher I'd swim upstream. I took a huge breath and began the first big test of my life.

I thrashed with my legs and pumped with my arms and refused to surface. My lungs were bursting, my temples aching and my cheeks bulging. I flogged my body to keep going. It was only the thought that I might have swum so far that I was out into the river that finally prompted me to give up. I stood up, completely disoriented in the shallow water, and was greeted with a great shout of laughter from the assembled school. It took me some time to realise that I was standing several yards further back from where I had begun!

The river had won that contest. I had taken on too strong a competitor and from that day, competition has held no attraction for me. You'll agree I'm sure, that this is hardly the yarn to tell someone who has just told you how he won a bronze medal in swimming at the British Empire Games in the 1950s!

Often the storytelling is at its fondest when recalling school-days. Recently I was part of an exchange about the respective textbooks we used back in the 1930s, each one of us quite secure in the belief that we had had the benefit of the best one. We took the pun as a case in point and recalled the example that was given in our respective English textbooks to teach this figure of speech. I thought mine was going to be hard to beat. It had illustrated the pun very satisfactorily for me at the time and was good enough to be remembered for seventy years.

> *The cat upon the garden wall*
> *Much cause have I to hate her,*
> *So often doth she mew till late*
> *That I could mutilate her!*

I was a little disconcerted to feel I'd been bettered by the example from the book used in a particular boys' school.

Ben Battle was a soldier bold
Used to war's alarms
A cannon ball blew off his legs
So he laid down his arms!

That kind of thing often happens with the swapping of yarns. It transpires that the other person has the better tale to tell, but a good yarn is a good yarn no matter who tells it. It's just that the telling is sweeter when that person happens to be you.

We all decided though that the best puns are not always the ones found in books, but rather the spontaneous ones of a good punster. My brother, Barry was addicted to the pun. It has to be admitted that his play on words ranged from the excruciating to the brilliant, but he counted every groan from his family as worth it if at other times he could also hear their spontaneous laughter.

I've always been inclined to think that the very best puns are the ones we make unconsciously, no matter how disconcerted we may feel at the laughter we have unwittingly provoked. When I was a young teacher in the 1940s I was reading to a Form Three class the story of Mr Edmond, the creator of Edmond's baking powder, and of his struggle to perfect his raising agent. He worked for years in a shed in his back yard experimenting with his ingredients and he ended up with one of the most successful business enterprises in New Zealand. As I closed the journal I said to my class by way of encouragement, 'Look at that now. See how that man rose in the world.' I can still remember my bewilderment as the class gave one delighted roar of laughter. 'Very clever, Sister!' I heard one girl say. At the time, I had no idea what I'd said, but whatever it was, I was grateful for the few extra Brownie points it had given me with a difficult class.

It seems to me from the anecdotal evidence of other old-timers, that for every unconscious pun we make in life we chalk up at least three spoonerisms. That delightful mental aberration by which we unconsciously transpose the initial letter of words one to the other is often attributed to mental tiredness or to absentmindedness or to scholarly abstraction. Whatever the cause it's a treachery of the tongue that generally produces a lot of laughter at the speaker's expense. We have only to think of the usher who hears herself saying politely, 'May I sew you to your sheet?' or the man who speaks proudly of his scoop of trouts, to get an idea of what our own fate might be when the day comes.

Of course, it's the Reverend Dr Spooner himself who is supposed to have made an endearing habit of this verbal transposition. 'The Lord,' he intoned once to his startled congregation, 'is indeed a shoving leopard!'

It was believed that when he found it necessary to be stern, he was particularly susceptible to these gaffes that have made him famous. But then we need to take into consideration that good stories often lose nothing in the telling. One has to be a little suspicious of the account given by a recalcitrant student at Oxford who claimed he reproached her with, 'You have tasted two whole worms, you have hissed all my mystery lectures and you have been caught fighting a liar in the quad!' Whatever the credibility of that one, it seems quite within the realm of possibility that he did call Queen Victoria 'a queer old dean!' He deserved to have his name go down in history although I'm inclined to think that the reverend doctor would not always approve of the more racy uses to which the spoonerism (not to mention the pun) is often put.

The contribution I generally make to spoonerism yarns comes from my memory bag marked sixties. It was still in a time when British history dominated the curriculum. To try to arouse some interest in nineteenth-century England in a class of New Zealand sixteen-year-olds and to reassure them that Mr Gladstone was indeed human, I used to introduce the topic of Anglo-Irish relations with a story. It is recorded that when the news that he had won the election of 1867 was brought to Gladstone at his country estate at Hawarden, he was engaged in his favourite pastime of cutting down trees. It is said that he leaned on his axe and made the admirable if optimistic statement: 'My mission is to pacify Ireland!' It was warm in the classroom that particular afternoon so I'll lay claim to mental tiredness rather than scholarly abstraction. I turned and wrote on the blackboard, 'My passion is to mystify Ireland.' The fact that my unconscious transposition could be considered a mild form of prophecy is no excuse. As it was, no one in the class noticed anything amiss. Why should they? One obscure observation is as good as another in a history class. It was only later when I walked to the back of the room that I saw what I had done. It was with some relief all round that I left Mr Gladstone to his own ponderous devices and turned to the vastly more entertaining observations of the Reverend Dr Spooner.

24

nly the years can tell the story that the days do not know. You have to live to be old to come to an understanding of that saying. The changes that happen within ourselves and in society at large are too imperceptible for the days to recognise them as they are happening. They are like a tableau being slowly assembled on stage behind the curtain until suddenly one day the curtain goes up and the picture is revealed.

Take the relationship between Maori and pakeha in New Zealand as it has evolved in my lifetime. For the first thirty years of my life, it was still acceptable in New Zealand to recount and to print what were known as Hori jokes. Hori was the character presented as the stereotype of the Maori. He inevitably came out of those lampoons as lazy, dirty, drinking and good for nothing. It was a personification of the Maori that suited the pakeha down to the ground, as it were. Hori made it possible to possess Maori land with a clear conscience. After all, Hori was not really fit to own it, was he? Fifty years later, who would dare hold to such a caricature? Yet the days could never tell us how or when in that fifty years the climate changed. Only the years can reveal that, and only a long span of years can tell the story of a sea change.

When I was at primary school in the 1920s in a part of the West Coast where there were no Maori, the indigenous people of the country were rendered virtually invisible to us. We believed that most of them lived in the North Island where they sang for tourists, but we knew little else and our curiosity was never aroused to know more. In the rudimentary history we were taught there was very little reference to our own country. I always thrilled to history, but it was not my own. In my first years at school an inspired teacher printed out history cards to supplement our primer reading books. I loved those history cards: *Alfred and the cakes. The geese that saved Rome. The first Prince of Wales. Bruce and the spider. Horatio on the bridge. Drake and the Golden Hind. Lord Nelson's blind eye.* There was a little nod in the direction of women with *Elizabeth Fry and the prisoners* and *Florence Nightingale and the lamp.* But of the Maori there was no sign and

of New Zealand, not a word. Before we left primary school we'd
heard about the Treaty of Waitangi, but not as a contract signed
and sealed between the Crown and the Maori, rather as a kind
of public relations exercise that had no serious impact on our
history and certainly not on our lives.

It has to be one of the most rewarding compensations for the
inconvenience of being old, to be able to remember how things
used to be and to see how they have evolved. The best thing of
all though is to know with the certainty of experience that there
can be no turning back. No child can say today that they do not
know that the Maori are the tangata whenua by a margin of
several centuries, that the British came and entered into a Treaty
with them in 1840 and that Aotearoa New Zealand is officially a
bicultural and a bilingual country. No adult can say it either for
that matter. The reactionaries would wish it not to be so, they
might try to turn back history, they might rage about the steps
taken to repair the injustices of the past, but they can do no more
than put obstacles on the line. They might be able to stop the
train for a time, but they cannot turn it back. History is not on
their side.

What I find most mysterious about all this is that these changes
have taken place inside me and I did not even notice them
happening. I cannot pinpoint the moments when I changed. I only
know that one day I felt ashamed of my gross mispronouncing of
Maori place names, that I had the first stirrings of mistrust of
the New Zealand history I'd been exposed to, that I decided to
go to Polytech to try to learn Maori, that our community began
saying part of our daily prayer in Maori, that I made my first
visit to a marae, that I began to take the Treaty of Waitangi

seriously. I have no idea what the particular catalyst was in each case, but I can see that I was part of a climate of change in the country catalysed by the Maori themselves and developing so subtly that I scarcely knew it was happening. I had to wait for the years to tell me the story that the days did not know.

I don't want to leave this significant dimension of old age without one more example. I've chosen this one because I believe I can pinpoint the decade when change began to take effect. I grew up in an age when virtually every man I knew smoked. It was still considered a very daring thing for a woman to do. Smoking for a woman in the 1920s was on a par with rolling your stockings. In other words it was quite shocking. There was a popular song at the time that lauded such practices and encouraged a nice disrespect of our elders at the same time. My memory brings back something like:

> *Roll 'em girls, roll 'em*
> *Go ahead and roll 'em!*
> *Don't let grandma tell you that it's shocking*
> *Paint a pretty picture on your stocking,*
> *Laugh at Ma, laugh at Pa*
> *Give them all the ha, ha, ha*
> *Roll 'em girlies, go ahead and roll 'em!*

It was not considered a nice song. Nor was smoking cigarettes considered nice, not for women. By the time I was in my late teens at the end of the thirties, it was still considered naughty enough to mark you as a modern woman and in proof of that I smoked right up to the last minute before I went in the convent gate.

But for men it was different. They smoked anywhere and everywhere, outside the house and inside the house, their own and other people's, they smoked in pubs and tearooms (the restaurant had still to be discovered), they smoked in hospitals and picture theatres, they smoked at dances and concerts, at funerals and in maternity homes. About the only place where it was not considered acceptable to smoke was in church although there were always some who were known to slip out during the sermon to have a few puffs in the porch. In my childhood, smoking for men was as socially acceptable as breathing and almost as necessary for their survival. Nice men smoked Craven A and Capstan, what were known as the tailored cigarette, but the real man rolled his own.

For some, rolling your own was an art form. The expert could do it with one hand. He held the cigarette paper delicately with the tips of his fingers, cradled the tobacco in the ball of the same hand, used his unoccupied fingers to work on it and then with the dexterity of long practice, transferred it in an even line along the paper; he then rolled the thin tissue, Zig Zag was the approved brand, ran his tongue along the edge, sealed it, pinched one end and put it in his mouth. At this point he took a box of matches from his pocket, extracted a match, struck it on the sole of his boot, still with one hand mark you, lit the cigarette and drew the smoke deep into his lungs, all in a matter of seconds and all in a manner that suggested that any fool could do it if he had a mind to. It made a big impression on me as a child and having gazed in wonder at such virtuoso performances, I have in later years always found the concept of a one-armed paper-hanger eminently plausible.

My father smoked a pipe. He lit up only once a day after the evening meal. The whole process followed a ritual in which the preparation was as important as the smoke itself. While the pipe was still cold, a pipe-cleaner was drawn through the stem. Then the pipe was put to one side while the tobacco was made ready. He smoked cut plug. He would bring out the plug of near-black tobacco and open his penknife. This was used to shave fine slivers from the solid block. The knife would then be wiped on the side of his trousers and he would begin methodically working the tobacco using the side of one hand to roll it back and forth in the palm of the other. When it was soft and malleable enough he would fill the bowl of his pipe with much pressing down of the thumb as the tobacco was added little by little. He would then take from a glass on the mantelpiece a long, slim taper rolled from newspaper, hold it to a flame in the open fireplace and begin the process of lighting the pipe.

The point of the newspaper tapers was twofold: it took much longer to light a pipe than a match flame could sustain. That was the practical reason. The other reason was vastly less effective. The intention was to demonstrate to his children how thrifty their father was in the vain hope that they would go and do likewise.

Then began the patient procedure of holding the light to the bowl of the pipe, pressing down the tobacco, applying the light again, pressing again, all done several times and all accompanied by strategic puffing until at last, the whole bowl was burning. It only remained to put out the taper and return what remained, still in the name of economy, to its container. Throughout this entire operation, we knew better than to speak to him, but once smoking he presented such a picture of utter contentment as to make everyone else in the room feel at peace.

It was into a social context such as this that the first whispers began to spread that smoking was bad for your health. The reaction was fierce and universal, the whole idea ludicrous. Such talk was the fabrication of some left-wing cranks. One of the first of these cranks to raise his voice publicly in New Zealand was Rolland O'Regan, my cousin. In the early 1950s he attended a medical conference in Paris and on his return he was reported in all the daily papers as saying that research now proved that smoking was connected with cancer. I have never forgotten the embarrassment of it as angry letters poured in to the papers denouncing him and people asked me, between furious draws on their fags, if I was related to this fellow.

Cousin or no cousin, my own brothers continued to smoke, sadly to their ultimate cost. One of them, visiting me from the Coast, rolled his own during the visit and began to smoke. Convent parlours were no more exempt than anywhere else. I began very tentatively. Had he heard, I wondered mildly, that smoking could cause lung cancer? Yes, he'd heard it, he said. Was I aware, he asked with equal mildness, that Mrs Walker had died of lung cancer? Had I ever, by any chance, ever seen Mrs Walker smoking a cigarette? He was talking about a neighbour of our childhood who would never have let tobacco touch her hands let alone her lips. I stared at him in disbelief. It seemed to me that if an intelligent man could present such logic in defence of his habit, then there was little hope that the social climate would ever change.

But change it did. And when all the factors came together,

that change took place with remarkable rapidity. In fact, I believe I can pin down when it happened. It was in the 1970s, twenty years after my brother's visit. In 1973 I left the safe harbour of the convent school and moved into the more turbulent seas of a large, co-educational high school. That transition is another story, but this is a story of a staff room and cigarette smoking. In my first weeks at this new school, I had to become acclimatised to a room blue with smoke. The truth was, I quite liked it. It took me back to my own smoking days and at that time I was only vaguely aware of the dangers of passive smoking. The only negative comment came from the members of my own household as each day I came in reeking with the smell of tobacco. It clung to my clothes, shrieking its presence in the clean air and even leaving a faint reminder of itself amongst the other clothes in the washing machine. It was a new experience for all of us.

It never so much as crossed my mind at the time to raise any objection. But it did cross someone else's mind. She was recently arrived from England, she was a language teacher and she was brave. She objected to having to eat her lunch in a smoke-laden atmosphere and she was ready to say so. At her first staff meeting she put forward a remit that there be no smoking in the staff room for the first twenty minutes of lunch time. A shocked silence fell on the assembly. It was the calm before the storm. Some of those teachers had been in that staff room for twenty years or more. Who did she think she was? Where had she come from? Her nationality came into question and I have no doubt her parentage as well. For days afterwards, the air seemed taut with tension and anger. At the next meeting it was put to the vote and by the slightest possible margin it was passed.

Was I brave and confident in the face of what was after all a moral decision? I was not. Did I put my hand up boldly for all to see? I did not. By chance that day, I was sitting next to a teacher whom I liked and admired. She was a teacher who was utterly devoted to her students and worked incredibly hard for their good. It had always seemed to me that she was able to sustain her commitment by the constant comfort of a cigarette. Even though I am almost pathologically right-handed, I raised my left hand because it was on the side away from her. I desperately wanted her not to see it. I liked all the men too, and I knew they were making a mental note of every colleague who was daring to vote away their basic rights. I was a craven wimp, a reluctant reformer, wanting no one to see me on the side of right. Thirty years later, I blush at the memory.

All these events took place about 1975. I retired from teaching two years later. In that short time, the attitude towards smoking was changing at an amazing pace. The air in the staff room became cleaner by the week. Already, by 1977, it was being seen as socially unacceptable to smoke in company. The language teacher from England had gone on her way, her work for us was done it seemed, and it was not in the realm of teaching French. Some people continued to smoke, of course, but a remarkable change had taken place in the country and what had been a universal mind-set for generations, went under the hammer with amazing speed. All this seems to demonstrate that if the moment for change has come, even the most entrenched attitude can be turned around with such rapidity that even a decade can tell the story. When I think of such things as racism, sexism and ageism, I find the memory of what happened in that staff room very reassuring.

25

OST OFTEN IT TAKES A LIFETIME FOR THE story of change to unfold in our lives, and the more intimate and personal the experience, the longer it takes for us to see the full picture. That's why it's only now after eighty years that I have any real understanding of the gradual development that has taken place in my inner life, that part of me that is most completely myself, the place where I have an intimate relationship with God. My spirituality is too much a part of me not to include it in this book about the experience of old age. The truth is it's too much a part of all of us to be ignored just because we find it difficult to speak about it.

In my earlier years I worked hard at my love life with God. I thought you had to. I believed that I always had to be proving to God that I loved him. I constantly protested it in my prayer, I was always trying to do things to please God and for some reason that I couldn't define, most often I felt I was falling short of his expectations. I tended to see God as someone who had to be constantly appeased for some reason or other, someone who would love me less if I didn't please him. I acted as though it was all up to me. If I did things to please God, God would be kind to me as a reward and if I displeased him he would withdraw from me and show his displeasure.

A few years ago, I caught a glimpse of this misguided kind of spirituality in an unexpected place. It was in the theatre. A leading New Zealand actor was doing a brilliant, hugely funny, one-man performance as a passionate if somewhat lunatic follower of the All Blacks. The night before the big game he was trying to do nothing to displease the deity in case the All Blacks lost as a result. The punch-line came when he explained that he'd been careful not to piddle in the shower so they wouldn't lose! It was a winner with the audience. But there was a dimension to the laughter that intrigued me. People were not just laughing at the humour of it. It was the kind of laughter that has that unmistakable edge of recognition, the way we laugh when we're thinking, 'Well, I wouldn't take it that far, but I know what you're talking about.'

I can't say when I turned away from that spirituality except to know with profound gratitude that I did. I think the earnestness it called for, the shadow of guilt that it cast, the implication that I could somehow earn God's love by lots of prayers and good works, winning points like a good Girl Guide, became too hard to sustain in practice and too immature to embrace in theory. Most of all, I came to the certain awareness that just as no love affair between two people could grow in such a dysfunctional relationship, neither could a love affair between God and me.

The most important aspect of this change was the growing certainty that no one can earn God's love. That's the first thing. I can't make God love me more, for the simple reason that God already loves me to the wire and the wire is infinity. All that earnest bargaining, I'll do good things for you and in return, you'll do good things for me, is an affront to love. God loves me unconditionally and the only possible response to a love like that is to love in return. I'll still talk to God in prayer and try to live the best life I can, but it will be for love, not for a reward. But how can I show God that I love him? Saying 'I love you' is not enough. Just as in love between two human beings, words of love have to have substance.

Jesus gave me one litmus test for my love of God. It is that I love my neighbour. He told us that whatever we do to others, we do to him. That's how closely he identifies himself with each one of us. *Love your neighbour as yourself.* It's a reassuring note, that one. He tells me I must love myself first and that's the benchmark for loving the other. God does not expect us to like every other person, he never asks the impossible. Loving them means to wish them well and be ready to stand beside them in their need.

I certainly don't expect everyone to like me but I have no doubt that God likes me. It's always been my experience that you like what you create, otherwise you would have created it differently. As the psalmist says so insightfully, *he knit me together in my mother's womb,* and Saint Paul wrote lyrically and confidently that I am *God's work of art.* God conceived of me, unique that I am, therefore he both likes me and loves me. Simple.

That's it really. Simplicity is at the heart of the spiritual life, the simplicity of a little child who never doubts for a moment that her mother and father love her. That's got to be what Jesus had in mind when he asked us to become as little children. So, here I am in old age, desperately hoping not to show any signs of second childhood in my mental life, but in my spiritual life, wanting more than anything else in the world to become like a little child, full of trust in God's love for me.

There's an important difference, of course. Children might be naughty but they can't sin. I can sin and I do, right on into old age. My sins, which used to weigh so heavily on me when I was younger, are now rather precious to me when I'm old. Much as I regret them for the hurt they do to others and to myself, I also value them for the opportunity they give to God to demonstrate the extent of his compassion and forgiveness. If I have no sins, I deprive God of the opportunity to show how limitless his love for me is. Saint Therese of Lisieux, bless her, was the first I heard saying it as bluntly as that. There's no reason why I should be less loving of myself than God is. It follows that if God's so ready to forgive me my sins, then I can surely forgive myself. It's good, sound psychology, but it's even better spirituality.

There's a nice touch of pomposity in the way we refuse to

forgive ourselves and cling to the guilt. It's as though we are saying that my sins are far too important to be forgiven so easily! We secretly think we should be taken more seriously, our sins included, and if God won't do it then we'll have to do it ourselves. It's hard to maintain this interior stance though, after you read the Gospel story about the prodigal son.

Jesus told these marvellous extended metaphors called parables to teach us important things about God. In this story of a father and son, God is the father and I am the son. The son, brash young blade that he was, asks the father to give him his inheritance in advance and he gets it. Then, being a young man with too much money for his own good, he proceeded to live 'riotously'. Not much detail is given except for the mention of drink and women. In due course, he'd spent it all and he'd done it all. From being a treasured son he degraded himself to become a swineherd so near starvation that he would have eaten the pigs' food gladly. He decided to return to his father and ask for forgiveness.

What happened next is the crux of the matter. The father saw him coming and ran down the road to meet him, arms extended to embrace him and kiss him and welcome him home. All this happened before the son had the chance to make his little prepared speech. There were no reproaches. Only wild excitement. He was back! Quick, sandals for his feet! The finest cloak! A ring for his finger! The fatted calf, kill it for a feast! This, according to Jesus, is the way God acts with the sinner who asks for forgiveness. Completely over the top! No wonder the faithful son who'd stayed home and done everything right felt slighted.

I've heard Luke's account of that parable hundreds of times and I love it, but in the end it was a real-life story that had the greater impact on me. It was a friend's mother who reflected most profoundly for me God's foolish love for each one of us. The son in this story, like the one in the Gospel, was prodigal in every sense of the word, her youngest. She had a large family and in her old age she had a home on the family farm where she was loved and cherished. But she knew that her family had lost patience with their spendthrift, alcoholic brother and he might not continue to feel welcome on the rare occasions when he chose to come home. It was a risk she was not prepared to take. To the dismay of all her children she left the comfort and care of the homestead and bought a little cottage about five miles away in the township to live by herself. Night or day, she never locked her door. That door was to be found open if and when her wayward son returned. And he did return when it suited him and when he was out of money. Like the older brother in the Gospel story, her other children had a point. She was lacking in common sense, she was encouraging him, she was putting herself at risk. There's no doubt she was doing all those things, but for one person at least she has been a mirror of God's way of loving and I'm deeply grateful to her.

The course of my relationship with God has developed so gradually that I scarcely noticed it happening. I've been much more aware of the development of my relationship with other people. In 1973, I moved with two other Sisters to live in a much-reviled street in Christchurch. Before we moved, kind people warned us of what we would experience. They spoke of violence, drugs, drunkenness and poverty. Sure, once there we came on all these things, but alongside them we found goodness that touched us to the core. In our innocence, if not our arrogance, we had hoped to bring the spirit of Christ to this neighbourhood. To our lasting enlightenment, and we hope our humility, we found Christ already there waiting to reveal himself to us in our neighbours. To people who'd always implicitly associated godliness with the practice of religion, this was news indeed. God was alive and well outside church and in the hearts of people who might say they didn't even believe in him. Where did this leave the church? We were on a learning curve that was a spiritual roller-coaster.

To explain what I'm saying I'll tell you about Fred. He was an alcoholic in the process of drying out. He wanted to have nothing to do with nuns. He lived in a unit that was attached to ours and that fact always seemed to be a matter of considerable regret to him. Like us at that time, he had three people in his household. He'd given a home to a Maori, a friendly man who'd confided to us that he had bouts of violence that placed his family at risk, and a man who was sent to 'live in the community' from a psychiatric hospital. They both became our close friends.

One night without warning, Fred died and the other two came banging on our door at five o'clock in the morning. We stayed with them all day and the Maori was in great distress, needing the house to be blessed before nightfall. He asked us to do it and in preparation, we joined him in scrubbing out and cleaning every room. That's how we came to be making the beds. It was winter and the bed that Fred had died in had two threadbare blankets. When we came to the next room we found a bed with two brand new blankets. Fred had bought them for him, he said, when he'd moved into the house. We were stunned. We had never done such a selfless thing in our lives. You can see what I mean about being surprised by godliness.

It was not long after this that I was going to a refresher course and was given a ride from Wellington to Palmerston North by the late Cardinal Delargey. He talked to his priest-driver for a time and then out of the blue, he turned to me and put an unexpected question. 'In this new life you're living,' he said, 'what has had the biggest impact on you?' I told him that it was experiencing the presence of God amongst people who didn't go to church and might even have never known God. There was a prolonged silence. I was just beginning to fear I'd trodden on his theological toes when he finally spoke. He said thoughtfully, 'You know we shouldn't be surprised at that. God lives in every person. We Christians just have the great good fortune to know that this is so and it's our mission in the world to tell this good news to everyone.'

I can't remember if I thanked him, but what he said was important to me. It brought into sharp focus what I had always believed, that everyone in the world is my sister and brother in a very real sense. We all share the one life of God. As this element of my spirituality grew and strengthened, one of its effects was to drive out irrational fear of others. One of the houses near us was occupied by a gang. Their tattoos, their patches, their apparent belligerence dovetailed neatly with my own prejudice to make me fearful of them. Now, when I met one of them on the street my interior voice told me, this is your brother. To begin with my greeting was met with surprise and a certain suspicion, but when it happened the next time and the next, they would grin and give me 'good day' and we were both relaxed enough to accept each other.

That was thirty years ago and now that I'm an old woman I count it as the most basic part of my spirituality that I see everyone as my sister and brother, on the bus, in the street, at a concert, at a film, in church, everywhere. I'm not claiming there's anything singular about my spirituality in this matter, it's just that I'm old and I want to testify to the way this has transformed my life. What happens is that this conviction of spiritual kinship with every other person, helps one to reach out in friendship and then comes the wonderful discovery that every single human being is worth knowing.

As for the place of the church in all this, I have remained a committed member because it brings me every Sunday into a community of local people with whom I feel completely at home and with whom I offer praise and thanks to God who is the source of all the goodness in life. It is here with this community too that I break the word of Scripture and the bread of Eucharist which give my spirit the food it needs to sustain it on the journey.

As I look back over the years, I am amazed at the place that change has played in the development of my spiritual life. I am speaking here specifically of those changes that I myself have initiated which have upset the pattern of my life. Not that I can lay claim to these changes as entirely my own. In each case, they've been made in the company of my community and the truth is that it's highly unlikely I ever would have made them of my own accord. They needed collective wisdom to generate the first inspiration, they need systematic discernment to reach a decision and most of all, they needed mutual support to carry them out. No, I couldn't have done any of them alone.

The process of change for our small community always begins with one of us floating an unlikely idea. The first reaction is invariably a cautious one. It is too radical, too impracticable, too daring altogether. Sorry, but we can't agree. All this, being interpreted, generally means it would cause too much upheaval, would be too upsetting of the even tenor of our lives. But we are a community as committed to method as any devoted follower of John Wesley, so we always go ahead with the process of discernment. And it's this process that inevitably has carried us, at different times, towards change.

I was in my fiftieth year when I decided on the biggest change of direction in my life. It was 1971 and I was comfortably established in convent life as the Superior of my community. I'd survived the junior status of my twenties, the doubts of my thirties, the burn-out of my forties. At fifty, I liked the attractive prospect of senior status ahead. But, it was not to be. The Second Vatican Council had just given a good shake-up to the Catholic Church and to nuns along with it. There was an unsettling call for change. Those in religious life were asked to study the needs of their contemporary society and discern in what ways, if any, they could help bind up the wounds of the modern world. The benchmark was to be the life of Christ and the life of the founder of their particular Order. It proved a disconcerting exercise. Neither life favoured comfort.

So, that was how I found myself leaving the wooded lawns and relative peace of Villa Maria convent and, together with Sister Teresa and Sister Helen, living in a State house in a suburban wasteland of graffiti and litter and constant noise – and of humanity – wonderful, struggling, courageous humanity. My spiritual and emotional life burst into new growth with the whole health-giving experience. I dread to ponder that I might not have made that change thirty years ago.

Ten years later I was sixty. We had settled into suburban life and I was just starting to feel comfortably at home there, when someone floated an idea! Our new life, taken up ten years before, had not always been understood. There were people, many of whom had been friends of an earlier era, who saw what we had done as a betrayal of the Catholic school system and of the Catholic parents who had given it so much loyalty. There was much speculation about what had prompted this unaccountable change of life for the three of us. The most likely one seemed to be that we were suffering from some kind of collective menopause, certainly a mid-life crisis. Some members of religious Orders, our own included, also felt that we were 'doing our own thing' and offering a kind of reproach to them for having remained faithful to their traditional way of life. We deeply regretted all this and we told each other that people would understand our motivation if we had a chance to explain ourselves. 'We should write a book!' It was said almost carelessly the first time, one day at a community meeting. Then it was said again later. It was ridiculous, of course. But we put it on the table and applied the method. The method we use is this: we get a long piece of newsprint and make a list of every conceivable reason why we should *not* do this particular thing. We then leave it for a time, sometimes an hour, sometimes a week, to allow for prayer and reflection and we come back to it. This time, we think of every possible reason why we should actually do this thing.

We allow more space and then meet to weigh up the negatives against the positives. At the end, each one says her *Yes* or *No* to the proposition or *Yes, but* . . . and with the discernment done, we come to a decision.

So, we decided to write a book! Easily said. But who exactly was going to write it? We looked speculatively at one another, Then someone said, 'You write a good letter, Pauline!' and after that the die was cast. My life had suddenly taken a fresh direction. It now entered an entirely new phase of isolation, self-doubt and the likelihood of failure. I couldn't even say I was writing it for my grandchildren. But out of it all gradually grew the wonderful awareness that I had a gift, hidden for sixty years. I could write! It had been there all that time waiting to be developed, so I wrote and I kept on writing for the next twenty years. As we are wont to say, with blithe, disregard for tautology, it was a new beginning.

And now, at eighty-one, I'm in the midst of another new beginning. We've moved house. Right now, we are adjusting to a much smaller living space than we've been used to, and to a new suburb, new streets, new neighbours on either side and to hundreds of friendly, wise, singularly silent neighbours directly across the road in an old Christchurch cemetery.

At the moment, with the trauma of the actual move still fresh in my mind, I am resolved that this will be the last move I'll undertake in a vertical position. Someone else will have to undertake the next one! But then again, I'm not really sure of that either. Change is like cholesterol. They tell us there is good cholesterol and bad cholesterol. And there's good change and bad change. If any proposed change of the future seems to be a good one, then I'll most surely embrace it. It will do for me what all past change has done. It will call on what resources I already have and it will call out new gifts I don't even know I have. Most of all, it will ask me to place my complete trust in God's abiding love for me, to trust in God's providence which, as the psalmist has said, has always been *a lamp at my feet*, shedding light on my path.

That's enough about my spirituality. There's more to it, but that's enough except for two final points. The first is that God is a spirit, neither male nor female. Because of the constraints of language, we have to give God a gender and for two millennia it has been traditional to use the male gender. I have done that here in speaking of God but I've done it because I think it will make most people feel more comfortable, more ready to hear what I'm saying. It's not my usual form of address. In my daily life I choose to give God the female gender in my prayer and in speaking of her. After a lifetime of perceiving of God as male, this change so enhances my perception of God that I'd like to suggest that this is a change whose moment is at hand. The other point is that my spiritual life plays a huge part in taking away my misgivings about what the future might hold and in abating my anxiety that, according to the law of averages, I have not a lot of time left. I'm coming to the end of what after all, was always a pilgrimage, and I intend to enjoy what remains of this journey as much as I've enjoyed what's gone before. It won't all be beer and skittles from now on, any more than it's always been that in the past, but I'm heading home to where I belong with a light enough step.

It's time to finish this book. The deadline is moving

dangerously close, but it's not the only deadline I have to meet. I have other commitments to see to before journey's end so I must be off. As the poet, Robert Frost would have it:

> *The woods are lovely, dark and deep*
> *But I have promises to keep*
> *And miles to go before I sleep*
> *And miles to go before I sleep.*